CISSP

Mandy Andress

CISSP Exam Cram

Copyright ©2001 The Coriolis Group, LLC. All rights reserved.

Limits of Liability and Disclaimer of Warranty

Trademarks

The Coriolis Group, LLC
14455 N. Hayden Road
Suite 220
Scottsdale, Arizona 85260

(480)483-0192
FAX (480)483-0193
www.coriolis.com

Library of Congress Cataloging-in-Publication Data
Andress, Mandy.
    CISSP / by Mandy Andress.
        p. cm. -- (Exam cram)
    Includes index.
    ISBN 1-58880-029-6
    1. Electronic data processing personnel--Certification. 2. Computer networks--Examinations--Study guides. I. Title. II. Series.

QA76.3 .A53 2001
005.8--dc21
                                2001042418
                                CIP

President and CEO
Roland Elgey

Publisher
Steve Sayre

Associate Publisher
Katherine R. Hartlove

Acquisitions Editor
Sharon Linsenbach

Product Marketing Manager
Jeff Johnson

Project Editor
Sharon McCarson

Technical Reviewer
Seyoum Zegiorgis

Production Coordinator
Todd Halvorsen

Cover Designer
Laura Wellander

Layout Designer
April Nielsen

Printed in the United States of America
10 9 8 7 6 5 4 3 2 1
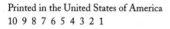

The Coriolis Group, LLC • 14455 North Hayden Road, Suite 220 • Scottsdale, Arizona 85260

A Note from Coriolis

Our goal has always been to provide you with the best study tools on the planet to help you achieve your certification in record time. Time is so valuable these days that none of us can afford to waste a second of it, especially when it comes to exam preparation.

Over the past few years, we've created an extensive line of *Exam Cram* and *Exam Prep* study guides, practice exams, and interactive training. To help you study even better, we have now created an e-learning and certification destination called **ExamCram.com**. (You can access the site at **www.examcram.com**.) Now, with every study product you purchase from us, you'll be connected to a large community of people like yourself who are actively studying for their certifications, developing their careers, seeking advice, and sharing their insights and stories.

We believe that the future is all about collaborative learning. Our **ExamCram.com** destination is our approach to creating a highly interactive, easily accessible collaborative environment, where you can take practice exams and discuss your experiences with others, sign up for features like "Questions of the Day," plan your certifications using our interactive planners, create your own personal study pages, and keep up with all of the latest study tips and techniques.

We hope that whatever study products you purchase from us—*Exam Cram* or *Exam Prep* study guides, *Personal Trainers, Personal Test Centers*, or one of our interactive Web courses—will make your studying fun and productive. Our commitment is to build the kind of learning tools that will allow you to study the way you want to, whenever you want to.

Visit ExamCram.com now to enhance your study program.

Help us continue to provide the very best certification study materials possible. Write us or email us at **learn@examcram.com** and let us know how our study products have helped you study. Tell us about new features that you'd like us to add. Send us a story about how we've helped you. We're listening!

Good luck with your certification exam and your career. Thank you for allowing us to help you achieve your goals.

ExamCram.com Connects You to the Ultimate Study Center!

Look for these related products from The Coriolis Group:

CCSA Exam Cram
By Tony Piltzecker

MCSE Windows 2000 Security Design Exam Cram
By Phillip Schein

MCSE Windows 2000 Security Design Exam Cram Personal Trainer
By Phillip Schein

MCSE Windows 2000 Security Design Exam Prep
By Richard McMahon and Glen Bicking

Also recently published by Coriolis Certification Insider Press:

Oracle 8i DBA: Backup and Recovery Exam Cram
By Debbie Wong

CCNP Routing Exam Cram Personal Trainer
By Jeremy McGrew

MCSE Exchange 2000 Design Exam Prep
By Michael Shannon and Dennis Suhanovs

Citrix CCEA MetaFrame 1.8 for Windows Exam Cram
By Anoop Jalan, Gene Beaty, and Travis Guinn

Server+ Exam Prep
By Drew Bird and Mike Harwood

I would like to dedicate this book to Heather,
whose patience and understanding
throughout the process of writing this book
kept me sane.

૨૦

About the Author

Mandy Andress is founder and president of ArcSec Technologies. Before founding ArcSec Technologies, Mandy worked for Exxon USA and several Big 5 accounting firms, including Deloitte & Touche and Ernst & Young. After leaving the Big 5, Mandy worked as Director of Security for Privada, Inc., a privacy startup in San Jose, and Chief Security Officer for Evant, an ASP startup in San Francisco.

Mandy has written numerous security product and technology reviews for *InfoWorld* and other publications including *Information Security Magazine, Network World, Federal Computer Week, Internet Security Advisor*, and *IBM DeveloperWorks*. She is also a frequent presenter at conferences, including Networld+Interop, BlackHat, SANS, and TISC. She is also the author of *Surviving Security*.

Mandy holds a Bachelor's of Business Administration in Accounting and a Master's of Science in MIS from Texas A&M University.

Acknowledgments

I would like to thank everyone at Coriolis who worked on this project for their help and patience, including Sharon McCarson, Deb Doorley, Paula Kmetz, Todd Halvorsen, Laura Wellander, April Nielsen, and Melanie Koehler. I would especially like to thank Sharon Linsenbach for her help and understanding when dealing with some of the issues that arose during this project.
—*Mandy Andress*

Contents at a Glance

Table of Contents

Introduction

Welcome to *CISSP Exam Cram*! Whether this is your first or your fifteenth *Exam Cram* book, you'll find information here and in Chapter 1 that will help ensure your success as you pursue knowledge, experience, and certification. This book aims to help you get ready to take—and pass—the CISSP exam. This Introduction explains ISC2's certification programs in general and talks about how the *Exam Cram* series can help you prepare for the CISSP exam.

Exam Cram books help you understand and appreciate the subjects and materials you need to pass the exam. *Exam Cram* books are aimed strictly at test preparation and review. They do not teach you everything you need to know about a topic. Instead, I present and dissect the questions and problems I've found that you're likely to encounter on a test. I've worked to bring together as much information as possible about the CISSP exam.

Nevertheless, to completely prepare yourself for any test, I recommend that you begin by taking the Self-Assessment included in this book immediately following this Introduction. This tool will help you evaluate your knowledge base against the requirements for the CISSP certification.

Based on what you learn from that exercise, you might decide to begin your studies with some classroom training or some background reading.

The Certified Information Systems Security Professional (CISSP) Certification

The CISSP certification is becoming the de facto security certification for security professionals. Many organizations require candidates have this certification and are encouraging existing employees to obtain the certification. The exam covers the following ten domains:

➤ Access Control Systems and Methodology

➤ Operations Security

➤ Cryptography

➤ Application and Systems Development

➤ Business Continuity and Disaster Recovery Planning

➤ Telecommunications and Network Security

➤ Security Architecture and Models

➤ Physical Security

➤ Security Management Practices

➤ Law, Investigation, and Ethics

To obtain the CISSP certification, you must pass a 250-question exam, agree to abide by the ISC2 Code of Ethics, and have three years of work experience in one or more of the ten test domains (listed above).

Recertification is required at three-year intervals by earning 120 hours of Continuing Professional Education (CPE) credits. These credits can be obtained in a variety of ways such as reading books, attending conferences, attending training classes, and writing articles.

The primary goal of the *Exam Cram* test preparation books is to make it possible, given proper study and preparation, to pass the CISSP exam on the first try.

Taking a Certification Exam

Once you've prepared for your exam, you need to register for the exam with ISC2. The CISSP exam is given several times a year throughout the world. You can find the latest schedule here: **www.isc2.org/cgi-bin/display_exam_control_file.cgi**. You can travel to an exam location or wait until the exam is given near you. The cost of the exam is $450 U.S. If you register less than 21 days in advance of the test date, you will be charged a $100 U.S. late registration fee. Also, if you need to reschedule your exam date, you will be charged a $150 U.S. rescheduling administration fee.

To sign up for a test, you must complete the exam registration form available at **www.isc2.org/Documents/CISSP_Exam_Registration_Form.doc**.

Once you register for the exam, you will receive a confirmation notice that you must bring to the exam site as well as a photo ID.

All exams are completely closed-book. In fact, you will not be permitted to take anything with you into the testing area, but you will be able to use the exam booklet as scratch paper.

Tracking CISSP Status

Once you complete the exam, you will wait approximately six weeks until the results are mailed to the address you listed when you registered. If you pass the exam, your certification is effective from the date of the exam.

When you receive notification that you passed, you will receive a certificate number, certification plaque, and certification card to carry with you.

How to Prepare for an Exam

Preparing for the CISSP exam requires that you obtain and study materials designed to provide comprehensive information about security. The following list of materials will help you study and prepare:

➤ The CISSP Study Guide, available at **www.isc2.org/cissp_studyguide**.

➤ The security books and resources also listed at **www.isc2.org/cissp_studyguide**.

➤ A CISSP review course, offered by ISC2, to help prepare you for the exam. Additionally, some people form study groups with colleagues or other people in the area studying for the exam.

About this Book

Each topical *Exam Cram* chapter follows a regular structure, along with graphical cues about important or useful information. Here's the structure of a typical chapter:

➤ *Opening hotlists*—Each chapter begins with a list of the terms, tools, and techniques that you must learn and understand before you can be fully conversant with that chapter's subject matter. We follow the hotlists with one or two introductory paragraphs to set the stage for the rest of the chapter.

➤ *Topical coverage*—After the opening hotlists, each chapter covers a series of topics related to the chapter's subject title.

Note: If you are familiar with other Exam Crams, you may notice that this Cram differs somewhat from other Crams. Due to the strict nondisclosure and confidentiality agreements that all CISSPs must sign, Exam Alerts and specific references to the exam have been omitted from this book. Questions in the Sample Test are culled from previous end-of-chapter questions in another effort to preserve the confidentiality of the exam.

➤ *Practice questions*—Although we talk about test questions and topics throughout the book, a section at the end of each chapter presents a series of mock test questions and explanations of both correct and incorrect answers.

➤ *Details and resources*—Every chapter ends with a section titled "Need to Know More?". This section provides direct pointers to third-party resources offering more details on the chapter's subject. In addition, this section tries to rank or at least rate the quality and thoroughness of the topic's coverage by each resource. If you find a resource you like in this collection, use it, but don't feel compelled to use all the resources.

The bulk of the book follows this chapter structure slavishly, but there are a few other elements that we'd like to point out. Chapter 12 includes a sample test that provides a good review of the material presented throughout the book to ensure you're ready for the exam. Chapter 13 is an answer key to the sample test that appears in Chapter 12. In addition, you'll find a handy glossary and an index.

Finally, the tear-out Cram Sheet attached next to the inside front cover of this *Exam Cram* book represents a condensed and compiled collection of facts and tips that we think you should memorize before taking the test. Because you can dump this information out of your head onto a piece of paper before taking the exam, you can master this information by brute force. You might even want to look at it in the car or in the lobby of the testing center just before you walk in to take the test.

How to Use this Book

We've structured the topics in this book to correspond with the 10 domains for the CISSP exam. Therefore, you can focus on those domains where you feel more work is required and avoid the topics you feel you already adequately know. If you need to brush up on a topic or you have to bone up for a second try, use the index or table of contents to go straight to the topics and questions that you need to study. Beyond helping you prepare for the test, we think you'll find this book useful as a tightly focused reference to some of the most important aspects of security.

Given all the book's elements and its specialized focus, we've tried to create a tool that will help you prepare for—and pass—the CISSP exam. Please share your feedback on the book with us, especially if you have ideas about how we can improve it for future test-takers. We'll consider everything you say carefully, and we'll respond to all suggestions.

Send your questions or comments to us at **learn@examcram.com**. Please remember to include the title of the book in your message; otherwise, we'll be forced to guess which book you're writing about. And we don't like to guess—we want to *know*! Also, be sure to check out the Web pages at **www.examcram.com**, where you'll find information updates, commentary, and certification information.

Thanks, and enjoy the book!

Self-Assessment

The reason I included a Self-Assessment in this *Exam Cram* book is to help you evaluate your readiness to tackle the CISSP certification. It should also help you understand some of the basics of computer security. But before you tackle this Self-Assessment, let's talk about concerns you may face when pursuing the CISSP certification and what an ideal CISSP candidate might look like.

CISSPs in the Real World

In the next section, I describe an ideal CISSP candidate, knowing full well that only a few real candidates will meet this ideal. In fact, my description of that ideal candidate might seem downright scary. But take heart: Although the requirements to obtain the CISSP certification may seem formidable, they are by no means impossible to meet. However, be keenly aware that it does take time, involves some expense, and requires real effort to get through the process.

Increasing numbers of people are attaining the CISSP certification, so the goal is within reach. You can get all the real-world motivation you need from knowing that many others have gone before, so you will be able to follow in their footsteps. If you're willing to tackle the process seriously and do what it takes to obtain the necessary experience and knowledge, you can take—and pass—the certification exam on the first try.

The Ideal CISSP Candidate

Just to give you some idea of what an ideal CISSP candidate is like, here are some relevant statistics about the background and experience such an individual might have. Don't worry if you don't meet these qualifications, or don't come that close—this is a far from ideal world, and where you fall short is simply where you'll have more work to do.

➤ Academic or professional training in security theory, concepts, and operations. This includes everything from networking media and transmission techniques through encryption, operating systems, services, and applications.

➤ Three-plus years of professional security experience, including experience with networking, implementation, policy development, and review.

➤ A thorough understanding of key security protocols, such as IPSec, SSL, SLIP, CHAP, and SSH.

➤ A thorough understanding of computer operations, physical security, and disaster recovery planning.

➤ Familiarity with key laws and regulations as they relate to computer security.

➤ An understanding of how to implement security for key network data.

➤ Working knowledge of perimeter security mechanisms such as firewalls, screening routers, and intrusion detection systems.

Fundamentally, this boils down to a possible bachelor's degree in computer science, plus three years' experience working in a position involving security design, installation, configuration, and maintenance. I believe that well under half of all certification candidates meet these requirements, and that, in fact, most meet less than half of these requirements—at least, when they begin the certification process. But because all the people who already have been certified have survived this ordeal, you can survive it too—especially if you heed what the Self-Assessment can tell you about what you already know and what you need to learn.

Put Yourself to the Test

The following series of questions and observations is designed to help you figure out how much work you must do to pursue the CISSP certification and what kinds of resources you may consult on your quest. Be absolutely honest in your answers, or you'll end up wasting money on exams you're not yet ready to take. There are no right or wrong answers, only steps along the path to certification. Only you can decide where you really belong in the broad spectrum of aspiring candidates.

Two things should be clear from the outset, however:

➤ Even a modest background in computer science will be helpful.

➤ Hands-on experience with security products and technologies is an essential ingredient to certification success.

Educational Background

1. Have you ever taken any security-related classes? [Yes or No]

   If Yes, proceed to Question 2; if No, proceed to Question 4.

2. Have you taken any classes on designing and operating security architectures? [Yes or No]

If Yes, you will probably be able to handle the CISSP exam's architecture and security component discussions. If you're rusty, brush up on basic operating system concepts, especially virtual memory, multitasking regimes, user mode versus kernel mode operation, and general computer security topics.

If No, consider some basic reading in this area. I strongly recommend a good general security book, such as *Computer Security Basics* by Deborah Russell (O'Reilly and Associates, ISBN 0937175714).

3. Have you developed any security policies, performed security audits, or developed response plans? [Yes or No]

If Yes, you will probably be able to handle the majority of the CISSP exam questions. If you're rusty, brush up on basic security policy, the requirements of a basic disaster recovery plan, what should be reviewed in a security audit, and so on.

If No, you might want to read one or two books in this topic area. The two best books that I know of are *Information Security Policies Made Easy*, by Charles Cresson Wood (Baseline Software, ISBN 1881585069) or *CISSP Examination Textbooks Volume 1: Theory* and *CISSP Examination Textbooks Volume 2: Practice* by SRV Professional Publications.

Testing Your Exam-Readiness

Whether you attend a formal class to get ready for an exam or use written materials to study on your own, some preparation for the CISSP certification exams is essential. At $450 a try, pass or fail, you want to do everything you can to pass on your first try. That's where studying comes in.

I have included a practice exam in this book, so if you don't score that well on the test, you can study more and then tackle the test again.

For any given subject, consider taking a class if you've tackled self-study materials, taken the test, and failed anyway. The opportunity to interact with an instructor and fellow students can make all the difference in the world, if you can afford that privilege. For information about review classes, visit the ISC2 page at **www.isc2.org**.

4. Have you taken a practice exam on your chosen test subject? [Yes or No]

If Yes, and you scored 70 percent or better, you're probably ready to tackle the real thing. If your score isn't above that threshold, keep at it until you break that barrier.

If No, obtain all the free and low-budget practice tests you can find and get to work. Keep at it until you can break the passing threshold comfortably.

Onward, through the Fog!

Once you've assessed your readiness, undertaken the right background studies, and reviewed the many sources of information to help you prepare for a test, you'll be ready to take a round of practice tests. When your scores come back positive enough to get you through the exam, you're ready to go after the real thing. If you follow our assessment regimen, you'll not only know what you need to study, but when you're ready to register for a test date.

The CISSP Certification Exam

. . . .

Terms you'll need to understand:

✓ Multiple-choice question formats

✓ Exam strategy

Techniques you'll need to master:

✓ Assessing your exam readiness

✓ Practicing (to make perfect)

✓ Budgeting your time

✓ Guessing (as a last resort)

Exam taking is not something that most people anticipate eagerly, no matter how well prepared they may be. In most cases, familiarity helps offset test anxiety. In plain English, this means the more you know about the exam and the more prepared you feel, the more relaxed you will be.

Understanding the details of taking the new exams (how much time to spend on questions, the environment you'll be in, and so on) will help you concentrate on the material rather than on the setting. Likewise, mastering a few basic exam-taking skills should help you recognize—and perhaps even outfox—some of the tricks and snares you're bound to find in some exam questions.

This chapter, besides explaining the exam environment, describes some proven exam-taking strategies that you should be able to use to your advantage.

Assessing Exam-Readiness

I strongly recommend that you read through and take the Self-Assessment included with this book (it appears just before this chapter, in fact). This will help you compare your knowledge base to the requirements for obtaining the CISSP certification, and it will also help you identify parts of your background or experience that may be in need of improvement, enhancement, or further learning. If you get the right set of basics under your belt, obtaining the CISSP will be that much easier.

Once you've gone through the Self-Assessment, you can remedy those domain areas where your background or experience may not measure up to an ideal certification candidate. But you can also tackle subject matter for other domains at the same time, so you can continue making progress while you're catching up in some areas.

Once you've worked through an *Exam Cram*, have read the supplementary materials, and have taken the practice test, you'll have a pretty clear idea of when you should be ready to take the real exam. Although I strongly recommend that you keep practicing until your scores top the 75 percent mark, 80 percent would be a good goal to give yourself some margin for error in a real exam situation (where stress will play more of a role than when you practice). Once you hit that point, you should be ready to go. You'll find more pointers on how to study and prepare in the Self-Assessment. But now, on to the exam itself!

The Exam Situation

When you arrive at the location of the exam, you will need to sign in. You will be asked to show your exam ticket and photo identification. After you've signed in, find a seat, get comfortable, and wait for the exam to begin.

The exam is completely closed book. In fact, you will not be permitted to take anything with you into the testing area, but you will be able to use the exam booklet as scratch paper.

Typically, the exam room will contain a number of tables. Some exam locations are more cramped than others, but ISC2 does try to make the candidates as comfortable as possible. You will also have the opportunity to complain about any issues you have with the testing environment at the completion of the exam.

The CISSP exam is timed. All candidates have up to six hours to complete the 250 question exam. This should provide plenty of time to complete the exam and even provide some time to go back and review your answers. The exam moderator will also keep you informed as to how much time you have left to complete the exam.

All questions on the exam are multiple choice and the exam contains 250 questions. 25 of these questions are for research purposes, so only 225 questions are actually scored for certification. The research questions are not identified, so you must answer all questions to the best of your ability. The exam questions are developed by an ISC2 committee and they are always updating and changing them.

In the next section, you'll learn more about how CISSP test questions look and how they must be answered.

Multiple-Choice Question Format

All exam questions require you to select a single answer from given choices. The following multiple-choice question requires you to select a single correct answer. Following the question is a brief summary of each potential answer and why it is either right or wrong.

Question 1

Which service usually runs on port 21?

○ a. DNS

○ b. HTTP

● c. FTP

○ d. SMTP

Answer c is correct because FTP services typically run on port 21. Answer a is incorrect because DNS typically runs on port 53. Answer b is incorrect because HTTP typically runs on port 80. Answer d is incorrect because SMTP typically runs on port 25.

Exam Strategy

A well-known principle when taking fixed-length exams is to first read over the entire exam from start to finish while answering only those questions you feel absolutely sure of. On subsequent passes, you can dive into more complex questions more deeply, knowing how many such questions you have left.

As you read each question, if you answer only those you're sure of and mark for review those that you're not sure of, you can keep working through a decreasing list of questions as you answer the trickier ones in order.

 There's at least one potential benefit to reading the exam over completely before answering the trickier questions: Sometimes, information supplied in later questions sheds more light on earlier questions. At other times, information you read in later questions might jog your memory about earlier questions. Either way, you'll come out ahead if you defer those questions about which you're not absolutely sure.

Here are some question-handling strategies that apply to fixed-length and short-form tests. Use them if you have the chance:

➤ When returning to a question after your initial read-through, read every word again—otherwise, your mind can fall quickly into a rut. Sometimes, revisiting a question after turning your attention elsewhere lets you see something you missed, but the strong tendency is to see what you've seen before. Try to avoid that tendency at all costs.

➤ If you return to a question more than twice, try to articulate to yourself what you don't understand about the question, why answers don't appear to make sense, or what appears to be missing. If you chew on the subject awhile, your subconscious might provide the details you lack, or you might notice a "trick" that points to the right answer.

As you work your way through the exam, it's wise to budget your time by making sure that you've completed one-quarter of the questions one-quarter of the way through the exam period, and three-quarters of the questions three-quarters of the way through.

If you're not finished when only five minutes remain, use that time to guess your way through any remaining questions. Remember, guessing is potentially more valuable than not answering, because blank answers are always wrong, but a guess may turn out to be right. If you don't have a clue about any of the remaining questions, pick answers at random, or choose all a's, b's, and so on. The important thing is to submit an exam for scoring that has an answer for every question.

At the very end of your exam period, you're better off guessing than leaving questions unanswered.

Question-Handling Strategies

For those questions that take only a single answer, usually two or three of the answers will be obviously incorrect, and two of the answers will be plausible—of course, only one can be correct. Unless the answer leaps out at you (if it does, reread the question to look for a trick; sometimes those are the ones you're most likely to get wrong), begin the process of answering by eliminating those answers that are most obviously wrong.

Almost always, at least one answer out of the possible choices for a question can be eliminated immediately because it matches one of these conditions:

➤ The answer does not apply to the situation.

➤ The answer describes a nonexistent issue, an invalid option, or an imaginary state.

After you eliminate all answers that are obviously wrong, you can apply your retained knowledge to eliminate further answers. Look for items that sound correct but refer to actions, commands, or features that are not present or not available in the situation that the question describes.

If you're still faced with a blind guess among two or more potentially correct answers, reread the question. Try to picture how each of the possible remaining answers would alter the situation. Be especially sensitive to terminology; sometimes the choice of words ("remove" instead of "disable") can make the difference between a right answer and a wrong one.

Only when you've exhausted your ability to eliminate answers, but remain unclear about which of the remaining possibilities is correct, should you guess at an answer. An unanswered question offers you no points, but guessing gives you at least some chance of getting a question right; just don't be too hasty when making a blind guess.

Mastering the Inner Game

In the final analysis, knowledge breeds confidence, and confidence breeds success. If you study the materials in this book carefully and review all the practice questions at the end of each chapter, you should become aware of those areas where additional learning and study are required.

After you've worked your way through the book, take the practice exam in the back of the book. Taking this test will provide a reality check and help you identify areas to study further. Make sure you follow up and review materials related to the questions you miss on the practice exam before taking the real exam. Only when you've covered that ground and feel comfortable with the whole scope of the practice exam should you set an exam appointment. Only if you score 80 percent or better should you proceed to the real thing (otherwise, obtain some additional practice tests so you can keep trying until you hit this magic number).

Armed with the information in this book and with the determination to augment your knowledge, you should be able to pass the certification exam. However, you need to work at it, or you'll spend the exam fee more than once before you finally pass. If you prepare seriously, you should do well. We are confident that you can do it!

The next section covers other sources you can use to prepare for the CISSP exam.

Additional Resources

A good source of information about CISSP exam resources comes from ISC2 itself. The CISSP study guide is available for download at **www.isc2.org/newsisc2guide.html**.

Access Control Systems and Methodology

Terms you'll need to understand:

- ✓ Access control
- ✓ Accountability
- ✓ Discretionary access control
- ✓ Mandatory access control
- ✓ Lattice-based access control
- ✓ Rule-based access control
- ✓ Role-based access control
- ✓ Brute force attack
- ✓ Denial of service attack
- ✓ Spoofing attack
- ✓ Man-in-the-middle attack
- ✓ Spamming
- ✓ Sniffers
- ✓ Crackers
- ✓ Intrusion detection

Techniques you'll need to master:

- ✓ Understanding access control techniques
- ✓ Understanding access control administration
- ✓ Understanding access control models
- ✓ Understanding identification and authentication techniques
- ✓ Understanding access control methodologies
- ✓ Identifying methods of attack
- ✓ Understanding intrusion detection

Access control is at the core of security and provides the means to control the behavior, use, and content of a system. It allows an administrator or manager to specify what systems users can access, which resources they can use or see, and which actions they can perform.

For the CISSP exam, you need to fully understand access control concepts and methodologies.

Accountability

Access control helps provide accountability to users. Identification and authentication techniques allow individual user actions to be logged and/or monitored. This control enables security officers and management to see what each individual user does in order to hold the individual accountable for his or her actions. Without accountability, you do not know who performed which action, who accessed which resource, and so on. For example, having multiple administrators accessing a single system as root, Administrator, or other superuser account, does not provide any accountability. You may know the root user performed an action, but you do not know which person was logged in as root when the action was performed.

Access Control Techniques

Access control techniques define ways to implement access control solutions. Various techniques exist and are useful in different environments.

Discretionary Access Control (DAC)

Discretionary access control (DAC) restricts a user's access to an object (i.e., a file). The owner of the file controls other users' access. In theory, resources left unprotected (i.e., without an owner) are freely accessible to all users.

Many risks are inherent in the DAC technique because there is no centralized administration. Each file owner controls his or her own access levels. Some owners may not be security-conscious and may allow everyone to modify any file. Production data can be updated by unauthorized users without appropriate controls; application software can be executed or updated by unauthorized personnel; confidentiality and integrity of information can be accidentally or deliberately compromised by users who were not intended to have access to it; auditing of file and resource accesses may be difficult or impossible; and finally, some resources—by their names, storage locations, and degree of access protection—provide a focus for attack.

Mandatory Access Control (MAC)

Mandatory access control (MAC), also known as *multilevel security*, is non-discretionary. All users and resources are classified and assigned a security label. Access requests are denied if the requestor's security label does not match that of the resource. MAC is most applicable to computer systems carrying defense information (and most other government information) or other data with extremely high security requirements.

Lattice-Based Access Control

Lattice-based access control systems were developed to deal with information flow in multiuser computer systems. They are commonly used in databases.

For example, given two objects with different security labels (classifications), what is the minimum security label a user must have to be allowed access to both objects? Given two users, what is the maximum label an object can have so it can be accessed by both users? A lattice is a mathematical structure that holds unique answers to these questions.

Rule-Based Access Control

With *rule-based access control*, the system intercepts every access request and compares the resource-specific access conditions with the rights of the user in order to make an access decision. Access control lists are an implementation of rule-based access control.

Role-Based Access Control

Role-based access control (RBAC) is an alternative to DAC and MAC. RBAC gives security officers the ability to specify and enforce enterprise-specific security policies in a way that maps naturally to an organization's structure. Each user is assigned one or more roles, and each role is assigned one or more privileges that are given to users in that role.

Access Control Lists

An *access control list (ACL)* is a table that tells a system which access rights each user has to a particular system object, such as a file directory or an individual file. Each object has a security attribute that identifies its access control list. The list has an entry for each system user (or privilege) with access privileges. The most common privileges include the ability to read a file (or all the files in a directory), to write to the file or files, and to execute the file (if it is an executable file or program). Windows NT- and Unix-based systems are among the operating systems that use access control lists. Lists are implemented differently by each operating system.

Access Control Administration

Access control administration can be a time-consuming process. Accounts need to be created, logged, and monitored. Additionally, access rights must be established and maintained.

Account Administration

Administering user accounts is a straightforward process. Accounts should be created when needed and when the proper approvals are received. Accounts should be removed as soon as they are no longer needed. Administrators run into problems when they do not delete accounts in a timely fashion.

Account, Log, and Journal Monitoring

Account accesses, especially superuser accounts such as Administrator and root, should be logged and monitored. Monitoring will help identify suspicious activity that should be investigated. Without account logging and monitoring, you have no way of knowing when accounts are being used. If an employee is consistently logging in late at night, that might be a sign that the account has been compromised or that the employee perhaps needs to log in when no one is around to copy confidential data or perform other suspicious activity. In either case, the situation should be investigated if it falls out of normal operations.

Access Rights and Permissions

Access rights and permissions determine who can access which resources. This technique is one of the most complex component of access control. First, access rights and permissions need to be established (i.e., authorization for access must be given). This authorization can be achieved in three ways: through file and data owners; through the principle of least privilege; or through segregation of duties and responsibilities.

File and Data Owners

Each resource should be assigned an owner who is responsible for administering and maintaining the resource's rights and permissions. Without known owners and custodians, data and objects are not being controlled. With ownership, responsibility is defined and users know who to contact with problems or questions.

Principle of Least Privilege

The *principle of least privilege* says that every user should be given the minimum level of permissions required to do his job. For example, if a user does not need write access to a specific directory, he should not be given that access.

Separation of Duties and Responsibilities

Separation of duties should be implemented to provide checks and balances, and to keep one person (or several people) from gaining too much power. For example, the same person should not be able to approve account creation, assign access rights, and physically create the account.

Once the account is created and access rights have been assigned, the account must be maintained throughout its existence in the system. The main elements that need to be addressed are the rights and permissions assigned to the account. As users progress in their careers, access needs change. Each user's account needs to be continuously updated to reflect these changes.

Finally, when an employee (or contractor) leaves the company or is terminated, his account must be immediately disabled. Additionally, temporary accounts, such as testing or demo accounts, should be deleted immediately when they are no longer needed. Unused accounts on the system leave easily opened doors for attackers.

Access Control Models

Access control models are theoretical representations of access control techniques. These models were developed to help quantify the need for concrete, scientifically based access control. The most common models are Bell-LaPadula, Biba, Clark-Wilson, and non-interference.

Bell-LaPadula

This model was proposed by Bell and LaPadula for enforcing access control in government and military applications. In these applications, subjects and objects are often partitioned into different security levels. A subject can only access objects at certain levels determined by the subject's security level. For instance, the following are two typical access specifications: "Unclassified personnel cannot read data at confidential levels," and "Top-secret data cannot be written into files at unclassified levels." This kind of access control disclosure model is also called *mandatory access control.*

The Bell-LaPadula model supports mandatory access control by determining the access rights from the security levels associated with subjects and objects. It also supports discretionary access control by checking access rights from an access matrix.

Each object is associated with a security level of any given form (i.e., classification level and set of categories). Each subject is also associated with a maximum and current security level, which can be changed dynamically. The set of classification levels is ordered by a < (less than) relationship. For instance, the relationship for the set "top-secret, secret, confidential, unclassified," looks like this:

unclassified < confidential < secret < top-secret

A category is a set of names such as Nuclear and Missile. Security level A dominates B if and only if A's classification set is a superset of B's. For instance, top-secret {Missile, NATO} dominates secret {NATO} because top-secret > secret and the set {Missile, NATO} contains {NATO}.

Biba

The first model to address integrity in computer systems was based on a hierarchical lattice of integrity levels defined by Biba in 1977. The *Biba integrity model* is similar to the Bell-LaPadula model for confidentiality in that it uses subjects and objects; in addition, Biba controls object modification in the same way that Bell-LaPadula controls disclosure.

Biba's integrity policy consists of three parts. The first part specifies that a subject cannot execute objects that have a lower level of integrity than the subject has. The second part specifies that subjects cannot modify objects that have a higher level of integrity than their current access levels. The third part specifies that a subject may not request service from subjects that have a higher integrity level.

Clark-Wilson

The *Clark-Wilson model*, published in 1987 and updated in 1989, involves two primary elements for achieving data integrity—the well-formed transaction and the separation of duties. Well-formed transactions prevent users from manipulating data, thus ensuring its internal consistency. Separation of duties prevents authorized users from making improper modifications, thus preserving the external consistency of data by ensuring that data in the system reflects the real-world data it represents.

The Clark-Wilson model differs from the other models that are subject- and object- oriented by introducing a third access element—programs—resulting in what is called an *access triple*, which prevents unauthorized users from modifying data or programs. In addition, this model uses integrity verification and transformation procedures to maintain internal and external consistency of data. The verification procedures confirm that the data conforms to the integrity specifications at the time the verification was performed. The transformation procedures are designed to take the system from one valid state to the next.

Non-Interference Model

For the development of highly secure systems, it is crucial that all information flowing through the system is understood. In particular, covert channels or unexpected information flows can be particularly damaging to a secure system that is attempting to maintain a high level of confidentiality. For example, a top-secret process should not—under normal situations—be able to send or otherwise signal any information to a secret process. *Non-interference* is a mathematical technique that allows a system model to be analyzed for this information.

Identification and Authentication Techniques

Before you can enforce access rights, you need to know that the user is actually the person who belongs to the username (or userid) in question. Identification and authentication provide this functionality. Knowledge-based authentication, characteristic-based authentication, tokens, and tickets are the most common forms of identification and authentication.

Knowledge-Based Authentication

The first type of authentication is *knowledge-based authentication*. Here, users enter an item of information that they know, such as a password, passphrase, or PIN. Passwords and the other knowledge-based authentication methods are easy to implement, but they are also fairly easy to break. Users often do not select strong passwords, so attackers can easily guess them and gain unauthorized access to sensitive information.

A strong password meets the following criteria:

➤ At least seven characters long

➤ Contains upper- and lowercase letters

➤ Contains at least one number

➤ Contains at least one special character (!@#$%^&*)

➤ Is *not* a dictionary word, proper name, or any tidbit of information that can be deduced about you (like your phone number, birth date, children's names, and so on)

Characteristic-Based Authentication

Characteristic-based authentication depends on the identification of a personal characteristic of the user. Biometrics, such as fingerprint scanners or voice recognition devices, is the best example of characteristic-based authentication. Some advanced systems can even detect users by their behavior, such as typing patterns.

Tokens

Tokens, such as RSA's SecurID or Rainbow's USB token, are hardware devices that store information about the user. The user information can be a certificate or a password. Often, these tokens are combined with passwords to enforce multi-factor authentication.

Tokens are often used as one-time passwords. RSA's SecurID changes the user's password every 60 seconds.

Tickets

Tickets are used in the Kerberos authentication system. Kerberos (created by MIT) is a network authentication protocol that uses secret-key cryptography to provide strong authentication for client/server applications.

Kerberos allows a client to prove its identity to a server (and vice versa) over an insecure network. After a client and server have used Kerberos to prove their identity, they can also encrypt all of their communications to assure privacy (confidentiality) and data integrity.

Kerberos is typically implemented when a user on a network is attempting to access a network service, and the service wants assurance that the user is who he says he is. The user presents a *ticket* that is issued by the Kerberos *authentication server* (AS), similar to presenting a driver's license issued by the DMV. The service then examines the ticket to verify the identity of the user. If everything checks out, the user is accepted and allowed to access the service.

This Kerberos ticket must contain information linking it unequivocally to the user. The ticket must demonstrate that the bearer knows something only its intended user would know, such as a password. Furthermore, there must be safeguards against an attacker stealing the ticket and using it later.

Access Control Methodologies and Implementation

Access control can be centralized or decentralized. Depending on the organization's environment and culture, one methodology usually works best. For closely managed corporations, centralized access control works best. For more distributed organizations, decentralized access control works best.

Centralized Access Controls

In general, *centralized access control* means a company is maintaining userids, rights, and permissions at one central location.

Remote Authentication Dial-In User Service (RADIUS)

Remote Authentication Dial-In User Service (RADIUS) is client/server protocol and software that enables remote access servers to communicate with a central server in order to authenticate dial-in users and authorize access to the requested system or service. RADIUS maintains user profiles in a central database that all remote servers can share. It provides better security, allowing a company to set up a policy that can be applied at a single administered network point.

Terminal Controller Access Control System (TACACS)

Terminal Controller Access Control System (TACACS) is an older authentication protocol common to Unix that allows a remote access server to forward a user's logon password to an authentication server to determine whether access can be allowed to a given system. TACACS is an unencrypted protocol. Today, TACACS has been replace by TACACS+, an entirely new protocol that uses TCP.

Decentralized Access Control

With decentralized access control, userids, rights, and permissions are stored on different computer systems throughout the network. Windows NT uses this approach.

Domains

Domains are the central units of management for a Windows NT network. A domain is a collection of computers and user accounts managed by a central authority. Domains help break up large networks into smaller groups of resources that are easier to manage. Domains are administrative as well as security entities. When a user logs into an account, they log into a domain and have access to resources in that domain—if their accounts have been given permission. Users may have accounts in other domains on the network.

Trust

Users in one domain cannot access resources in another domain unless trust relationships are specifically established by administrators of the domains. A trusting domain enables another domain (the trusted domain) to access its resources. After a trust relationship is established, a list of users from the trusted domain can access resources on the trusting domain.

Methods of Attack

Several methods of attack exist to compromise access control mechanisms. Some of the more common attacks include brute force, denial of service, dictionary, spoofing, and spamming.

Brute Force Attack

In a *brute force* attack, the attacker tries all possible words and character combinations to try and find the correct password, passphrase, or PIN.

Denial of Service (DoS) Attack

A *denial of service (DoS)* attack occurs when a user or organization is deprived of the services of a resource they would normally expect to have. Typically, the loss of service is the inability to access a particular network service, such as email. Although usually intentional and malicious, a denial of service attack can sometimes happen accidentally.

Buffer Overflow Attack

The most common kind of DoS attack is simply to send more traffic to a network address than the programmers who planned its data buffers anticipated. The attacker may be aware that the target system has a weakness that can be exploited, or the attacker may simply try the attack in the hope that it might work. When the system receives a large amount of data that it cannot handle, the system may crash, keeping users from accessing its resources.

SYN Attack

The *Syn* attack is another type of DoS attack. When a session is initiated between the Transmission Control Program (TCP) client and server in a network, a very small buffer space exists to handle the usually rapid "handshaking" exchange of messages that set up the session. The session-establishing packets include a SYN field that identifies the sequence in the message exchange. An attacker can send a number of connection requests very rapidly and then fail to respond to the reply. This attack leaves the first packet in the buffer so that other, legitimate connection requests can't be accommodated. Although the packet in the buffer is dropped after a certain period of time without a reply, the effect of receiving many of these bogus connection requests is to make it difficult for legitimate requests for a session to get established. In general, this kind of attack depends on the operating system providing correct settings or allowing the network administrator to tune the size of the buffer and the timeout period.

Teardrop Attack

A *teardrop* attack (another DoS attack) exploits the way that the Internet Protocol (IP) divides large packets into fragments. The fragment packet identifies an offset to the beginning of the first packet, thus enabling the entire packet to be reassembled by the receiving system. In the teardrop attack, the attacker's IP puts a confusing offset value in the second (or later) fragment. If the receiving operating system does not have a plan for this situation, the system can crash.

Smurf Attack

In a *smurf* attack, the perpetrator sends an IP ping (or "echo my message back to me") request to a receiving site. The ping packet specifies that it be broadcast to a number of hosts within the receiving site's local network. The packet also indicates that the request is from another site, the target site that is to receive the denial of service. (Sending a packet with someone else's return address in it is called spoofing the return address.) The result will be a lot of ping replies flooding back to the innocent, spoofed host. If the flood is great enough, the spoofed host will no longer be able to receive or distinguish real traffic.

Dictionary Attack

In a *dictionary* attack, the attacker uses a predefined list of dictionary words and tries each entry to see if it matches a user's password.

Spoofing Attack

A *spoofing* attack occurs when a user appears to be someone else or manipulates packets so they appear to come from another system or network. Examples include spoofing an internal network IP address and spoofing a source or return email address. Spoofing can be used in many ways to create DoS attacks, such as sending a flood of UDP packets with a spoofed source address.

Man-in-the-Middle Attack

A *man-in-the-middle* attack occurs when the attacker places himself in the flow of traffic and intercepts communications.

Spamming

Spamming attacks occur when a user receives unsolicited email messages.

Sniffers

Sniffers are placed on a network to capture packets and their contents. With sniffers, attackers can easily find userid and password combinations that can be used to gain unauthorized access to a system and its resources.

Crackers

Crackers are programs that break passwords. Crackers can use brute force, dictionary, or another attack specific to the application at hand. L0phtcrack, one of the most famous crackers, quickly breaks passwords for Windows NT/2000.

Monitoring

Monitoring is the process of reviewing system and network activity on a continuous or periodic basis to ensure system availability, integrity, and confidentiality. Intrusion Detection Systems are the most common monitoring tools used today.

Intrusion Detection Systems (IDS)

Intrusion Detection Systems (IDS) monitor networks and computer systems for signs of intrusion or misuse. *Intrusion* refers to unauthorized users attacking resources. *Misuse* refers to authorized users doing something they should not be doing, as documented in a security policy.

Intrusion Detection Systems work in the background, continuously monitoring network traffic and system log files for suspicious activity. When they find something, whether it be an attack, suspicious activity, or just abnormal traffic, alerts are sent to the appropriate individuals, often by email, page, or SNMP trap.

Intrusions can originate from inside or outside your network. The strength of an IDS lies in the fact that it can help detect malicious activity from internal users.

Categories of Intrusion Analysis

Intrusions can be categorized into two main classes: signature and statistical analysis.

Signature Intrusions

Signature intrusions look for specific attacks against known weak points of a system. They can be detected by watching for certain actions being performed on certain objects.

The majority of commercial IDS products examine network traffic and look for well-known patterns of attack. This means that for every recognized attack technique, the product developers code what is usually referred to as a *signature* into the system. The signature can be as simple as a pattern match (such as "/cgi-bin/phf?") that might indicate someone attempting to access the vulnerable CGI script on a Web server, or as complex as a security state transition written as a formal mathematical expression.

To use these signatures, the IDS performs signature analysis on the information it obtains. *Signature analysis* is pattern-matching of system settings and user activities against a database of known attacks. Commercial IDS products include databases that contain hundreds (or thousands) of attack signatures.

Statistical Intrusion Analysis

Statistical intrusion analysis is based on observations of deviations from normal system usage patterns. These deviations are detected by defining a profile of the system being monitored and detecting significant deviations from this profile.

The idea behind this approach is to measure a baseline of statistics such as CPU utilization, disk activity, user logins, file activity, and so on. Then, the system can alert you when there is a deviation from this baseline. The benefit of this approach is that it can detect anomalies without having to understand the underlying cause. For example, let's say you monitor traffic from individual workstations. One day, each system starts sending information to an external site at 3 A.M. This deviation is interesting to note and should be investigated. The transferred information could be key log files, password lists, sensitive documents, and so on.

Anomalous intrusions are detected by observing significant deviations from normal behavior. The classic model for anomaly detection, developed by Denning, contains metrics that are derived from system operation. A *metric* is defined as a random variable x representing a quantitative measure accumulated over a period. These metrics are computed from available system parameters such as average CPU load, number of network connections per minute, and number of processes per user.

An anomaly may be a symptom of a possible intrusion. Given a set of metrics which can define normal system usage, you can assume that exploitation of a system's vulnerabilities involves abnormal use of the system; therefore, security violations could be detected from abnormal patterns of system usage.

Anomalous intrusions are hard to detect. There are no fixed patterns that can be easily identified. Ideally, you would like a system that combines human-like pattern-matching capabilities with the vigilance of a computer program. It would always monitor systems for potential intrusions, but would be able to ignore false intrusions if they resulted from legitimate user actions.

To create the baseline, many intrusion detection systems rely on the analysis of operating system audit trails. This data forms a *footprint* of system usage over time, and is readily available on most systems. From this baseline and continuous observation, the IDS will compute metrics about the system's overall state and decide whether an intrusion is occurring.

An IDS may also perform its own system monitoring. It may keep aggregate statistics that give a system usage profile. These statistics can be derived from a variety of sources such as CPU usage, disk I/O, memory usage, activities by users, and number of attempted logins. These statistics must be continually updated to reflect the current system state. They are correlated with an internal model that allows the IDS to determine if a series of actions constitute a potential intrusion. This model may describe a set of intrusion scenarios or use the profile of a clean system as a baseline.

Practice Questions

Question 1

> Which of the following is a knowledge-based authentication mechanism?
>
> ○ a. Smart card
>
> ○ b. Token
>
> ○ c. Password
>
> ○ d. Biometrics

Answer c is correct. A password is a knowledge-based authentication mechanism. Answers a and b are incorrect because smart cards and tokens are token-based authentication devices. Answer d is incorrect because biometrics is a characteristic-based authentication device.

Question 2

> Which of the following is a centralized access control methodology?
>
> ○ a. RADIUS
>
> ○ b. Lattice
>
> ○ c. DAC
>
> ○ d. MAC

Answer a is correct. RADIUS is a centralized access control methodology. Answer b is incorrect because lattice is an access control model. Answers c and d are incorrect because DAC and MAC are access control techniques.

Question 3

> What is it called when an attacker sends unsolicited communications?
>
> ○ a. Sniffers
>
> ○ b. Crackers
>
> ○ c. Spoofing
>
> ○ d. Spamming

Answer d is correct. Spamming is sending unsolicited communications. Answer a is incorrect because sniffers allow attackers to read network traffic. Answer b is incorrect because crackers allow an attacker to break passwords. Answer c is incorrect because spoofing allows attackers to imitate a different user or system.

Question 4

Which of the following allows attackers to break passwords?

○ a. Sniffers

○ b. Crackers

○ c. Spoofing

○ d. Spamming

Answer b is correct. Crackers allow attackers to break passwords. Answer a is incorrect because sniffers allow attackers to read network traffic. Answer c is incorrect because spoofing allows attackers to imitate a different user or system. Answer d is incorrect because spamming is the process an attacker uses to send unsolicited communications, such as email.

Question 5

Which of the following allows attackers to imitate a different user or system?

○ a. Sniffers

○ b. Crackers

○ c. Spoofing

○ d. Spamming

Answer c is correct. Spoofing allow attackers to imitate a different user or system. Answer a is incorrect because sniffers capture network packets. Answer b is incorrect because crackers allow attackers to break passwords. Answer d is incorrect because spammers send unsolicited email messages.

Question 6

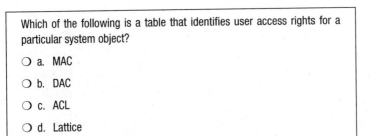

Which of the following is a table that identifies user access rights for a
particular system object?

○ a. MAC

○ b. DAC

○ c. ACL

○ d. Lattice

Answer c is correct. ACL is a table that identifies user access rights for a particular system object. Answers a and b are incorrect because MAC and DAC are access control techniques that use security classification or file owner listings as access rights. Answer d is incorrect because lattices deal with information flow in multiuser environments.

Question 7

Which access control technique allows security officers to specify access
security policies based on an organization's structure?

○ a. MAC

○ b. DAC

○ c. Lattice

○ d. RBAC

Answer d is correct. RBAC allows security officers to specify access security policies based on an organization's structure. Answers a and b are incorrect because MAC and DAC are access control techniques that use security classification or file owner listings as access rights. Answer c is incorrect because lattices deal with information flow in multiuser environments.

Question 8

> Which access control technique allows a resource owner to control other user's access to an object?
>
> ○ a. MAC
>
> ○ b. DAC
>
> ○ c. Lattice
>
> ○ d. RBAC

Answer b is correct. DAC allows a resource owner to control other user's access to an object. Answer a is incorrect because MAC is a nondiscretionary access control technique that uses defined security classifications. Answer c is incorrect because lattices deal with information flow in multiuser environments. Answer d is incorrect because RBAC allows security officers to specify access security policies based on an organization's structure.

Question 9

> Which access control technique is nondiscretionary?
>
> ○ a. MAC
>
> ○ b. DAC
>
> ○ c. Lattice
>
> ○ d. RBAC

Answer a is correct. MAC is nondiscretionary. Answer b is incorrect because DAC is discretionary access control. Answer c is incorrect because lattices deal with information flow in multiuser environments. Answer d is incorrect because RBAC allows security officers to specify access security policies based on an organization's structure.

Question 10

Which technique monitors networks and computer systems for signs of intrusion or misuse?

- ○ a. IDS
- ○ b. MAC
- ○ c. Bell-LaPadula
- ○ d. TACACS

Answer a is correct. IDS monitors networks and computer systems for signs of intrusion or misuse. Answer b is incorrect because MAC is an access control technique. Answer c is incorrect because Bell-LaPadula is an access control model. Answer d is incorrect because TACACS is a centralized access control methodology.

Need to Know More?

 http://kedem.cs.duke.edu/cps296/Lectures/Lecture12.pdf features a great discussion on access control techniques and methodologies.

 www.list.gmu.edu/confrnc/esorics/html_ver/abs_e96rbac.html features an excellent discussion on RBAC.

 www.securityfocus.com is an excellent resource for all security topics.

Telecommunications and Network Security

Terms you'll need to understand:

- ✓ Open Systems Interconnection (OSI) layers and characteristics
- ✓ IPSec
- ✓ Secure Remote Procedure Call (S-RPC)
- ✓ Serial Line Internet Protocol (SLIP)
- ✓ Point-to-Point Protocol (PPP)
- ✓ Virtual Private Network (VPN)
- ✓ Firewalls
- ✓ Challenge-Handshake Authentication Protocol (CHAP)
- ✓ Password Authentication Protocol (PAP)
- ✓ High-Level Data Link Control (HDLC)
- ✓ Synchronous Data Link Control (SDLC)
- ✓ Integrated Services Digital Network (ISDN)
- ✓ Tunneling
- ✓ Network Address Translation (NAT)
- ✓ Transparency
- ✓ Hash
- ✓ Address Resolution Protocol (ARP)

Techniques you'll need to master:

- ✓ Understanding the seven layers of the OSI model
- ✓ Understanding communications and network security
- ✓ Understanding Internet/intranet/extranet devices, services, and protocols
- ✓ Understanding email security techniques
- ✓ Understanding network attacks and countermeasures

The Telecommunications and Network Security domain includes the structures, transmission methods, transport formats, and security measures used to provide integrity, availability, authentication, and confidentiality for transmissions over private and public networks.

For the CISSP exam, you need to fully understand network security relating to voice and data communications, as well as the management techniques to help prevent, detect, and recover from security incidents.

Open Systems Interconnection (OSI) Layers and Characteristics

The Open Systems Interconnection (OSI) model has seven layers that help define network operations. From bottom to top, the layers are: Physical, Data Link, Network, Transport, Session, Presentation, and Application.

Physical

The Physical layer moves the final completed frame from the computer's memory location to the network transmission medium. It is not involved with any further packaging operations on the packet such as headers and control fields. Physical layer protocols only deal with the mechanical, electrical, functional, and procedural aspects of this process.

Data Link

The Data Link layer is the last layer in the protocol suite that treats the data as a logical data string held in the computer's main memory and processed by the communication software. Final sequence numbering, addressing data, and the primary error control data must be provided before data can be passed to the Physical layer for actual transmission. The trailer is added at this point to identify the end of the transmission frame.

Network

The packet (handled by the upper layers) has completed the logical packaging of the application data. The remaining packaging done by the Network and lower layers involves the addressing and final preparation of the transmission block. The Network layer's packaging processes are constrained by the physical transmission protocols that will be used. The original message, which may already have been partitioned at higher levels, will often be broken into even smaller packets.

Transport

The Transport layer provides the interface between the lower level physical networking controls and the higher levels that are concerned with logical application data handling. If the message is long, it may be partitioned into a series of smaller message units.

Session

The Session layer provides control over the orderly exchange of data during the period when the sender and receiver are communicating. Login passwords and the exchange of user IDs may be handled at the Session layer. Accounting operations, as well as aspects of flow control, may also be determined at this layer.

Presentation

The Presentation layer provides control over the way the data will be encoded to allow proper handling when it is presented to the receiver's application.

Application

The Application layer is the layer that the end user sees and is familiar with. The original user data is the meaningful content that will be communicated to the receiver. It is stored in main memory, where each layer of the protocol suite will contribute to its packaging and hand it to the next lower level.

Physical Media Characteristics

Each physical medium, such as *unshielded twisted pair (UTP)* or *coaxial cable*, has its own unique characteristics and capabilities. Understanding these capabilities helps administrators identify and implement the best network cabling for their environment.

Unshielded Twisted Pair (UTP)

The quality of UTP can vary from telephone-grade wire to extremely high-speed cable. The cable has four pairs of wires inside the jacket. Each pair is twisted with a different number of twists per inch (but the same number of twists for all pairs in a jacket) to help eliminate interference from adjacent pairs and other electrical devices. The Electronic Industry Association/Telecommunication Industry Association (EIA/TIA) has established standards of UTP and rated five categories of wire. Table 3.1 shows the types of UTP and their uses.

One difference between the various categories of UTP is the tightness of the twisting of the copper pairs. The tighter the twisting, the higher the supported transmission rate and the greater the cost per foot.

Table 3.1 Categories of UTP.	
Type	**Use**
Category 1	Voice only (telephone wire)
Category 2	Data to 4 Mbps (LocalTalk)
Category 3	Data to 10 Mbps (Ethernet)
Category 4	Data to 20 Mbps (16 Mbps Token Ring)
Category 5	Data to 100 Mbps (fast Ethernet)

If you are designing a 10 Mbps Ethernet network and are considering the cost savings of buying Category 3 wire instead of Category 5, remember that the Category 5 cable will provide more room to grow as transmission technologies improve. Both Category 3 and Category 5 UTP have a maximum segment length of 100 meters. 10BaseT refers to the specifications for UTP cable (Category 3, 4, or 5) carrying Ethernet signals.

The standard connector for UTP cabling is an *RJ-45 connector*, a plastic connector that looks like a large telephone-style connector. A slot allows the RJ-45 to be inserted only one way. RJ stands for Registered Jack, implying that the connector follows a standard borrowed from the telephone industry. This standard designates which wire goes with each pin inside the connector.

Shielded Twisted Pair (STP)

A disadvantage of UTP is that it may be susceptible to radio and electrical frequency interference. *Shielded twisted pair (STP)* is suitable for environments with electrical interference; however, the extra shielding can make the cables quite bulky. STP is often used on networks using Token Ring topology.

Coaxial Cable

Coaxial cabling has a single copper conductor at its center. A plastic layer provides insulation between the center conductor and a braided metal shield. The metal shield helps to block any outside interference from fluorescent lights, motors, and other computers.

Although coaxial cabling is difficult to install, it is highly resistant to signal interference. In addition, it can support greater cable lengths between network devices than twisted pair cable. The two types of coaxial cabling are thick coaxial and thin coaxial.

Thin coaxial cable is also called *thinnet*. 10Base2 refers to the specifications for thin coaxial cable carrying Ethernet signals. The 2 refers to the approximate maximum segment length of 200 meters. In fact, the maximum segment length is 185 meters. Thin coaxial cable is popular in school networks, especially linear bus networks.

Thick coaxial cable is also called *thicknet*. 10Base5 refers to the specifications for thick coaxial cable carrying Ethernet signals. The 5 refers to the maximum segment length of 500 meters. Thick coaxial cable has an extra protective plastic cover that helps keep moisture away from the center conductor. This extra protection makes thick coaxial a great choice when running longer lengths in a linear bus network. One disadvantage of thick coaxial is that it does not bend easily and is therefore difficult to install.

The most common type of connector used with coaxial cables is the *Bayone-Neill-Concelman (BNC)* connector. Different types of adapters are available for BNC connectors, including a T-connector, barrel connector, and terminator.

Fiber Optic Cable

Fiber optic cabling consists of a center glass core surrounded by several layers of protective materials. This cable transmits light rather than electronic signals, eliminating the problem of electrical interference, and making it ideal for environments with large amounts of electrical interference. Fiber optic cable is also the standard for connecting networks between buildings becasue of its immunity to the effects of moisture and lighting.

Fiber optic cable has the ability to transmit signals over much longer distances than coaxial or twisted pair. It also has the capability to carry information at vastly greater speeds. This capacity broadens communication possibilities to include services such as video conferencing. The cost of fiber optic cabling is comparable to copper cabling; however, fiber optic cabling is more difficult to install and modify. 10BaseF refers to the specifications for fiber optic cable carrying Ethernet signals.

Fiber optic cables have:

➤ Outer insulating jackets made of Teflon or PVC

➤ Kevlar fiber, which helps to strengthen the cable and prevent breakage

➤ Plastic coatings, used to cushion the fiber center

➤ Centers (cores) made of glass or plastic fibers

The most common connector used with fiber optic cable is an *ST connector*. It is barrel-shaped, similar to a BNC connector. A newer connector, the SC, is becoming more popular. Table 3.2 summarizes cable types and their maximum lengths.

Table 3.2 Cable type summary.		
Specification	**Cable Type**	**Maximum Length**
10BaseT	UTP	100 meters
10Base2	Thin coaxial	185 meters
10Base5	Thick coaxial	500 meters
10BaseF	Fiber optic	2000 meters

Network Topologies

Network topologies define the design of a network. The topology of a network greatly influences which security processes, procedures, and technologies are implemented. For example, networks, with their shared medium, need to be protected from packet sniffers.

Star Topology

A *star topology* is designed with each node (file server, workstations, and peripherals) connected directly to a central network hub or concentrator.

Data on a star network passes through the hub or concentrator before continuing to its destination. The hub or concentrator manages and controls all functions of the network. It also acts as a repeater for the data flow. This configuration is common with twisted pair cable; however, it can also be used with coaxial cable or fiber optic cable.

The protocols used with star configurations are usually Ethernet. Token Ring uses a similar topology, called the *star-wired ring*, as shown in Figure 3.1.

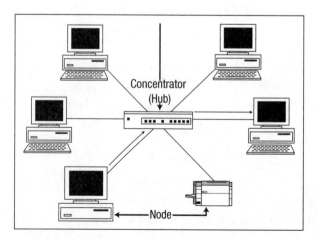

Figure 3.1 The star topology uses a central hub to manage traffic.

The advantages of a star topology are:

➤ Easy to install and wire

➤ No disruptions to the network when connecting or removing devices

➤ Easy to detect faults and to remove parts

The disadvantages of a star topology are:

➤ Requires more cable length than a linear topology

➤ Nodes are disabled if the hub or concentrator fails

➤ More expensive than linear bus topologies because of the cost of the concentrators

Bus Topology

A linear *bus topology* consists of a main run of cable with a terminator at each end. All nodes (file server, workstations, and peripherals) are connected to the linear cable. Ethernet networks use a linear bus topology, as shown in Figure 3.2.

The bus topology consists of one single communications line.

The advantages of a linear bus topology are:

➤ Easy to connect a computer or peripheral to a linear bus

➤ Requires less cable length than a star topology

The disadvantages of a linear bus topology are:

➤ Entire network shuts down if there is a break in the main cable

➤ Terminators are required at both ends of the backbone cable

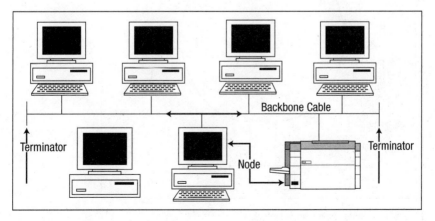

Figure 3.2 Use of a linear bus topology.

➤ Difficult to identify the problem if the entire network shuts down

➤ Not meant to be used as a standalone solution in a large building

Ring Topology

The *ring topology* is a physical closed loop consisting of point-to-point links. In Figure 3.3, you can see how each node on the ring acts as a repeater. It receives a transmission from the previous node and amplifies it before passing it on.

The ring topology consists of a closed communications loop.

The advantages of ring topology are:

➤ Very little signal degradation occurs because each repeater duplicates the data signals.

The disadvantages of ring topology are:

➤ A break in the ring can disable the entire network. Many ring designs incorporate extra cabling that can be switched in if a primary cable fails.

➤ Because each node must have the capability of functioning as a repeater, the networking devices tend to be more expensive.

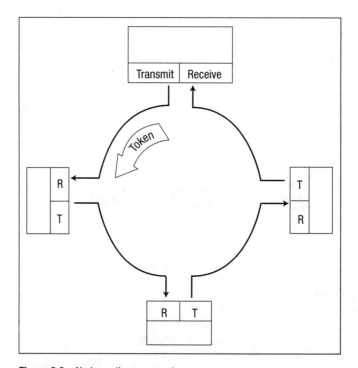

Figure 3.3   Nodes acting as repeaters.

IPSec

IPSec provides interoperable, high-quality, cryptographically based security. The set of security services offered includes connectionless integrity, data origin authentication, replay protection, confidentiality (encryption), and limited traffic flow confidentiality. These services are offered at the Network layer and provide security in three cases:

➤ Host to host

➤ Host to subnet

➤ Subnet to subnet

Information travels unencrypted over the internal network but is encrypted at the router before traveling on to the external network. IPSec allows the user (or system administrator) to control the granularity at which a security service is offered.

These objectives are met through the use of two traffic security protocols, the *Authentication Header (AH)* and the *Encapsulating Security Payload (ESP)*, and through the use of cryptographic key management procedures and protocols.

Authentication Header (AH)

The AH provides connectionless integrity, data origin authentication, and an optional anti-replay service.

Encapsulating Security Payload (ESP)

The ESP protocol provides confidentiality (encryption) and limited traffic flow confidentiality. It also provides connectionless integrity, data origin authentication, and an anti-replay service. Both AH and ESP are vehicles for access control, based on the distribution of cryptographic keys and the management of traffic flows relative to these security protocols.

Key Exchange

The *Internet Key Management Protocol* is an Application layer protocol that supports public key-based techniques and support of Key Distribution Centers such as those used by Kerberos.

Modes

IPsec provides two modes for ensuring confidentiality: tunnel mode and transport mode. Each method has its pros and cons, discussed next.

Tunnel Mode ESP

In *tunnel mode*, the original IP datagram (including header) is encrypted. The entire ESP frame is placed within a new datagram that has an unencrypted IP header. All additional unencrypted information (such as routing headers) are placed between the IP header and the encapsulated security payload. The receiver strips off the cleartext IP header and decrypts the ESP.

This mode allows unencrypted traffic on the internal network and encryption performed at the router.

Transport Mode ESP

In *transport mode*, only the payload is encrypted. The IP header and the IP options are unencrypted and are used for routing the packet. The receiver decrypts the ESP and uses the unencrypted header as an IP header if necessary.

The transport mode ESP provides approximately the same capabilities as the SSL protocol, except that it provides its services to all packets, not only to defined port addresses like SSL (port 443).

Transmission Control Protocol/Internet Protocol (TCP/IP)

Transmission Control Protocol/Internet Protocol (TCP/IP) is a two-layered program. The higher layer, TCP, manages the assembling of a message or file into smaller packets that are transmitted over the Internet and received by a TCP layer that reassembles the packets into the original message. The lower layer, IP, handles the address part of each packet so that it gets to the right destination.

TCP/IP communication is primarily point-to-point, meaning each communication is from one point (or host computer) in the network to another point or host computer. TCP/IP and the higher-level applications that use it are collectively said to be *connectionless* because each client request is considered a new request unrelated to any previous one. Being connectionless frees network paths so that everyone can use them continuously. (Note that the TCP layer itself is not connectionless as far as any one message is concerned. Its connection remains in place until all packets in a message have been received.)

IP

IP is a connectionless datagram delivery protocol that performs addressing, routing, and control functions for transmitting and receiving datagrams over a network. As a connectionless protocol, IP does not require a predefined path associated with a logical network connection. As packets are received by the router,

IP addressing information is used to determine the best "next hop" a packet should take en route to its final destination. As a result, IP does not control data path usage. If a network device or line becomes unavailable, IP provides the mechanism needed to route datagrams around the affected area.

IP datagrams begin with a packet header. The header identifies the version of IP used to create the datagram, the header length, the type of service required for the datagram, the length of the datagram, the datagram's identification number, fragmentation control information, the maximum number of hops the datagram can be transported over the network, the protocol format of the data field, the source and destination addresses, and potential IP options.

TCP

TCP provides a reliable, connection-oriented, Transport layer link between two hosts. Using a two-way handshaking scheme, TCP provides the mechanism for establishing, maintaining, and terminating logical connections between hosts using IP as its transport protocol. Additionally, TCP provides protocol ports to distinguish multiple programs executing on a single device by including the destination and source port number with each message. TCP performs functions such as reliable transmission of byte streams, data flow definitions, data acknowledgments, lost or corrupt data retransmissions, and multiplexing multiple connections through a single network connection. Furthermore, TCP is responsible for encapsulating information into a datagram structure.

Local Area Network (LAN)

A *local area network (LAN)* is a network of interconnected workstations sharing the resources of a single processor or server within a relatively small geographic area, for example, a small office building. Usually, the server has applications and data storage that are shared in common by multiple workstation users. A LAN may serve as few as four or five users or as many as several thousand.

Wide Area Network (WAN)

A *wide area network (WAN)* is a geographically dispersed telecommunications network (the term distinguishes a broader telecommunication structure from a LAN). A WAN may be privately owned or rented, but the term usually connotes the inclusion of public (shared user) networks. An intermediate form of network, in terms of geography, is a *metropolitan area network (MAN)*.

Virtual Private Network (VPN)

A *virtual private network (VPN)* is a private data network that uses the public telecommunication infrastructure, maintaining privacy through the use of a tunneling protocol and security procedures. A VPN can be contrasted with a system of owned or leased lines that can only be used by one company. The VPN gives a company the same capabilities, at a much lower cost, by using the shared public infrastructure rather than a private one. Phone companies have provided secure shared resources for voice messages; VPN makes it possible to have the same secure sharing of public resources for data. Companies today are looking at using private VPNs for both extranets and wide-area intranets.

Using a VPN involves encrypting data before sending it through the public network, and decrypting it at the receiving end. An additional level of security involves encrypting not only the data, but also the originating and receiving network addresses. IPSec is the standard VPN protocol.

Secure Remote Procedure Call (RPC)

Remote Procedure Call (RPC) is a protocol that one program can use to request a service from a program located in another computer in a network without having to understand network details. (A procedure call is also sometimes known as a *function call* or a *subroutine call*.) RPC uses the client/server model. The requesting program is a client and the service-providing program is the server. Like a regular or local procedure call, an RPC is a synchronous operation requiring the requesting program to be suspended until the results of the remote procedure are returned. However, using lightweight processes or threads that share the same address space allows multiple RPCs to be performed concurrently.

When program statements that use RPC are compiled into an executable program, a stub is included in the compiled code that acts as the representative of the remote procedure code. When the program is run and the procedure call is issued, the stub receives the request and forwards it to a client runtime program in the local computer. The client runtime program knows how to address the remote computer and server application and sends the message across the network that requests the remote procedure. Similarly, the server includes a runtime program and stub that interface with the remote procedure itself. Results are returned the same way.

There are several RPC models and implementations. A popular model and implementation is the Open Software Foundation's Distributed Computing Environment (DCE). The IEEE defines RPC in its ISO Remote Procedure Call Specification, ISO/IEC CD 11578 N6561, ISO/IEC, November 1991.

RPC spans the Transport layer and the Application layer in the OSI model of network communication. RPC makes it easier to develop an application that includes multiple programs distributed in a network.

Remote Authentication Dial-In User System (RADIUS)

Remote Authentication Dial-In User Service (RADIUS) is a client/server protocol and software that enables remote access servers to communicate with a central server to authenticate dial-in users and authorize their access to the requested system or service. RADIUS maintains user profiles in a central database that all remote servers can share. It provides better security, allowing a company to set up a policy that can be applied at a single administered network point. Having a central service also means that it's easier to track usage for billing and network statistics. RADIUS is a de facto industry standard and is a proposed IETF standard.

Network Monitors and Packet Sniffers

Network monitors and *packet sniffers* help you monitor network traffic for problems or security incidents. These tools can help you detect rogue servers running on your network as well as examine the information passing through your network in plaintext.

Network Monitor

A *network monitor* is an intelligent packet sniffer. The monitor analyzes packets in an attempt to identify malicious activities. If the monitor detects such activity, it can send alarms. Intrusion detection systems are network monitors.

Packet Sniffer

A *sniffer* is nothing more than hardware or software that hears (and does not ignore) all packets sent across the wire. To use your machine as a sniffer, you need either special software (a promiscuous driver for the Ethernet card) or a version of networking software that allows promiscuous mode. A sniffer must be located within the same network block as the network it is intended to sniff.

Firewalls

A *firewall* is a collection of components placed between two networks. There are three main techniques used in firewalls today—packet filters, circuit gateways, and application proxies.

Packet Filtering

With *packet filtering*, decisions are based on examination of TCP or UDP packet information. One important limitation of packet filters is that they cannot tell good users from bad ones; they can only tell good packets from bad packets. Packet filtering works best in networks that have very black-and-white security policies.

Circuit Gateways

Circuit gateways are used when the actual information passed by the network application is not important, but the user of the application is. A circuit gateway is best thought of as a tunnel, built through the firewall that links selected systems on one side to selected systems on the other. Circuit gateways are not very different from packet filters, but are commonly joined to an out-of-band authentication scheme that adds some additional information.

Application Proxies

Application proxies are used when the actual content or data stream in an application is important and needs to be controlled. For example, an application proxy could be used to limit FTP users so that they could only get files from the Internet but never push them to the Internet. The problem with application proxies is that they are specific to a particular application, which makes them difficult to maintain. Application proxies for user programs typically also include authentication information in the application data stream. Many firewalls that include applications proxies also use circuit gateways for new applications, or for applications that aren't considered a security risk.

Firewall Architectures

Fitting a firewall in a network architecture can be a complex process. Some of the more common architectures include using screening routers, stateful filters, or application gateways.

Router Architecture

Router architecture uses packet filtering. A packet-filtering router can stop connections from flowing across the firewall boundary, and can do so effectively and inexpensively. The filtering rules define which packets are passed and which are dropped. For security policies that do not require examining data at higher layers (such as the Application layer), the packet-filtering router provides security simply by prohibiting connection. This architecture runs on Layer 3, the Network layer.

A packet filter cannot be used safely for certain kinds of traffic, such as X Window System connections that appear at unpredictable high-numbered (unprivileged) ports. Packet filters also cannot support certain types of security policies, such as per-user or time-of-day restrictions.

The security in a router that is acting as a packet filter is based on a *filter rule set*. These filter rules describe TCP and UDP packets in terms of source and destination addresses and application port numbers. To protect services inside the firewall, a network manager establishes rules that permit or deny access to packets flowing through the firewall to each service.

One major disadvantage of using a router as a firewall is that attacks on the network can go undetected because routers have little or no logging or printing capability.

Stateful Packet Filters Architecture

Stateful packet filters provide more powerful security measures than the router architecture because a router has no state information. This means that it examines each packet individually without any knowledge of other packets that have existed before. For example, it is not possible to permit DNS responses (which use connectionless UDP) to pass through the firewall only in response to DNS queries. State information comes from the protocol model of a finite state machine. Stateful packet filters use this information to intelligently analyze packets. For example, a user sends out an FTP request. The stateful packet filter will analyze incoming FTP packets to see if they relate to the previous outbound request.

Application Gateways Architecture

Application gateway firewalls are expensive, difficult to install, and complex, but they offer much more security than the previously discussed architectures. Application gateway firewalls take an active part in each connection between the Internet and the corporate network. The firewall maintains state information and builds either transport-level or application-level gateways between the internal and external networks. This architecture runs on Layer 4 (the Transport layer) or higher.

Firewalls of this type enable authentication information for users wishing to use Internet services. These firewalls are considered intrusive because they require either application-level changes on internal users' systems or procedural changes (such as logging onto the firewall before any external access is allowed).

Application gateway firewalls cannot protect all Internet services because each application has to have special code written to support the firewall. New services might not have such support developed.

One advantage of application gateway firewalls is that internal network information (i.e., IP addresses) can be completely hidden from the outside world.

Repeated/Switched/Routed Networks

Repeaters, switches, and routers are the backbone of any network. Without them, we would not be able to communicate with each other. Understanding the role and functionality of these devices in a network is crucial to seeing the important role they play in a security infrastructure.

Repeated Networks

Repeaters are devices used to boost the strength of a signal. They are spaced at intervals throughout the length of a communication circuit.

Switched Networks

A *switch* connects more than two LAN segments that use the same data link and network protocol. Switches operate at the Data Link layer. They may connect the same or different types of cable.

Packet-switched networks are those in which relatively small units of data, called packets, are routed through a network based on the destination address contained within each packet. Breaking communication down into packets allows the same data path to be shared among many users in the network. This type of communication between sender and receiver is known as *connectionless* (rather than dedicated). Most traffic over the Internet uses packet switching, and the Internet is basically a connectionless network.

Contrasted with a packet-switched network is a *circuit-switched network*, a type of network such as the regular voice telephone network in which the communication circuit (path) for the call is set up and dedicated to the participants in that call. For the duration of the connection, all resources on that circuit are unavailable for other users. Voice calls using the Internet's packet-switched system are possible. Each end of the conversation is broken down into packets that are reassembled at the other end.

Another common type of digital network that uses packet switching is the *X.25 network*, a widely installed commercial WAN protocol. Internet protocol packets can be carried on an X.25 network. The X.25 network can also support virtual circuits in which a logical connection is established for two parties on a dedicated basis for some duration. A *permanent virtual circuit (PVC)* reserves the path on an ongoing basis and is an alternative for corporations to a system of leased lines. A PVC is a dedicated logical connection, but the actual physical resources can be shared among multiple logical connections or users.

Routed Networks

In general, routers connect two or more LANs that use the same or different (usually different) data link protocols, but the same network protocol. They may connect the same or different types of cable. Routers operate at the Network layer and forward only those messages that need to go to other networks.

Transport Layer Security (TLS) and Secure Sockets Layer (SSL)

Secure Sockets Layer (SSL) and *Transport Layer Security (TLS)* provide Transport layer security. SSL is a Session layer protocol that works with reliable transport protocols only (such as TCP). SSL has a specific port number assigned that is dependent on the application protocol where SSL is located in the next lower layer. Only three ports have been assigned: HTTP, NNTP, and SMTP.

In contrast to IPsec, SSL can only provide host-to-host, or typically host-to-server, confidentiality and authenticity.

SSL has built-in key exchange capabilities. It supports server key-exchange messages as well as client key-exchange messages. It provides a secure communication where the server does not need knowledge a priori of the client's public key. The client can have a limited set of server public keys that are trusted by the client (approved by an authority). After the request to make a secure connection, the client encrypts its public key with the use of the server's public key. The server decrypts the client's public key by using his own private key. From this point, the secure connection can be established by using both keys.

Secure Electronic Transactions (SET)

Secure Electronic Transaction (SET) is a system for ensuring the security of financial transactions on the Internet. It was supported initially by Mastercard, Visa, Microsoft, Netscape, and others. With SET, a user is given an electronic wallet (digital certificate) and a transaction is conducted and verified using a combination of digital certificates and digital signatures among the purchaser, a merchant, and the purchaser's bank in a way that ensures privacy and confidentiality. SET is not often used today.

Here's how SET works. Assume that a customer has a SET-enabled browser (such as Netscape or Microsoft's Internet Explorer) and that the transaction provider (bank, store, or so on) has a SET-enabled server.

1. The customer opens a Mastercard or Visa bank account. Any issuer of a credit card is some kind of bank.

2. The customer receives a digital certificate. This electronic file functions as a credit card for online purchases or other transactions. It includes a public key with an expiration date. It has been digitally signed by the bank to ensure its validity.

3. Third-party merchants also receive certificates from the bank. These certificates include the merchant's public key and the bank's public key.

4. The customer places an order over a Web page, by phone, or by some other means.

5. The customer's browser receives the merchant's certificate and confirms that the merchant is valid.

6. The browser sends the order information. This message is encrypted with the merchant's public key, the payment information that is encrypted with the bank's public key (which can't be read by the merchant), and information that ensures the payment can only be used with this particular order.

7. The merchant verifies the customer by checking the digital signature on the customer's certificate. This may be done by referring the certificate to the bank or to a third-party verifier.

8. The merchant sends the order message along to the bank. This message includes the bank's public key, the customer's payment information (which the merchant can't decode), and the merchant's certificate.

9. The bank verifies the merchant and the message. The bank uses the digital signature on the certificate with the message and verifies the payment part of the message.

10. The bank digitally signs and sends authorization to the merchant, who can then fill the order.

Privacy-Enhanced Mail (PEM)

Privacy-Enhanced Mail (PEM) is an Internet standard that provides for secure exchange of electronic mail. PEM employs a range of cryptographic techniques for confidentiality, sender authentication, and message integrity. The message integrity aspects allow the user to ensure that a message hasn't been modified during transport from the sender. The sender authentication allows a user to verify that the PEM message that he has received is truly from the person who claims to have sent it. The confidentiality feature allows a message to be kept secret from people to whom the message was not addressed.

Originator Authentication

In RFC 1422 [2], an authentication scheme for PEM is defined. It uses a hierarchical authentication framework-compatible X.509, "The Directory—Authentication Framework." Central to the PEM authentication framework are certificates, which contain items such as the digital signature algorithm used to sign the certificate, the subject's Distinguished Name (DN), the certificate issuer's DN, a validity period indicating the starting and ending dates the certificate should be considered valid, and the subject's public key along with the accompanying algorithm. This hierarchical authentication framework has four entities.

The first entity is a central authority called the *Internet Policy Registration Authority (IPRA)*, acting as the root of the hierarchy and forming the foundation of all certificate validation in the hierarchy. It is responsible for certifying and reviewing the policies of the entities in the next lower level. These entities are called *Policy Certification Authorities (PCAs)*, and are responsible for certifying the next lower level of authorities. The next lower level consists of *Certification Authorities (CAs)*, responsible for certifying both subordinate CAs and also individual users. Individual users are on the lowest level of the hierarchy.

This hierarchical approach to certification allows one to be reasonably sure that certificates coming from users, assuming one trusts the policies of the intervening CAs and PCAs and the policy of the IPRA itself, actually came from the person whose name is associated with it. This hierarchy also makes it more difficult to spoof a certificate because it is likely that few people will trust or use certificates that have untraceable certification trails. In order to generate a false certificate, one would need to subvert at least a CA and possibly the certifying PCA and the IPRA itself.

Message Confidentiality

Message confidentiality in PEM is implemented with standardized cryptographic algorithms. RFC 1423 [3] defines both symmetric and asymmetric encryption algorithms to be used in PEM key management and message encryption.

Data Integrity

In order to provide data integrity, PEM implements a concept known as a *message digest*. Essentially both algorithms take arbitrary-length "messages," which could be any message or file, and produce a 16-octet value. This value is then encrypted with whichever key management technique is currently in use. When the message is received, the recipient can also run the message digest on the message, and if it hasn't been modified in transit, the recipient can be reasonably assured that the message hasn't been tampered with maliciously. Message digests are used because they're relatively fast to compute, and finding two different meaningful messages that produce the same value is nearly impossible.

Challenge-Handshake Authentication Protocol (CHAP)

Challenge-Handshake Authentication Protocol (CHAP) is a more secure procedure for connecting to a system than the *Password Authentication Protocol (PAP)*. Here's how CHAP works:

1. After the link is made, the server sends a challenge message to the connection requestor. The requestor responds with a value obtained by using a one-way hash function.

2. The server checks the response by comparing it with its own calculation of the expected hash value.

3. If the values match, the authentication is acknowledged; otherwise, the connection is usually terminated.

At any time, the server can request that the connected party to send a new challenge message. Because CHAP identifiers are changed frequently and because authentication can be requested by the server at any time, CHAP provides more security than PAP. RFC1334 defines both CHAP and PAP.

Password Authentication Protocol (PAP)

Password Authentication Procedure (PAP) is a procedure used by PPP servers to validate a connection request. PAP works as follows:

1. After the link is established, the requestor sends a password and an ID to the server.

2. The server either validates the request and sends back an acknowledgement, terminates the connection, or offers the requestor another chance.

Passwords are sent without security and the originator can make repeated attempts to gain access. For these reasons, a server that supports CHAP will offer to use that protocol before using PAP. PAP protocol details can be found in RFC 1334.

Serial Line Internet Protocol (SLIP)

Serial Line Internet Protocol (SLIP) is a TCP/IP protocol used for communication between two machines that are configured for communication with each other. For example, your Internet service provider may provide you with a SLIP connection so that the provider's server can respond to your requests, pass them on to the Internet, and forward your requested Internet responses back to you. Your dial-up connection to the server is typically on a slower serial line rather than on the parallel or multiplex lines (such as a T1 line) of the network you are hooking up to.

Point-to-Point Protocol (PPP)

Point-to-Point Protocol (PPP) is a protocol for communication between two computers using a serial interface, typically a personal computer connected by phone line to a server. For example, your Internet server provider may provide you with a PPP connection so that the provider's server can respond to your requests, pass them on to the Internet, and forward your requested Internet responses back to you. PPP uses IP and is designed to handle others. It is sometimes considered a member of the TCP/IP suite of protocols. Relative to the OSI reference model, PPP provides Layer 2 (Data Link layer) service. Essentially, it packages your computer's TCP/IP packets and forwards them to the server where they can actually be put on the Internet.

PPP is a full-duplex protocol that can be used on various physical media, including twisted pair, fiber optic lines, or satellite transmission. It uses a variation of *High Level Data Link Control (HDLC)* for packet encapsulation.

PPP is usually preferred over the earlier de facto standard SLIP because it can handle synchronous as well as asynchronous communication. PPP can share a line with other users, and it has error detection that SLIP lacks. When a choice is possible, PPP is preferred.

High-Level Data Link Control (HDLC)

HDLC is a group of protocols or rules for transmitting data between network points (sometimes called *nodes*). In HDLC, data is organized into a unit (called a frame) and sent across a network to a destination that verifies its successful arrival. The HDLC protocol also manages the flow or pacing at which data is sent. HDLC is one of the most commonly used protocols in Layer 2 of the OSI model. Layer 1, as previously mentioned, is the detailed Physical level that involves actually generating and receiving the electronic signals. Layer 3 is the higher level that has knowledge about the network, including access to router tables that indicate where to forward or send data. On sending, Layer 3 creates a frame that usually contains source and destination network addresses. HDLC (Layer 2) encapsulates the Layer 3 frame, adding data link control information to a new, larger frame.

Now an ISO standard, HDLC is based on IBM's *Synchronous Data Link Control (SDLC)* protocol, which is widely used by IBM's large customer base in mainframe computer environments. In HDLC, the protocol that is essentially SDLC is known as *Normal Response Mode (NRM)*. In NRM, a primary station (usually at the mainframe computer) sends data to secondary stations that may be local or may be at remote locations on dedicated leased lines in what is called a *multidrop* or *multipoint* network. (This is not the network we usually think of; it's a nonpublic closed network. In this arrangement, communication is usually half-duplex.)

Variations of HDLC are also used for the public networks that use the X.25 communications protocol and for frame relay, a protocol used in both LANs and WANs, public and private.

In the X.25 version of HDLC, the data frame contains a packet. (An X.25 network is one in which packets of data are moved to their destination along routes determined by network conditions as perceived by routers and reassembled in the right order at the ultimate destination.) The X.25 version of HDLC uses peer-to-peer communication with both ends able to initiate communication on duplex links. This mode of HDLC is known as *Link Access Procedure Balanced (LAPB)*.

Table 3.3 summarizes the HDLC variations and who uses them.

Frame Relay

Frame relay is a telecommunication service designed for cost-efficient data transmission for intermittent traffic between LANs and between endpoints in a WAN. Frame relay puts data in a variable-sized unit called a frame and leaves any necessary error correction (retransmission of data) up to the endpoints, which speeds up overall data transmission. For most services, the network provides a PVC, which means that the customer sees a continuous, dedicated connection without having to pay for a fulltime leased line, while the service provider figures out the route each frame travels to its destination and can charge based on usage. An enterprise can select a level of service quality—prioritizing some frames and making others less important. Frame relay is offered by a number of service providers. Frame relay is provided on fractional or full T1 carriers. Frame relay complements and provides a midrange service between ISDN (which offers bandwidth at 128 Kbps), and *Asynchronous Transfer Mode (ATM)*, which operates in somewhat similar fashion to frame relay but at speeds from 155.520 Mbps or 622.080 Mbps.

Frame relay is based on the older X.25 packet-switching technology which was designed for transmitting analog data, such as voice conversations. Unlike X.25,

Table 3.3 HDLC variations.	
HDLC Subset	**Uses**
NRM (Normal Response Mode)	Multipoint networks that typicaly use SDLC
LAP (Link Access Procedure)	Early X.25 implementations
LAPB (Link Access Procedure, Balanced)	Current X.25 implementations
LAPD (Link Access Procedure for the ISDN D) Channel	ISDN D channel and frame relay
LAPM (Link Access Procedure for Modems)	Error-correcting modems (specified as part of V.42)

which was designed for analog signals, frame relay is a fast-packet technology, which means that the protocol does not attempt to correct errors. When an error is detected in a frame, it is simply dropped (thrown away). The end points are responsible for detecting and retransmitting dropped frames. (However, the incidence of error in digital networks is extraordinarily small relative to analog networks.)

Frame relay is often used to connect LANs with major backbones, and is also used on public WANs and in private network environments with leased lines over T1 lines. It requires a dedicated connection during the transmission period. It's not ideally suited for voice or video transmission, which requires a steady flow of transmissions. However, under certain circumstances, it is used for voice and video transmission.

Frame relay moves packets at the Data Link layer of the OSI model rather than at the Network layer. A frame can incorporate packets from different protocols such as Ethernet and X.25. It is variable in size and can be as large as a thousand bytes or more.

Synchronous Data Link Control (SDLC)

Synchronous Data Link Control (SDLC) is a transmission protocol developed by IBM in the 1970s as a replacement for its binary synchronous (BSC) protocol. SDLC is equivalent to Layer 2 of the OSI model of network communication. This level of protocol makes sure that data units arrive successfully from one network point to the next and flow at the right pace.

SDLC uses the primary station–secondary station model of communication. Typically, in mainframe networks, the host mainframe is the primary station and workstations and other devices are secondary stations. Each secondary station has its own address. Typically, multiple devices or secondary stations are attached to a common line in what is known as a *multipoint* or *multidrop* arrangement. SDLC can also be used for point-to-point communication. SDLC is primarily for remote communication on corporate wide-area networks.

SDLC was the basis for the International Organization for Standardization standard data link protocol, HDLC. SDLC essentially became one of several variations of HDLC, the NRM. Although SDLC (and normal response mode) are efficient protocols for closed private networks with dedicated lines, other modes of HDLC serve X.25 and frame relay protocols that manage packets on shared-line switched networks (like those used by the Internet).

SDLC became part of IBM's Systems Network Architecture and the more comprehensive Systems Application Architecture, and its more recent Open Blueprint. SDLC is still commonly encountered, and is probably the most prevalent data link protocol in today's mainframe environment.

Integrated Services Digital Network

Integrated Services Digital Network (ISDN) is a set of CCITT/ITU (Consultative Committee for International Telegraph/International Telecommunications Union) standards for digital transmission over ordinary telephone copper wire as well as over other media. Home and business users who install an ISDN adapter in place of a modem can see highly graphic Web pages arriving very quickly (up to 128 Kpbs). ISDN requires adapters at both ends of the transmission, so your access provider also needs an ISDN adapter. ISDN is generally available from your phone company in most urban areas in the United States and Europe.

There are two levels of service: the Basic Rate Interface (BRI), intended for the home and small enterprise, and the Primary Rate Interface (PRI), for larger users. Both rates include a number of B-channels and D-channels. Each B-channel carries data, voice, and other services. Each D-channel carries control and signaling information.

The Basic Rate Interface consists of two 64 Kbps B-channels and one 16 Kbps D-channel. Thus, a Basic Rate user can have up to 128 Kbps service. The Primary Rate consists of 23 B-channels and one 64 Kpbs D-channel in the United States or 30 B-channels and 1 D-channel in Europe.

ISDN, in concept, is the integration of both analog (voice data) with digital data over the same network. Although the ISDN you can install is integrating these on a medium designed for analog transmission, broadband ISDN (BISDN) will extend the integration of both services throughout the rest of the end-to-end path using fiber optic and radio media. BISDN will encompass frame relay service for high-speed data that can be sent in large bursts, the Fiber Distributed-Data Interface (FDDI), and the Synchronous Optical Network (SONET). BISDN will support transmission from 2 Mbps up to much higher, but as yet unspecified, rates.

X.25

The *X.25 protocol*, adopted as a standard by the CCITT, is a commonly-used network protocol. The X.25 protocol allows computers on different public networks (such as CompuServe, Tymnet, or a TCP/IP network) to communicate through an intermediary computer at the Network layer level. X.25 protocols correspond closely to the Data Link and Physical layer protocols defined in the OSI communication model.

Tunneling

Relative to the Internet, *tunneling* is using the Internet as part of a private secure network. The "tunnel" is the particular path that a given company message or file might travel through the Internet.

A protocol or set of communication rules called *Point-to-Point Tunneling Protocol (PPTP)* makes it possible to create a virtual private network (VPN) through "tunnels" over the Internet. This means that companies no longer need their own leased lines for wide-area communication, but can securely use the public networks.

PPTP, sponsored by Microsoft and other companies, and Layer 2 Forwarding, proposed by Cisco Systems, are now combined to form L2TP, a new IETF standard.

Network Address Translation (NAT)

Network Address Translation (NAT) is the translation of an IP address used within one network to a different IP address known within another network. One network is designated the inside network and the other is the outside. Typically, a company maps its local inside network addresses to one or more global outside IP addresses and unmaps the global IP addresses on incoming packets back into local IP addresses. This mapping helps ensure security because each outgoing or incoming request must go through a translation process that also offers the opportunity to qualify or authenticate the request or match it to a previous request. NAT also conserves the number of global IP addresses that a company needs, and it lets the company use a single IP address in its communication with the world.

NAT is included as part of a router and is often part of a corporate firewall. Network administrators create a NAT table that does the global-to-local and local-to-global IP address mapping. NAT can also be used in conjunction with policy routing. NAT can be statically defined or it can be set up to dynamically translate from and to a pool of IP addresses.

Transparency

Transparency relates to how intrusive the firewall is to system users. Packet filtering routers are the most transparent; users may not even know a firewall sits between them and the external network because they never need to take any action. Application gateway firewalls are the most intrusive because they require users to sign on to the firewall directly and/or configure applications to go through the firewall.

Hash Function

Hashing is the transformation of a string of characters into a (usually) shorter fixed-length value or key that represents the original string. Hashing is used to index and retrieve items in a database because it is faster to find the item using the shorter hashed key than to find it using the original value. It is also used in many encryption algorithms.

The hashing algorithm is called the *hash function* (and probably the term is derived from the idea that the resulting hash value can be thought of as a "mixed up" version of the represented value). In addition to faster data retrieval, hashing is also used to encrypt and decrypt digital signatures (used to authenticate message senders and receivers). The digital signature is transformed with the hash function, and then both the hashed value (known as a *message digest*) and the signature are sent in separate transmissions to the receiver. Using the same hash function as the sender, the receiver derives a message digest from the signature and compares it with the message digest it received. They should be the same.

The hash function is used to index the original value or key and then used later each time the data associated with the value or key is to be retrieved. Thus, hashing is always a one-way operation. There's no need to "reverse engineer" the hash function by analyzing the hashed values. In fact, the ideal hash function can't be derived by such analysis. A good hash function should not produce the same hash value from two different inputs. If it does, this is known as a *collision*. A hash function that offers an extremely low risk of collision may be considered acceptable.

Fax Security

For secure faxes, you need to focus on four main areas:

➤ Secure phone lines

➤ Confidential cover letters

➤ Protected physical location

➤ Encrypted fax data when sending over phone lines

Securing phone lines, encrypting the fax data, and classifying sensitive faxes as confidential will help reduce the chance of an unauthorized user seeing the contents of the fax. One additional measure would be to place the fax machine in a secure room, accessible only to those that have clearance to see the information.

Address Resolution Protocol (ARP)

Address Resolution Protocol (ARP) is a protocol for mapping an Internet protocol address to a physical machine address that is recognized in the local network. For example, in IP Version 4 (the most common level of IP in use today) an address is 32 bits long. In an Ethernet local area network, however, addresses for attached devices are 48 bits long. (The physical machine address is also known as a Media Access Control or MAC address.) A table, usually called the ARP cache, is used to maintain a correlation between each MAC address and its corresponding IP address. ARP provides the protocol rules for making this correlation and providing address conversion in both directions.

When an incoming packet destined for a host machine on a particular local area network arrives at a gateway, the gateway asks the ARP program to find a physical host or MAC address that matches the IP address. The ARP program looks in the ARP cache and, if it finds the address, provides it so that the packet can be converted to the right packet length and format and sent to the machine. If no entry is found for the IP address, ARP broadcasts a request packet in a special format to all the machines on the LAN to see if one machine knows that it has that IP address associated with it. A machine that recognizes the IP address as its own returns a reply so indicating. ARP updates the ARP cache for future reference and then sends the packet to the MAC address that replied.

Flooding

In a network, *flooding* is the forwarding by a router of a packet from any node to every other node attached to the router except the node from which the packet arrived. Flooding is a way to distribute routing information updates quickly to every node in a large network. It is also sometimes used in multicast packets (from one source node to many specific nodes in a real or virtual network).

The Internet's *Open Shortest Path First (OSPF)* protocol, which updates router information in a network, uses flooding.

PBX Fraud and Abuse

The best method of eliminating fraud and abuse is to eliminate remote access to your PBX and replace it with telephone credit cards for authorized personnel. If this is not an option, try one of the following suggestions:

➤ Limit the number of employees who use remote access.

➤ Use an unpublished number for remote access lines instead of 800 numbers.

➤ Use a delayed electronic call response to provide added security. Your PBX should be programmed to wait at least five rings before answering a call.

➤ Use a voice recording or silent prompt instead of a tone. A steady tone used as a remote access prompt leaves your system vulnerable to perpetrators' automatic dialing programs.

➤ Tailor access to your PBX to conform to the needs of your business. Block access to international and long-distance numbers your company does not call. If this isn't practical, consider using time-of-day routing features to restrict international calls to daytime hours only.

➤ Whenever possible, limit remote PBX access to local calling during normal business hours. Be sure to restrict access after hours and on weekends.

➤ Delete all authorization codes that were programmed into your PBX.

Practice Questions

Question 1

> Which layer of the OSI model handles TCP?
>
> ○ a. Physical
>
> ○ b. Network
>
> ● c. Transport
>
> ○ d. Data Link

Answer c is correct. TCP works at the Transport layer. Answers a and d are incorrect because the Physical and Data Link layers deal with getting data packets to the physical communications medium. Answer b is incorrect because IP works at the Network layer.

Question 2

> Which of the following is a protocol that one program can use to request a service from a program on another computer?
>
> ● a. Secure RPC
>
> ○ b. CHAP
>
> ○ c. SLIP
>
> ○ d. PPTP

Answer a is correct. Secure RPC is a protocol that one program can use to request a service from a program on another computer. Answer b is incorrect because CHAP is a password authentication protocol. Answer c is incorrect because SLIP is a TCP/IP protocol used for communication between two machines configured for communication with each other. Answer d is incorrect because PPTP is a tunneling protocol.

Question 3

> Which of the following is a tunneling protocol?
>
> ○ a. Secure RPC
> ○ b. CHAP
> ○ c. SLIP
> ● d. PPTP

Answer d is correct. PPTP is a tunneling protocol. Answer a is incorrect because Secure RPC is a protocol that one program can use to request a service from a program on another computer. Answer b is incorrect because CHAP is a secure procedure for connecting to a system. Answer c is incorrect because SLIP is used for communications between machines, such as your system and your ISP.

Question 4

> Which of the following allows or denies traffic based only on protocol/port information?
>
> ● a. Packet filtering
> ○ b. Circuit gateways
> ○ c. Application proxies
> ○ d. Switch

Answer a is correct. Packet filtering allows or denies traffic based only on protocol/port information. Answer b is incorrect because circuit gateways are more tunnel oriented. Answer c is incorrect because application proxies create a break in the communication process. Answer d is incorrect because switches are networking devices.

Question 5

> Which of the following creates a break in the communication process?
>
> ○ a. Packet filtering
> ○ b. Circuit gateways
> ● c. Application proxies
> ○ d. Switch

Answer c is correct. Application proxies create a break in the communication process. Answer a is incorrect because packet filters allow or deny traffic based only on protocol/port information. Answer b is incorrect because circuit gateways are more tunnel oriented. Answer d is incorrect because switches are networking devices.

Question 6

Firewalls often use which technology to help "hide" internal network IP addresses?

● a. NAT

○ b. PAP

○ c. SLIP

○ d. CHAP

Answer a is correct. Firewalls often use NAT to help hide internal network IP addresses. Answers b and d are incorrect because PAP and CHAP are authentication protocols. Answer c is incorrect because SLIP is a communications protocol.

Question 7

Which cabling method uses an RJ-45 connector?

○ a. Coaxial cable

● b. UTP

○ c. Fiber optic cable

○ d. Wireless

Answer b is correct. UTP uses an RJ-45 connector. Answer a is incorrect because coaxial cable uses a BNC connector. Answer c is incorrect because fiber optic cable uses an SC connector. Answer d is incorrect because wireless networks do not have specific connectors.

Question 8

An Ethernet network often uses which type of topology?

○ a. Star

○ b. Ring

● c. Bus

○ d. Diamond

Answer c is correct. An Ethernet network often uses a bus topology. Answer a is incorrect because star topologies are used in switched environments. Answer b is incorrect because ring topology is often used in Token Ring implementations. Answer d is incorrect because diamond is not a network topology.

Question 9

Which of the following is not a transmission protocol?

○ a. PPP

○ b. SLIP

○ c. Frame Relay

● d. ARP

Answer d is correct. ARP is not a transmission protocol. Answer a is incorrect because PPP is a protocol for communication between two computers using a serial interface. Answer b is incorrect because SLIP is used for communications between machines, such as your system and your ISP. Answer c is incorrect because Frame Relay is a telecommunications service.

Question 10

Which protocol maps an IP address to a physical machine address?

○ a. PPP

○ b. SLIP

○ c. Frame Relay

● d. ARP

Answer d is correct. ARP maps an IP address to a physical machine address. Answer a is incorrect because PPP is a protocol for communication between two computers using a serial interface. Answer b is incorrect because SLIP is used for communications between machines, such as your system and your ISP. Answer c is incorrect because Frame Relay is a telecommunications service.

Need to Know More?

 www.ja.net/CERT/Bellovin/TCP-IP_Security_Problems.html features an excellent discussion on security problems in the TCP/IP protocol suite.

 www.securityfocus.com is a great overall security resource.

 http://webopedia.internet.com/TERM/O/OSI.html is a useful resource for information on the OSI model.

Security
Management Practices

Terms you'll need to understand:

✓ Confidentiality
✓ Integrity
✓ Availability
✓ Authorization
✓ Authentication
✓ Nonrepudiation
✓ Layering
✓ Data hiding

Techniques you'll need to master:

✓ Understanding security management concepts and principles
✓ Managing change control
✓ Understanding employment policies and practices

The Security Management Practices domain covers the identification of an organization's information assets and the development, documentation, and implementation of policies, standards, and procedures that ensure confidentiality, integrity, and availability.

For the CISSP exam, you need to fully understand the planning, organization, and roles of individuals in identifying and securing an organization's information assets. Your understanding should include developing policies and procedures, awareness training, and employee hiring and termination practices.

Security Management Concepts and Principles

In security, specific concepts must be addressed by any solution. The main concepts are availability, integrity, and confidentiality, which are discussed next in detail. Without addressing these three concepts, security solutions do not provide the complete package.

Availability

Protecting the *availability* of data means ensuring that it is accessible to those who use the data when they need to use it. This area was not emphasized until the denial of service (DoS) attacks hit the Internet in February 2000. Prior to these attacks, problems with availability were caused mainly by technology issues or maintenance problems. The DoS attacks of 2000 showed that the Internet could be brought to its knees by a few determined individuals. For an e-commerce site, where revenue is obtained from online orders or ad impressions displayed, any downtime (when the site is not accessible to customers) can cost the company millions of dollars.

Integrity

Protecting the *integrity* of data means ensuring that the data has not been modified in any way, whether in transit or in storage. If a company sends payroll data to a processing center over the Internet, how would the payroll department like a zero added to the amount paid to the HR Director while the data is in transit, changing the amount to be paid from $5,000 to $50,000? Or what if a zero is added to each salary field in the HR database, increasing everyone's salary by a magnitude of 10? Protecting data integrity prevents these kinds of errors.

Confidentiality

Protecting the *confidentiality* of data means ensuring that only the authorized people have the ability to see the data. Access controls and authorization models help define who can see what, whereas cryptography helps prevent data being seen by tools (such as sniffers) as it travels over public networks.

When most people think about security, they focus on confidentiality. Secrecy is important, but the availability and integrity of data is just as critical. A software company might lose millions of dollars if the source code to its applications is found and leaked to the public. But the company might also lose millions of dollars if it is the victim of a DoS attack, and customers cannot access the Web site to order products. Additionally, if the source code is modified slightly when being transferred from one machine to another, causing the application to crash the system instead of functioning properly, customers will not continue to buy the software, and word will spread quickly about the poor quality of the product.

Security Services and Mechanisms

The ISO developed Document 7498-2, "Information Processing Systems – Open Systems Interconncection – Basic Reference Model – Part 2: Security Architecture," to explain security architecture concepts such as security services and security mechanisms.

Security Services

The ISO standard defines several key security services, defined here in Table 4.1, that you will learn more about in later chapters.

Confidentiality, integrity, and availability are often combined and referred to as the *CIA triad*.

Table 4.1 Definitions of security services.	
Term	**Definition**
Identification and authentication	Authentication is the process of proving that you are who you say you are—establishing proof of identity. This can be achieved through passwords, smart cards, biometrics, or a combination thereof.
Access control or authorization	Access controls provide a means of determining who can access which system resources. After a user is authenticated to a system, defined access controls tell the system where the user can go. For example, ordinary system users should not have access to areas where account passwords are stored. Access control services prevent this from occurring.
Data confidentiality	Data confidentiality protects data from being viewed by unauthorized individuals.

(continued)

Table 4.1 Definitions of security services *(continued)*.	
Term	**Definition**
Data integrity	Data integrity protects data from being modified, retaining the consistency and original meaning of the information.
Nonrepudiation	Repudiation is the ability for an individual to deny participation in a transaction. If a customer places an order and a nonrepudiation security service is not built in to the system, the customer could deny ever making that purchase. Nonrepudiation services provide a means of proving that a transaction occurred, whether it was an order placed at an online store or an email message sent and received. Digital signatures are one means of providing nonrepudiation.

Security Mechanisms

ISO 7498-2 also defines *security mechanisms*. Security mechanisms are technologies, whether software or procedures, that implement one or more security services. The main security mechanisms are defined in Table 4.2.

Table 4.2 Definitions of security mechanisms.	
Term	**Definition**
Encryption	Encryption is the process of converting data to an unrecognizable form. This supports security services such as authentication, confidentiality, integrity, and nonrepudiation. Encryption technologies are described in further detail later in this chapter.
Digital signatures	Digital signatures help guarantee the authenticity of data, much like a written signature verifies the authenticity of a paper document. This supports security services such as authentication and nonrepudiation.
Access control	Access control is a process that ensures a person or system has the permission to use a requested resource. These controls can be built directly into the operating system, incorporated into applications, or implemented as add-on packages. One example of an access control mechanism is a firewall.
Data integrity checks	Data integrity checks include mechanisms such as parity checks and checksum comparisons. These checks support the data integrity service and require the sender and receiver to compare check sequences to ensure the data has not been modified.

(continued)

Table 4.2 Definitions of security mechanisms *(continued)*.	
Term	**Definition**
Authentication exchange	Authentication exchange is a communication mechanism between a requester and a verifier to assure the verifier of the requester's identity. This communication can occur between the sender and the receiver in the case of mutual authentication, or between the sender, receiver, and a third party in the case of third-party authentication.
Traffic padding	Traffic padding is a mechanism that disguises data characteristics to provide protection against traffic analysis. This mechanism can include the padding of data (adding irrelevant and unnecessary data to a message) or sending dummy messages to disguise traffic.

Specific vs. Pervasive Mechanisms

As defined by ISO, a security mechanism can be *specific* or *pervasive*. A specific security mechanism implements only one security service at a time. One example of a specific security mechanism is encryption. Although encryption can be used to implement data confidentiality, integrity, and nonrepudiation security services, the means of implementation requires a different security mechanism for each service.

A pervasive security mechanism implements multiple security services. Usually, pervasive mechanisms are lists of procedures. Examples of pervasive mechanisms include incident detection, response procedures, and audit logs.

Protection Mechanisms

Protection mechanisms are used in coding or database development to further protect data and resources. These mechanisms are required for higher-level government certification.

Layering

The concept of *layering* is required at TCSEC layers B3 or above and requires that:

➤ Layers know about the interfaces and depend on the services of layers below, but know nothing about—and do not depend on—the correct functioning of the layers above.

➤ Each layer is protected from tampering by the layers above.

➤ Layers cannot violate the portions of the security policy enforced by the layers below.

Layering not only facilitates the verification of the correctness of the application by allowing examination of one layer at a time, but it also simplifies future changes by allowing the higher layers to be modified (or perhaps even "chopped off" and replaced) for new releases without the need to redesign the lower layers.

Data Abstraction

Data abstraction is a fundamental premise of object-oriented programming. It is the process of defining user types and using these types only through a set of interface operations instead of directly manipulating their representations. The concept of data abstraction is also required at TCSEC layers B3 or above. For example, the design might make use of a stack object, with the operations **PUSH** and **POP**, so that the use of the stack is easier to understand than if the design described an array of words, a pointer, and the algorithms used to temporarily store words in the array.

Change Control and Management

Change control and management deals with the processes and procedures to properly approve, migrate, and deploy changes to applications, servers, network infrastructure, or any other critical function. Without change control, developers and programmers could create small programs that delete data, transfer funds, cause computation errors, and so forth. Proper change control procedures help minimize this risk by ensuring that only agreed-upon and approved changes are migrated to the production environment.

Best practice change control procedures should include the following:

1. Request for change should be documented on a standard change request form.

2. The form should then be submitted to the information systems department, where further information on the request, such as estimated completion time and cost, is added.

3. Change specifications should then be approved in advance by a supervisor.

4. Source or object code changes should be reviewed by a supervisor or quality assurance group in a testing area before being migrated to production.

Information/Data

For the exam, information/data focuses on *information valuation*. In general, when valuing information, you focus on how much it would cost to replace the lost data, often referred to as *cost-of-loss modeling*.

In cost-of-loss modeling, assets may have one or more of the following properties: substance, confidentiality, integrity, and service potential. The value of these properties can be determined by looking at the effect of adverse impacts such as deprivation, disclosure, modification, and unavailability.

There are at least six cost-of-loss models. The first four address consequences of adverse events. The other two models focus on transferring responsibility to another party or claiming that any amount of risk is unacceptable, so the cost-of-loss model is useless. The models are:

➤ *Replacement model*—Addresses deprivation.

➤ *Repair model*—Addresses restoration of system integrity eroded by unwanted modification.

➤ *Compromise model*—Addresses unauthorized disclosure of sensitive information and is highly speculative.

➤ *Service model*—Addresses the unavailability of system resources. Assigns a cost-per-unit time to the various services delivered by or to the system.

➤ *Transference model*—Deals with risk as transferred to another party, usually an insurance company.

➤ *Catastrophe model*—Any risk of catastrophic loss is unacceptable and cost-benefit analysis has no real role. If you cannot handle any loss, than you will take all necessary measures, regardless of cost.

Employment Policies and Practices

The employees (and people in general) are the weakest link in the security chain. After hiring strong, dependable people, security awareness training is the next step. The three components of a good *employee security awareness program* are:

➤ *Framework*—Appropriate organization structure, the requisite job descriptions, and lines of authority that provide for clear definitions of responsibilities and authority.

➤ *Hiring practices*—Performing background checks and completely understanding the person being hired.

➤ *Education operations*—Keeping employees informed and aware of security issues and their role in the security process.

Employee policies and practices help protect the organization from the following threats:

➤ Theft (outright removal of an asset of the company by an employee)

➤ Fraud (an employee obtaining assets of the organization through intentional misrepresentation or misapplication of information)

➤ Misuse of information (an employee releasing sensitive data to the public)

➤ Sabotage (an employee intentionally deleting or modifying data)

➤ Rule disobedience (an employee ignoring security policies)

➤ Physical accidents (an employee spilling a drink on a system, for example)

➤ Emergencies (an employee having an accident, causing a fire, finding a break-in, and so on)

Although it is virtually impossible for an organization to be completely immune to fraud, the only way it should be susceptible to fraud is if the collusion of two or more individuals occurs. If two or more individuals are working together, fraud is much harder to detect. By defining the organizational structure along functional lines, it is possible to prevent employees from entering areas where they do not belong; this is the standard *separation of duties* concept. However, an organization's structure can assist in the prevention of fraud only by preventing deliberate breaches of security such as theft, fraud, sabotage, and misuse of information.

A few organizational/functional structures that should be in place include:

➤ Segregating systems analysis and programming functions

➤ Segregating the systems development function from the systems maintenance

➤ Segregating the software maintenance organization from the operations functions

➤ Segregating the operations control functions from development activities

➤ Rotating software maintenance and computer operations personnel within their own areas

➤ Ensuring that family relationships do not exist between employees in sensitive components of the organization

The optimum corporate security structure to achieve maximum security levels would involve three independent groups:

➤ Corporate security chief

➤ Internal auditor

➤ EDP security officer

Hiring Practices

Hiring practices are an important part of the employment process. At a minimum, employers should perform reference checks and security background checks.

For reference checks, specific information that should be reviewed with the references other than work competence include information relating to the employee's habits, honesty, and educational record.

Background checks should look into the following areas:

➤ Special checks (check all available public records to determine whether the employee has any negative elements on his or her record)

➤ Military records

➤ Law enforcement records

➤ Drug testing

➤ Lie detector tests (seldom used except for highly sensitive security positions); illegal in some states

➤ Educational records

When an employee is terminated, all access should be immediately revoked and he should not be allowed to return to his desk unless accompanied by a manager or security guard. The organization should have a termination checklist to follow.

Employee Relationships

Care should be taken by an organization to make sure that its relationship with its employees is maintained at a reasonable level. The entire work force is generally loyal to the employing organization, and employee morale is a significant factor in the organization's security. Compensatory time, bonuses, and recognition of accomplishments are some of the tools available to management to maintain morale.

Operations

Company operations also have specific security policies and procedures that should be in place to ensure maximum security. One of the main processes that should be in place is job rotation, which helps prevent one employee from being in total control of a specific area. If job rotation is not possible, employees in sensitive areas should be given extended vacations and should be forced to take their vacations on contiguous days.

Access control is also an important area for operations. Each employee should have an ID card, and access to sensitive areas should be strictly controlled.

As always, continuous observation of the employees and their behavior is necessary.

Policies, Standards, Guidelines, and Procedures

A *policy* is a broad statement of management's views and position regarding a particular topic. Policies designate the computer security function as management's representation for ensuring that the appropriate protective steps are taken. The policy statement might conclude with a caveat that those who fail to comply may face sanctions. Policies must be both enforced and reinforced by standards, guidelines, and procedures.

Standards (or corporate standards) are mandatory activities, actions, rules, or regulations designed to provide the policies with the support, structure, and specific directions they require to be meaningful and effective. A standard may state that only authorized personnel can access this data. Or, the data must be backed-up and stored off-site.

Guidelines are more general statements that are also designed to achieve the policy's objectives by providing a framework within which to implement procedures. Standards connote specific, mandatory activities, actions, and rules, while guidelines contain more general approaches and flexible parameters within which to operate.

Procedures spell out the specifics of how the policy and the supportive standards and guidelines will actually be implemented in an operating environment. Active management support is critical to successfully implement computer security programs.

Risk Management

Risk management is the process of establishing and maintaining information technology security within an organization. Risk analysis is the means by which threats to systems are identified and assessed to justify security safeguards. Risk is the probability that a threat agent (cause) will exploit a system vulnerability (weaknesses) and thereby create an effect detrimental to the system.

Several types of risk exist. *Inherent risk* exists in all situations and does not take into account existing safeguards. *Present risk* currently exists and does take existing safeguards into account. *Residual risk* is what is left after all mitigating factors are implemented. It takes both existing and recommended safeguards into account.

Cost-Benefit Analysis

Although mitigating risk is important, the solution to mitigating the risk should not cost more than it would to replace the data or resource. The annualized cost of safeguards to defend against threats or to shield assets, or both, is compared with the expected cost of loss.

To perform the *cost-benefit analysis*, you need to understand the properties of threats that you can encounter, which include the likelihood of the threat, the number of times a year a particular threat can occur, the severity of the threat, and its consequences.

The value of an asset is either its cost (quantitative value) or its importance (qualitative value) to an organization. Irrespective of their value to an organization, some assets are more prone to loss than others. Exposure of an asset may justify spending more for safeguards than the cost of the asset would indicate in a cost-benefit analysis.

Risk Safeguards

There are several ways to reduce risk. *Risk avoidance* is the safest way and just requires you to avoid any scenario that would introduce risk. Even though this is the safest way, it is certainly not the most practical. *Risk transference* is an option that transfers risk to other parties, such as insurance companies. You can also mitigate the risk (most common safeguard) by implementing security controls, policies, and procedures.

When selecting safeguards, you need to be aware of any constraints that may affect the selection of a safeguard. Time constraints can occur that specify the time in which a solution can be selected or specify how a safeguard can affect processing time once implemented. Financial constraints are often encountered. *Return on Investment (ROI)* calculations are one of the standard measurements for information security controls selection. You can also encounter technical constraints, sociological constraints, environmental constraints, and legal constraints.

Roles and Responsibilities

Each employee, regardless of position or title, should have specific roles and responsibilities that are clearly defined and documented. As part of this documentation, security roles should be included.

Security awareness should also be included in the roles and responsibilities discussion. For senior management, security awareness is brief, but focused. For line management, more detailed coverage of standards, guidelines, and procedures should be discussed. Departmental security representatives and coordinators should be selected and made aware of specific policies, standards, guidelines, and procedures for their group.

Practice Questions

Question 1

> Which of the following concepts ensures that data and resources are accessible when they need to be?
>
> ○ a. Confidentiality
>
> ○ b. Integrity
>
> ● c. Availability
>
> ○ d. Authorization

Answer c is correct. Availability ensures data and resources are accessible when they need to be. Answer a is incorrect because confidentiality protects data from being viewed by unauthorized individuals. Answer b is incorrect because integrity protects data from being modified, retaining the consistency and original meaning of the information. Answer d is incorrect because authorization provides a means of determining who can access which system resources.

Question 2

> Providing a means of determining who can access which system resources describes which of the following concepts?
>
> ○ a. Confidentiality
>
> ○ b. Integrity
>
> ○ c. Availability
>
> ● d. Authorization

Answer d is correct. Authorization provides a means of determining who can access which system resources. Answer a is incorrect because confidentiality protects data from being viewed by unauthorized individuals. Answer b is incorrect because integrity protects data from being modified, retaining the consistency and original meaning of the information. Answer c is incorrect because availability ensures data and resources are accessible when they need to be.

Question 3

Protecting data from being viewed by unauthorized individuals describes
which of the following concepts?

- ⦿ a. Confidentiality
- ○ b. Integrity
- ○ c. Availability
- ○ d. Authorization

Answer a is correct. Confidentiality protects data from being viewed by unauthorized individuals. Answer b is incorrect because integrity protects data from being modified, retaining the consistency and original meaning of the information. Answer c is incorrect because availability ensures data and resources are accessible when they need to be. Answer d is incorrect because authorization provides a means of determining who can access which system resources.

Question 4

Confidentiality, integrity, and availability constitute which of the following?

- ○ a. Accountability
- ○ b. Nonrepudiation
- ○ c. Audit
- ⦿ d. CIA triad

Answer d is correct. Confidentiality, integrity, and availability constitute what is known as the CIA triad. Accountability, nonrepudiation, and audit are not part of the CIA triad. Answer a is incorrect because accountability binds an action to a specific individual. Answer b is incorrect because nonrepudiation keeps an individual from denying that a transaction took place. Answer c is incorrect because audit is the process of analyzing and reviewing configurations, policies, procedures, and so on.

Question 5

> Which of the following concepts describes binding an action to a specific individual?
>
> ◉ a. Accountability
> ○ b. Nonrepudiation
> ○ c. Audit
> ○ d. CIA triad

Answer a is correct. Accountability binds an action to a specific individual. Answer b is incorrect because nonrepudiation keeps an individual from denying that a transaction took place. Answer c is incorrect because audit is the process of analyzing and reviewing configurations, policies, procedures, and so on. Answer d is incorrect because the CIA triad is a combination of confidentiality, integrity, and availability.

Question 6

> Keeping an individual from denying that a transaction took place describes which of the following concepts?
>
> ○ a. Accountability
> ◉ b. Nonrepudiation
> ○ c. Audit
> ○ d. CIA triad

Answer b is correct. Nonrepudiation keeps an individual from denying that a transaction took place. Answer a is incorrect because accountability binds an action to a specific individual. Answer c is incorrect because audit is the process of analyzing and reviewing configurations, policies, procedures, and so on. Answer d is incorrect because the CIA triad is the combination of confidentiality, integrity, and availability.

Question 7

Which of the following is not ideal in an effective change control program?

- ○ a. Change requests must be formally documented.
- ○ b. All changes must be approved.
- ◉ c. Programmer moves code directly to production.
- ○ d. Code is approved before being migrated to production.

Answer c is correct. A programmer moving code directly to production is not an effective change control program. Answers a, b, and d are incorrect because they are all effective change control procedures.

Question 8

What should you not do after dismissing an employee?

- ○ a. Escort him out the door
- ◉ b. Let him return to his desk unsupervised
- ○ c. Disable all accounts and logons
- ○ d. Follow the termination checklist

Answer b is correct. After dismissing an employee, you should not let him return to his desk unsupervised. Answers a, c, and d are all steps of an effective termination policy.

Question 9

A(n) _____ can assist only in the prevention of deliberate breaches of security such as theft, fraud, sabotage, and misuse.

- ◉ a. Organization structure
- ○ b. Encapsulation
- ○ c. Training program
- ○ d. Change control

Answer a is correct. An organization's structure can assist only in the prevention of deliberate breaches of security such as theft, fraud, sabotage, and misuse. Answers b, c, and d are incorrect because encapsulation, training programs, and change control all help prevent other security breaches in addition to theft, fraud, sabotage, and misuse.

Question 10

Security awareness programs cannot:

- ○ a. Make employees aware of issues
- ○ b. Show them the proper procedures to follow
- ◉ c. Enforce security policy
- ○ d. Make them aware of risks

Answer c is correct. Awareness programs help educate, but they cannot enforce security policy. Answers a, b, and d are thus incorrect.

Need to Know More?

 www.ja.net/CERT/Bellovin/TCP-IP_Security_Problems.html describes some common security problems in the TCP/IP protocol suite.

 www.securityfocus.com is an excellent resource for general security information.

 http://webopedia.internet.com/TERM/O/OSI.html has detailed information on the OSI model.

Applications and Systems Development Security

Terms you'll need to understand:

✓ Distributed computing

✓ Agents

✓ Aggregation

✓ Inference

✓ Polyinstantiation

✓ Neural networks

Techniques you'll need to master:

✓ Understanding distributed and nondistributed computing environments

✓ Understanding databases and data warehousing

✓ Understanding the System Development Life Cycle (SDLC)

The Applications and Systems Development Security domain requires understanding the development process and the controls that should be included to help provide increased security levels. *Applications* refer to distributed or centralized agents, applets, software, databases, data warehouses, and knowledge-based systems.

For the CISSP exam, you need to fully understand the security and controls of the systems development process, system life cycle, application controls, change controls, data warehousing, data mining, knowledge-based systems, program interfaces, and concepts used to ensure data and application integrity, confidentiality, and availability.

Distributed Environment

In general, computing is said to be *distributed* when the computer programming, processing, and data that computers work on are spread out over more than one computer, usually over a network in a client-server environment. Computing prior to low-cost computer power on the desktop was organized in centralized *glass houses* (so called because the computers were often shown to visitors through picture windows). Although these centers still exist, large and small enterprises are moving applications and data where they can operate most efficiently in the enterprise, to some mix of desktop workstations, LAN servers, regional servers, Web servers, and other servers. A popular trend is *client-server computing*, which simply means that a client computer can provide certain capabilities for a user and request others from other computers that provide services for the clients (HTTP is an example of this idea).

The *Distributed Computing Environment (DCE)* is a particular industry standard for implementing a distributed computing environment. Today, major software makers are fostering an object-oriented view of distributed computing. As a distributed publishing environment with Java and other products that help companies create distributed applications, the World Wide Web is accelerating the trend toward distributed computing and the view that, as Sun Microsystem's slogan says, "The network is the computer."

In network computing, DCE is an industry-standard software technology for setting up and managing computing and data exchange in a system of distributed computers. DCE is typically used in large networks of computing systems that include different-sized servers scattered geographically, and it uses the client/server model. With DCE, application users can use applications and data on remote servers. Application programmers need not be aware of where their programs will run or where the data will be located.

Much of DCE setup requires the preparation of distributed directories so that DCE applications and related data can be located when they are being used.

DCE includes security support, and some implementations provide support for access to popular databases such as IBM's CICS, IMS, and DB2 databases.

DCE was developed by the Open Software Foundation (OSF) using software technologies contributed by some of its member companies.

Agents

On the Internet, an *agent* (also called an intelligent agent) is a program that gathers information or performs some other service on some regular schedule without your immediate presence. Typically, an agent program, using parameters you have provided, searches all or some part of the Internet, gathers information you're interested in, and presents it to you on a daily or other periodic basis. An agent is sometimes also called a *bot* (short for robot). The definitive site about bots is BotSpot (**http://botspot.com**). The practice or technology of having information brought to you by an agent is sometimes referred to as *push technology*. Security considerations for bots include knowing what data and programs are being pushed and who is providing them. A malicious user who could control a bot could easily send Trojans or viruses through the system to all users.

Other agents have been developed that personalize information on a Web site based on registration information and usage analysis. Other types of agents include specific site watchers that tell you when the site has been updated or that look for other events, and analyst agents that not only gather, but also organize and interpret information for you.

Applets

An *applet* is a small application program. Prior to the Internet, the built-in writing and drawing programs that came with Windows were sometimes called applets. On the Web, using Java (the object-oriented programming language), an applet is a small program that can be sent along with a Web page to a user. Java applets can perform interactive animations, immediate calculations, or other simple tasks without having to send a user request back to the server.

Sandboxing, a method of quarantining suspicious code as it enters a computer or network, is a security measure often used to protect systems from malicious applets. The application detains suspect code in a segregated area, monitors its attempted actions, and compares the actions to established security policies. Actions allowed by the policy are permitted to enter the system, whereas suspect and prohibited actions are blocked.

ActiveX

ActiveX is the name Microsoft has given to a set of object-oriented programming technologies and tools. The main technology is the *Component Object Model*

(COM). Used in a network with a directory and additional support, COM becomes the *Distributed Component Object Model (DCOM).* Your main objective when writing a program to run in the ActiveX environment is to create a component, a self-sufficient program that can be run anywhere in your ActiveX network. This component is known as an *ActiveX control.* ActiveX is Microsoft's answer to the Java technology from Sun Microsystems. An ActiveX control is roughly equivalent to a Java applet.

If you have a Windows operating system on your personal computer, you may notice a number of Windows files with the OCX file name suffix. OCX stands for Object Linking and Embedding control. *Object Linking and Embedding (OLE)* was Microsoft's program technology for supporting compound documents such as the Windows desktop. The COM now takes in OLE as part of a larger concept. Microsoft now uses the term *ActiveX control* instead of OCX for the component object.

One of the main advantages of a component is that it can be reused by many applications (referred to as *component containers*). A COM component object (ActiveX control) can be created using one of several languages or development tools, including C++, Visual Basic, PowerBuilder, or VBScript.

Java

Java is a programming language expressly designed for use in the distributed environment of the Internet. It was designed to have the look and feel of the C++ language, but it is simpler to use than C++ and enforces an object-oriented programming model. Java can be used to create complete applications that can run on a single computer or be distributed among servers and clients in a network. With Java, you can write the code once and be able to run it anywhere. It can also be used to build a small application module or applet for use as part of a Web page. Applets make it possible for a Web page user to interact with the page.

The majority of applets on the Web are unsigned. These applets may be assigned untrusted, high, or medium security. Table 5.1 discusses these levels. Signed applets contain a *signature*, a sequence of characters embedded in the applet's code. The signature tells who the applet comes from; it does not provide information about the content or quality of the applet. You cannot alter or duplicate the signature.

Objects

In object-oriented programming, *objects* are what you think about first in designing a program, and they are also the units of code that are eventually derived from the process. In between, each object is made into a generic class of object, and even more generic classes are defined so that objects can share models and reuse the class definitions in their code. Each object is an instance of a particular class

Table 5.1 Java security levels.	
Security Level	**Action**
Untrusted	Untrusted applets are not permitted to run.
High Security	Applets granted High Security run with safe constraints and are blocked from unsafe actions. They can't read, write, or delete files, and they can't access most WebView settings. They may connect to, and accept connections from, only the server of their origin. They may only listen on network ports above 1024. They cannot access the print queue or clipboard.
Medium Security	Applets granted Medium Security run with safe constraints. In most cases, if they attempt any of the actions listed under High Security, WebView gives a warning. You may grant permission for the action if you want. Medium Security applets cannot access the clipboard, even with a warning.
Low Security	Applets granted Low Security run with minimal constraints, without warning of potentially unsafe actions. WebView warns if the applet tries to launch local applications, but all the other actions listed above are permitted without warnings. Of all the possible default security settings, this setting carries the greatest risk.

or subclass with the class's own methods or procedures and data variables. An object is what actually runs in the computer.

Local/Nondistributed Environment

In a local/nondistributed environment, everything runs locally on the system. Unlike distributed computing, where processing can be shared with a remote system, a nondistributed environment keeps everything in-house, so to speak. Potential security concerns in a nondistributed environment include viruses, Trojan horses, logic bombs, and worms.

Viruses

A *virus* is a piece of programming code inserted into other programming to cause some unexpected and, for the victim, usually undesirable event. Viruses can be transmitted by downloading code from other sites, from email, or by using an infected diskette. The source of the file you're downloading, or of a diskette you've received, is often unaware of the virus. The virus lies dormant until circumstances cause its code to be executed by the computer. Some viruses are playful in intent and effect ("Happy Birthday, Ludwig!"), and some can be quite harmful, erasing data or causing your hard disk to require reformatting.

Generally, there are three main classes of viruses: file infectors, system or boot-record infectors, and macro viruses.

File Infectors

File infectors attach themselves to program files, usually selected COM or EXE files. Some can infect any program for which execution is requested, including SYS, OVL, PRG, and MNU files. When the program is loaded, the virus is loaded as well.

System or Boot-Record Infectors

System or boot-record infectors infect executable code found in certain system areas on a disk. They attach to the DOS boot sector on diskettes or the master boot record on hard disks. A typical scenario (familiar to the author) is to receive a diskette from an innocent source that contains a boot disk virus. When your operating system is running, files on the diskette can be read without triggering the boot disk virus. However, if you leave the diskette in the drive, and then turn the computer off or reload the operating system, the computer will look first in your A: drive, find the diskette with its boot disk virus, load it, and make it temporarily impossible to use your hard disk (allow several days for recovery). This is why you should make sure you have a bootable floppy.

Macro Viruses

Macro viruses are among the most common viruses, and they tend to do the least damage. They infect your applications, such as Microsoft Word, and typically insert unwanted words or phrases.

Trojan Horses

In computers, a *Trojan horse* is a program or virus in which malicious or harmful code is contained inside apparently harmless programming, data, or messages in such a way that it can get control and do its chosen form of damage, such as ruining the file allocation table on your hard disk. In one celebrated case, a Trojan horse was a program that was supposed to find and destroy computer viruses. A Trojan horse can be considered a virus if it is widely redistributed.

Logic Bombs

Logic bombs are code surreptitiously inserted into an application or OS that causes it to perform some destructive or security-compromising activity whenever specified conditions are met.

Worms

A *worm* is a type of virus or replicative code that situates itself in a computer system in a place where it can do harm. Like most computer viruses, worms usually come in Trojan horses.

Most users place far too much trust in files arriving from outside sources. Antivirus solutions are the best defense. Essentially, antivirus systems look for known undesirables on an ever-growing list. Some systems also add a profiling system that quarantines a suspect file and waits for user action. Profiling is also called "heuristics."

In general, most antivirus products are very similar in functionality. They all find virus attacks within a percentage point of each other. What separates the products are administrative features and enterprise functionality.

Databases and Data Warehousing

A *database* is a collection of data that is organized so that its contents can easily be accessed, managed, and updated. The most prevalent type of database is the *relational* database, a tabular database in which data is defined so that it can be reorganized and accessed in a number of different ways. A *distributed* database is one that can be dispersed or replicated among different points in a network. An *object-oriented* database is one that is congruent with the data defined in object classes and subclasses.

Databases contain aggregations of data records or files, such as sales transactions, product catalogs and inventories, and customer profiles. Typically, a database manager lets users control read/write access, specify report generation, and analyze usage. Databases and database managers are prevalent in large mainframe systems, but are also present in smaller distributed workstation and mid-range systems such as the AS/400 and personal computers. SQL is a standard language for making interactive queries from and updating a database such as Microsoft's SQL Server, Oracle, and Sybase.

A *data warehouse* is a central repository for all or significant parts of the data that an enterprise's various business systems collect. IBM sometimes uses the term "information warehouse." Typically, a data warehouse is housed on an enterprise mainframe server. Data from various online transaction processing (OLTP) applications and other sources is selectively extracted and organized in the data warehouse database for use by analytical applications and user queries. Data warehousing emphasizes the capture of data from diverse sources for useful analysis and access, but it does not generally start from the point of view of the end user or knowledge worker who may need access to specialized, sometimes local databases, also known as a *data mart*.

Aggregation

Aggregation is the process of combining small pieces of information to gain insight into the whole. An aggregation problem occurs whenever there is a collection of data items that is classified at a higher level than the levels of the individual data items by themselves. A classic example from a military context occurs when the location of individual ships in a fleet is unclassified, but the aggregate information concerning the location of all ships in the fleet is secret. Similarly, in the commercial sector, the individual sales figures for branch offices might be considered less sensitive than the aggregate sales figures for the entire company.

Data Mining

Data mining is the analysis of data for relationships that have not previously been discovered. For example, the sales records for a particular brand of tennis racket might, if sufficiently analyzed and related to other market data, reveal a seasonal correlation with the purchase—by the same parties—of golf equipment.

Data mining results include:

➤ *Associations*—correlating one event to another event (beer purchasers buy peanuts a certain percentage of the time)

➤ *Sequences*—finding that one event leads to another later event (a rug purchase followed by a purchase of curtains)

➤ *Classification*—recognizing patterns and new organizations of data (for example, profiles of customers who make purchases)

➤ *Clustering*—finding and visualizing groups of facts not previously known

➤ *Forecasting*—discovering patterns in the data that can lead to predictions about the future

Inference

An *inference* is a unilateral activity in which an unclassified user legitimately accesses unclassified information, and deduces secret information.

Even in multilevel secure DBMSs, it is possible for users to draw inferences from the information they obtain from the database. The inference could be derived purely from the data obtained from the database system, or it could depend on some prior knowledge obtained by users from outside the database system. An inference presents a security breach if higher-classified information can be inferred from lower-classified information.

Polyinstantiation

The technique of *polyinstantiation* is used to prevent inference violations. Essentially, it allows different versions of the same information item to exist at different classification levels. For example, an unclassified user wants to enter a row in a relation in which each row is labeled either S (secret) or U (unclassified). If the same key is already occurring in an S row, the unclassified user can insert the U row, gaining access to any information by inference. The classification of the row must therefore be treated as part of the relation key. Thus, U rows and S rows always have different keys because the keys have different security classes.

Several approaches have been proposed to address this problem. Each approach reflects some perspective about the meaning and the use of polyinstantiation and consequently has advantages and disadvantages. Some approaches aim at allowing polyinstantiation, while others aim at preventing it.

The approaches which allow polyinstantiation are based on the assumption that polyinstantiation is an inevitable part of the multilevel paradigm. Users at different levels may see different attribute values for the same real-world tuple (for example different salary values for the same employee), and thus the users must be allowed to update these values differently.

The SeaView and the Jajodia and Sandhu models are based on multilevel relations and support both tuple and attribute polyinstantiations. The models define the key of multilevel relation to be a combination of the original key attributes, their classifications, and the classifications of all other attributes in the relation. The two models control the proliferation of tuples caused by updates in different ways. In the SeaView model, an update/insert operation may introduce a number of tuples which are exponential in the number of non-key attributes in the relation. Jajodia and Sandhu argue that these tuples are spurious and, in their model, they revise the SeaView constraints to limit the tuple explosion caused by updates.

In the belief-based model, researchers distinguish between what a user sees and what a user believes. In particular, a user can see all data whose access class is dominated by the access class of the user. However, a user believes only in data that has an access class equal to the user's access class.

Some approaches have been proposed based on preventing polyinstantiation. One approach for preventing entity polyinstantiation is to require all key values to be classified at the lowest possible level so that they are visible to every user. Another possible approach for preventing entity polyinstantiation is to partition the domain of the primary key among the various levels so that each value of the primary key value has a unique possible classification. Attribute polyinstantiation can be prevented by introducing a special "restricted" value. Value "restricted" is used for an element at a given level when a value for the element exists at a higher level. However, all these approaches restrict the flexibility of the system.

Multilevel Security

Multilevel security focuses on confidentiality. Discretionary access controls pose a serious threat to confidentiality; mandatory access controls help eliminate these problems. Multilevel secure database systems enforce mandatory access controls in addition to the discretionary controls commonly found in most current products.

The use of multilevel security, however, can create potential conflicts between data confidentiality and integrity. Specifically, the enforcement of integrity rules can create covert channels for discovering confidential information, which even mandatory access controls cannot prevent.

With mandatory access controls, the granting of access is constrained by the system security policy. These controls are based on security labels associated with each data item and each user. A label on a data item is called a *security classification*, and a label on a user is called a *security clearance*. In a computer system, every program run by a user inherits the user's security clearance—that is, the user's clearance applies not only to the user, but to every program executed by that user. Once assigned, the classifications and clearances cannot be changed, except by the security officer.

Security labels in the military and government sectors have two components: a hierarchical component and a set of categories. The hierarchical component consists of the following classes, listed in decreasing order of sensitivity: top secret, secret, confidential, and unclassified. The set of categories may be empty, or it may consist of such items as nuclear, conventional, navy, army, or NATO.

Commercial organizations use similar labels for protecting sensitive information. The main difference is that procedures for assigning clearances to users are much less formal than in the military or government sectors. It is possible for security labels to dominate each other. For example, label X is said to dominate label Y if the hierarchical component of X is greater than or equal to the hierarchical component of Y, and if the categories of X contain all the categories of Y. That is, if label X is (TOP-SECRET, {NUCLEAR, ARMY}) and label Y is (SECRET, {ARMY}), then label X dominates label Y. Likewise, if label X is (SECRET, {NUCLEAR, ARMY}), it would dominate label Y. If two labels are exactly identical, they are said to dominate each other.

If two labels are not comparable, however, neither one dominates the other. For example, if label X is (TOP-SECRET, {NUCLEAR}) and label Y is (SECRET, {ARMY}), they are not comparable.

When a user signs on to the system, that user's security clearance specifies the security level of that session. That is, a particular program (e.g., a text editor) is run as a secret process when executed by a secret user, but is run as an unclassified process when executed by an unclassified user. It is possible for a user to sign on at a security level lower than the one assigned to that user, but not at one higher. For example, a secret user can sign on as an unclassified user, but an unclassified user may not sign on as a secret user. Once a user is signed on at a specific level, all programs executed by that user will be run at that level.

Knowledge-Based Systems

A *knowledge-based system* is a program for extending and/or querying a collection of knowledge expressed using some formal knowledge representation language. Many organizations use knowledge systems such as Lotus Notes to add papers, presentations, thoughts, and ideas of their employees. Other organizations develop their own knowledge-based systems to help employees make better decisions by automating the analysis process based on past experience and other factors. Expert systems and neural networks are two types of knowledge systems.

Expert Systems

An *expert system* is an artificial intelligence application that uses a knowledge base of human experience to aid in solving problems. The degree of problem solving is based on the quality of the data and rules obtained from the human expert. Expert systems are designed to perform at a human expert level. In practice, they will perform both well below and well above that of an individual expert.

The expert system derives its answers by running the knowledge base through an inference engine, a software program that interacts with the user and processes the results from the rules and data in the knowledge base.

Expert systems are used in applications such as medical diagnosis; equipment repair; investment analysis; financial, estate, and insurance planning; route scheduling for delivery vehicles; contract bidding; counseling for self-service customers; production control; and training.

Conventional programming languages, such as Fortran and C, are designed and optimized for the procedural manipulation of data (such as numbers and arrays). Humans, however, often solve complex problems using very abstract, symbolic approaches that are not well suited for implementation in conventional languages.

Although abstract information can be modeled in these languages, considerable programming effort is required to transform the information to a format usable with procedural programming paradigms.

Rule-based programming is one of the most commonly used techniques for developing expert systems. In this programming paradigm, rules are used to represent heuristics, or "rules of thumb," which specify a set of actions to be performed for a given situation. A rule is composed of an *if* portion and a *then* portion. The if portion of a rule is a series of patterns which specify the facts (or data) that cause the rule to be applicable. The process of matching facts to patterns is called pattern matching. The expert system tool provides a mechanism, called the inference engine, which automatically matches facts against patterns and determines which rules are applicable. The *if* portion of a rule can actually be thought of as the *whenever* portion of a rule since pattern matching always occurs whenever changes are made to facts. The *then* portion of a rule is the set of actions to be executed when the rule is applicable. The actions of applicable rules are executed when the inference engine is instructed to begin execution. The inference engine selects a rule, and then the actions of the selected rule are executed (which may affect the list of applicable rules by adding or removing facts). The inference engine then selects another rule and executes its actions. This process continues until no applicable rules remain.

Neural Networks

In information technology, a *neural network* is a system of programs and data structures that approximates the operation of the human nervous system. A neural network usually involves a large number of processors operating in parallel, each with its own small sphere of knowledge and access to data in its local memory. Typically, a neural network is initially "trained" or fed large amounts of data and rules about data relationships (for example, "A grandfather is older than a person's father"). A program can then instruct the network on how to behave in response to an external stimulus (for example, input from a computer user who is interacting with the network) or can initiate activity on its own (within the limits of its access to the external world).

Neural networks often use principles of fuzzy logic to make determinations. Neural networks are sometimes described in terms of knowledge layers, with, in general, more complex networks having deeper layers. In feed-forward systems, learned relationships about data can "feed forward" to higher layers of knowledge.

Current applications of neural networks include: oil exploration data analysis, weather prediction, the interpretation of nucleotide sequences in biology labs, and the exploration of models of thinking and consciousness.

Security considerations for neural networks include planning for what happens if someone tampers with the analysis code, along with the usual authentication and authorization application issues.

System Development Life Cycle (SDLC)

The *Systems Development Life Cycle (SDLC)* is an organized, structured, methodology for developing, implementing, and installing a new or revised *Computer Information System (CIS)*. Standard phases include investigation, analysis and general design, detailed design and implementation, installation, and review. Each phase is made up of activities and each activity is made up of tasks. An *activity* is a group of logically related tasks that lead to, and are defined by, the accomplishment of a specific objective. A *task* is the smallest unit of work that can be assigned and controlled through normal project management techniques, and it is normally performed by an individual person, usually in a matter of days.

Investigation

A project starts by the need or wish to satisfy an objective. The objective may vary a great deal in nature and form. For example, it may be required to develop a system for the control of large buildings, but the objective may also be expressed as the wish to provide an aid to building control.

Therefore, the first phase of a project concerns the expression of a need to satisfy objectives, which leads to expressing a concept and identifying essential constraints. This phase gives no indication about the manner of achieving these objectives. Different techniques can be used, particularly creativity and value analysis techniques (value engineering).

Although descriptions in the requirements definition may appear clear to the customer, this step normally contains few details, and is consequently inadequate for characterizing the complete project. During the definition phase, objectives are listed which must be satisfied by the final system. The purpose of the definition phase is to produce a detailed description of the external behavior of the system. This description describes functions to be fulfilled, constraints to be respected, interfaces to be used, and all complementary information specifying the system size, the execution speed, performance and other characteristics to be satisfied, and so on. The resulting document is called a *requirements specification*. Security considerations must be included in this process. By not discussing security objectives and requirements at the beginning, you will add time and money to the project later.

Analysis and General Design

The design work consists of going on from the requirements specification to an *implementation definition*—in other words, the documents necessary to undertake the implementation. Initially, the designer directly uses specifications to produce a decomposition in terms of internal functions. As decisions are made, refinement continues by expressing how each function—considered as a black box—contributes to achieving the objectives.

This is a simplified view, because design involves several intermediate stages. In each stage, every requirement is transformed into a corresponding implementation by a sequence of decisions.

Although this outline is now conventional, particularly for software projects, useful intermediate stages depend on the class of problems being processed. For real-time systems, the design must produce a simultaneous definition of hardware and software to be used (hardware/software codesign), so the process is more complicated.

The security considerations developed in the investigation stage should be further fleshed out in this step. Specific technologies and security controls, such as user authentication, authorization, encryption, and so on, should be discussed in detail.

Implementation

The implementation phase concerns hardware and software development, followed by the integration of the software into the hardware infrastructure. This implementation leads to a running system that can be reproduced and that satisfies all requirements.

Code reviews in this stage will help catch security issues before the product goes into production. Although code reviews can be costly and time-consuming, the resources spent to fix problems down the road may be much greater. Besides catching potential buffer overflows and format string attacks, code reviews can also find trap doors (back doors to the application) that a developer may have included.

Installation

The installation stage concerns experimentation on a prototype to evaluate its characteristics. Production is started after this evaluation. Complementary industrialization criteria are introduced at this stage.

In this stage, you can start the certification process. For example, operating systems usually go after the C2 certification, and firewalls try for the ICSA seal of approval.

Proper change management procedures should be followed during the installation process. A very detailed, thorough evaluation of the product should also be performed.

Review

When the product has been mass produced and marketed, it goes into operation. The exploitation phase starts, which implies maintenance.

Various types of maintenance are possible: corrective to eliminate residual errors, adaptive to take account of new requirements, and preventive to increase system reliability.

The last two phases do not necessarily form part of the project. However, regardless of the organization, the company is always responsible. For example, other groups or departments can be responsible for production and maintenance of developed products.

Practice Questions

Question 1

> When the computer programming, processing, and data that computers
> work on are spread out over more than one computer, you have imple-
> mented a(n) _____.
>
> ○ a. Distributed Computing Environment
>
> ○ b. Nondistributed computing environment
>
> ○ c. Agent
>
> ○ d. Applet

Answer a is correct. A Distributed Computing Environment is implemented
when the computer programming, processing, and data that computers work on
are spread out over more than one computer. Answer b is incorrect because a
nondistributed computing environment is one where the computer programming,
processing, and data are not spread out over more than one computer. Answer c is
incorrect because an agent is a program that gathers information or performs
some other service on some regular schedule without your immediate presence.
Answer d is incorrect because an applet is a small application program.

Question 2

> A program that gathers information or performs some other service on some
> regular schedule without your immediate presence is a(n) _____.
>
> ○ a. Applet
>
> ○ b. ActiveX control
>
> ○ c. Agent
>
> ○ d. C++ control

Answer c is correct. An agent is a program that gathers information or performs
some other service on some regular schedule without your immediate presence.
Answer a is incorrect because an applet is a small application program. Answers
b and d are incorrect because a control (ActiveX or C++) is a component of the
ActiveX language and environment.

Question 3

> Which programming language was developed for specific use on the Internet and on a wide variety of platforms?
>
> ○ a. Fortran
>
> ○ b. C++
>
> ○ c. C
>
> ○ d. Java

Answer d is correct. Java was developed for specific use on the Internet and on a wide variety of platforms. Answers a, b, and c are incorrect because these languages were not developed specifically for use over the Internet and for functionality on a wide variety of platforms.

Question 4

> An activity in which an unclassified user legitimately accesses unclassified information and deduces secret information refers to _____.
>
> ○ a. Inference
>
> ○ b. Polyinstantiation
>
> ○ c. Data mining
>
> ○ d. Aggregation

Answer a is correct. Inference is an activity in which an unclassified user legitimately accesses unclassified information and deduces secret information. Answer b is incorrect because polyinstantiation is used to prevent inference violations. Answer c is incorrect because data mining is the analysis of data for relationships that have not previously been discovered. Answer d is incorrect because aggregation is the process of combining small pieces of information to gain insight into the whole.

Question 5

> The analysis of data for relationships that have not previously been discovered is _____.
>
> ○ a. Inference
>
> ○ b. Polyinstantiation
>
> ○ c. Data mining
>
> ○ d. Aggregation

Answer c is correct. Data mining is the analysis of data for relationships that have not previously been discovered. Answer a is incorrect because inference is a unilateral activity in which an unclassified user legitimately accesses unclassified information and deduces secret information. Answer b is incorrect because polyinstantiation is used to prevent inference violations. Answer d is incorrect because aggregation is the process of combining small pieces of information to gain insight into the whole.

Question 6

> What technique is used to prevent inference violations?
>
> ○ a. Inference
>
> ○ b. Polyinstantiation
>
> ○ c. Data mining
>
> ○ d. Aggregation

Answer b is correct. Polyinstantiation is used to prevent inference violations. Answer a is incorrect because inference is a unilateral activity in which an unclassified user legitimately accesses unclassified information and deduces secret information. Answer c is incorrect because data mining is the analysis of data for relationships that have not previously been discovered. Answer d is incorrect because aggregation is the process of combining small pieces of information to gain insight into the whole.

Question 7

> A type of virus or replicative code that situates itself in a computer system
> in a place where it can do harm is a _____.
>
> ○ a. Worm
>
> ○ b. Trojan horse
>
> ○ c. Logic bomb
>
> ○ d. Denial of service attack

Answer a is correct. A worm is a type of virus or replicative code that situates
itself in a computer system in a place where it can do harm. Answer b is incorrect
because a Trojan horse is a program or virus in which malicious or harmful code
is contained inside apparently harmless programming, data, or message in such a
way that it can get control and do its chosen form of damage. Answer c is incorrect because a logic bomb is code or an application that is surreptitiously inserted
into an application or OS that causes it to perform some destructive or security-
compromising activity whenever specified conditions are met. Answer d is incorrect because a denial of service attack prohibits users from accessing data or a
service when needed.

Question 8

> Code surreptitiously inserted into an application or OS that causes it to per-
> form some destructive or security-compromising activity whenever speci-
> fied conditions are met is a _____.
>
> ○ a. Worm
>
> ○ b. Trojan horse
>
> ○ c. Logic bomb
>
> ○ d. Denial of service attack

Answer c is correct. A logic bomb is code surreptitiously inserted into an application or OS that causes it to perform some destructive or security-compromising
activity whenever specified conditions are met. Answer a is incorrect because a
worm is a type of virus or replicative code that situates itself in a computer system
in a place where it can do harm. Answer b is incorrect because a Trojan horse is a
program or virus in which malicious or harmful code is contained inside apparently harmless programming, data, or messages in such a way that it can get
control and do its chosen form of damage. Answer d is incorrect because a denial
of service attack prohibits users from accessing data or a service when needed.

Question 9

Which viruses infect executable code found in certain system areas on a disk?

- ○ a. Trap doors
- ○ b. Trojan horses
- ○ c. Macro viruses
- ○ d. Boot-sector viruses

Answer d is correct. Boot-sector viruses infect executable code found in certain system areas on a disk. Answer a is incorrect because a trap door is a back door to an application or system created by the developer. Answer b is incorrect because a Trojan horse is a program or virus in which malicious or harmful code is contained inside apparently harmless programming, data, or messages in such a way that it can get control and do its chosen form of damage. Answer c is incorrect because macro viruses infect applications such as Word and Excel by planting malicious macros.

Question 10

A backdoor application entry point added by the developer is a _____.

- ○ a. Trap door
- ○ b. Trojan horse
- ○ c. Macro virus
- ○ d. Boot-sector virus

Answer a is correct. A trap door is a backdoor application entry point added by the developer. Answer b is incorrect because a Trojan horse is a program or virus in which malicious or harmful code is contained inside apparently harmless programming, data, or messages in such a way that it can get control and do its chosen form of damage. Answer c is incorrect because macro viruses infect applications such as Word and Excel by planting malicious macros. Answer d is incorrect because a boot-sector virus infects executable code found in the master boot record.

Need to Know More?

 www.securityfocus.com is a great resource for general security information.

 www.symantec.com has excellent information on viruses and anti-virus countermeasures.

 www.usdoj.gov/jmd/irm/lifecycle/table.htm is the Web site of the Department of Justice SDLC Guidance, and provides detailed information on the System Development Life Cycle.

Cryptography

Terms you'll need to understand:

✓ Symmetric algorithms

✓ Asymmetric algorithms

✓ Message authentication

✓ Digital signature (DS)

✓ Hash function

✓ Public key infrastructure (PKI)

Techniques you'll need to master:

✓ Understanding cryptographic concepts, methodologies, and practices

✓ Understanding private and public key algorithms

✓ Understanding public key infrastructure (PKI)

The Cryptography domain addresses the principles, means, and methods of disguising information to ensure its integrity, confidentiality, and authenticity.

For the CISSP exam, you need to fully understand the basic concepts of cryptography, public and private key algorithms, key distribution and management, digital signatures, applications, and more.

Encryption Techniques and Technologies

Cryptography can be used to control access to computers and networks and involves the processes of encryption and decryption. Cryptography also involves securing the transmission and storage of data; its purpose is to protect data from the eyes of unintended viewers. Encryption protects data from attackers (a person or system that intends to compromise a system) by scrambling the information (or plaintext) into an unreadable form (or ciphertext). This scrambling process is based on algorithms that use various forms of substitution, transposition, or mathematical constructs to encrypt the message.

Rounds, Parallelization, and Strong Encryption

Algorithms make up the foundation of the encryption process. They are mathematical constructs that are applied to plaintext through various applications in order to encrypt transmissions or to store information. Decryption is the process of using the same algorithm used in the encryption process to restore the information into readable form.

An algorithm generally goes through several *rounds* when encrypting and decrypting data. A round is a discrete part of the encryption process; the higher the number of rounds, the better. Some algorithms, especially symmetric key algorithms, process encryption in blocks, using half the data in one round, the other half in a second round, and then combine everything in a final third round, making the encryption that much stronger. This separation also speeds up processing time.

Parallelization can also be used during the encryption/decryption process. It refers to the method of using multiple processes, processors, or machines working together to try and crack an algorithm. It can also be used to increase the speed of the encryption/decryption process by utilizing multiple processors.

Strong encryption refers to an encryption process that uses at least a 128-bit key. The major difference between strong encryption and other types of encryption is the size of the encryption key; the larger the key, the stronger the encryption. New technologies are always being developed to create longer keys, so this definition may need to change in the future. In the past, the United States government did not allow products containing strong encryption to be exported. As of January 2000, this policy has been changed to allow the export of products using strong encryption.

Symmetric (Private Key) Encryption

The *private key* method (or *symmetric* method) is an encryption process where one key is used for both encryption and decryption. This is different from public key encryption where a different key is used for encryption and decryption.

Private key encryption is fast and efficient, making it ideal for large data transmissions. Furthermore, private key encryption is effective when used in conjunction with public key encryption because it is much faster. Using public key encryption for key exchange and then using symmetric encryption for data transfer is commonly used. However, because the same key is used for both encryption and decryption, the sender and receiver must have the keys before the data transmission, which raises a critical problem. The private key must be transported over a secure channel to the receiver. But how is a channel secured? If a secure channel existed, encryption wouldn't be needed to begin with. So, the receiver and sender must devise a method for safely exchanging the key prior to transmission, such as through mail or a physical face-to-face exchange.

Also, the private key method requires a large number of keys. Usually, people transmit data to and receive data from more than one party. Each pair of senders and receivers must have a unique key, thus causing each party to maintain multiple keys, which can be difficult to manage. Many businesses interact with millions of one-time customers daily, making this solution impractical. Therefore, the private key method is best used in environments where the private key could be easily exchanged and where frequent communication exists between parties. For instance, the private key method is optimally used in internal communication between colleagues.

Symmetric Algorithms

Many symmetric algorithms exist, including the Data Encryption Standard (DES), Triple DES, RSA algorithms RC2, RC4, RC5, RC6, International Data Encryption Algorithm (IDEA), Blowfish and Twofish, Shipjack, MARS, Rijndael and Serpent, and Advanced Encryption Standard (AES).

Data Encryption Standard (DES)

DES is one of the most widely accepted, publicly available cryptographic systems today. It was developed by IBM in the 1970s but was later adopted by the U.S. government as a national standard. DES uses a 56-bit key (as compared to 40-128 bits); the larger the key, the more secure the transmission. DES processes 64-bit inputs into 64-bit ciphertext. Essentially, this algorithm goes through 16 iterations that interlace blocks of plaintext with values obtained from the key.

How does the DES algorithm work? Dividing the original message into 64-bit blocks starts the process. Each block is then permutated to change the order of its bits. Next, this plaintext block is split into two 32-bit blocks (the right and left blocks). Simultaneous to the division and permutation of the original message, the 56-bit key is divided into two 28-bit halves (the right and left half). Each half is circular-shifted to the left, reconnected, transposed, and enlarged to 48 bits. (The two key halves are saved and used for the following iteration.) Then, the right half of the plaintext blocks (32-bit) is expanded to 48-bits and is permutated. Next, the new 48-bit plaintext block is crossed over with the 48-bit key blocks. This result is then converted to 32-bits using a substitution function. This 32-bit block is crossed over with the left half of the plaintext block (the left half of the original 64-bit block) forming two new 32-bit halves. The process then starts again with the circular shifting of the new 32-bit halves. There are 15 more iterations of this sequence.

This is a simplified version of the many complex details involved with the DES algorithm. DES is a standard algorithm used in single key encryption; however, there are many alternatives. Two alternatives include International Data Encryption Algorithm (IDEA) and Ron Rivest's RC ciphers.

Triple DES

DES uses a 56-bit key and is not deemed sufficient to encrypt sensitive data. Triple DES goes through three iterations of DES, effectively encrypting the data with a 168-bit key strong enough to secure sensitive information. The data is first encrypted using a 56-bit DES key, decrypted with another 56-bit DES key, and finally encrypted again with the original 56-bit DES key.

Because Triple DES contains several levels of encryption, it can better protect against man-in-the-middle attacks.

DES is a very fast algorithm, and although Triple DES is a little slower, it is still faster than some other symmetric encryption algorithms. The biggest advantage for Triple DES, though, is that it is compatible with all software and hardware that support DES.

RSA Algorithms

Ron Rivest, Adi Shamir, and Leonard Adleman are best known for inventing the public-key RSA algorithm in 1977. They also developed the RC series of symmetric algorithms. This series uses variable-length keys up to 128 bits. RC2 and RC4 are the most commonly used symmetric key algorithms for commercial applications.

RC2 and RC5 were developed by Ron Rivest (Rivest Cipher No. 2). RC2 is a *block mode cipher*, meaning it encrypts data in 64-bit blocks. Because it is a variable-length key, it can use key lengths from zero to infinity. Of course, the larger the key length, the slower the encryption process.

RC5 is similar to RC2 because it is a block cipher, but RC5 uses a variable block size, key length, and number of processing rounds. The general recommendation for RC5 is to use a 128-bit key and 12 to 16 processing rounds for a secure algorithm.

RC4, developed by Ron Rivest in 1987, is a *stream cipher*, meaning it encrypts all the data in real time. This process differs from block ciphers that break the data into smaller chunks for processing. RC4 allows a variable key length, but a 128-bit key is standard.

RC6 is actually a new family of encryption algorithms developed in 1998. A theoretical weakness was discovered in RC5; RC6 was designed to fix this flaw.

IDEA

The *International Data Encryption Algorithm (IDEA)* was originally developed in 1990 as the Proposed Encryption Standard (PES). In 1992, it was renamed IDEA. IDEA is a block cipher that uses 64-bit data blocks and a 128-bit key. Even though some consider this a stronger algorithm than RC4 and Triple DES, it has not gained wide acceptance and usage in the market.

Blowfish and Twofish

Both Blowfish and Twofish were developed by Bruce Schneier, famed cryptographer, author of *Applied Cryptography*, and founder of Counterpane. Blowfish is a very flexible symmetric key algorithm often used in Secure Shell (SSH). It is a variable-round block cipher that can use a variable key length up to 448 bits.

Twofish is Schneier's latest algorithm. It uses a 128-bit block and is much faster than Blowfish. It supports 28-, 192-, and 256-bit keys and is designed to work on smart cards.

Skipjack

Skipjack is a symmetric key algorithm designed by the U.S. National Security Agency (NSA) and found in the Fortezza and Clipper chips. It uses an 80-bit key and 32 rounds on 64-bit data blocks. The math behind this algorithm is top secret.

MARS

MARS is a block cipher algorithm developed by IBM. It uses 128-bit blocks and supports keys longer than 400 bits. MARS provides stronger security and better performance speed over DES. Like Twofish, it is designed to work on smart cards.

Rijndael

The Rijndael algorithm is a block cipher that supports 128-, 192-, or 256-bit keys. This algorithm is designed to work quickly over ATM networks, ISDN lines, and high-definition television (HDTV). Rijndael was accepted as the new Advanced Encryption Standard (AES).

Serpent

Serpent is a 128-bit block cipher that supports key sizes up to 256 bits. It is comparable to DES, but it is optimized for Intel-based chips.

The Advanced Encryption Standard (AES)

The AES is the encryption algorithm that will replace DES as the national standard. Some feel DES and Triple DES are no longer adequate algorithms for our security needs. The National Institute of Standards and Technology (NIST) recently announced that the Rijndael algorithm will replace DES.

Asymmetric Key Encryption

A second method of encryption is *public key* or *asymmetric key* encryption. This form of cryptography involves two keys: a private key and a public key. Every user has a public key, which is distributed freely, and a private key, which is secret. For transmission, the data is first encrypted with the recipient's public key. Next, the data is sent to the recipient who decrypts it with their private key. Therefore, to send an encrypted message, according to the public key method, the sender must first obtain the intended recipient's public key.

The asymmetric technique itself is simple, yet producing two keys that work together to provide a high level of security can be complex. This added complexity, however, increases the use of public key cryptography. Messages and data can be exchanged without first communicating a private key. Also, because of the public key method, documents can contain digital signatures authenticating the data source. Due to the high level of security provided by this method, it is most often applied to electronic commerce. There are several public key schemas; however, the most popular and well-known technique involves RSA.

Asymmetric Algorithms

There are many asymmetric algorithms. Topics related to asymmetric algorithms include the RSA Algorithm, RSA implementation, the math of RSA, Diffie-Hellman, and digital signature algorithm (DSA).

The RSA Algorithm

The RSA algorithm randomly uses a very large prime public key. The algorithm uses this prime number to generate another—the private key. The private key is derived through complex mathematical functions. The RSA Algorithm is founded on four basic properties:

➤ *Property 1*—Deciphering (decrypting) an enciphered (encrypted) message yields the original message. This property is represented by the following equation:

D (E (M))=M

where D represents the action of deciphering, E represents the action of enciphering, and M represents the original message.

➤ *Property 2*—Relatively, E and D are easily computed.

➤ *Property 3*—Knowing E does not reveal an easy way to compute D. In other words, only the holder of D can decipher (decrypt) a message.

➤ *Property 4*—The converse of the first property is true. Therefore, a deciphered message can be encrypted to result in the original message.

These properties seem simple enough (and they are for small numbers of 10 to 20 digits); however, the RSA algorithm generally uses numbers up to 154 digits (512 bits) for each of the public and private keys. The RSA algorithm is based on a one-way, or trap door, function. A function is known as a trap door function if it meets the first three properties above. A trap door function is easy to compute in one direction but not the other. It is labeled a "trap door" function because the inverse of the function is easily computed only if you know the private (trap door) information (or, for encryption purposes, the private key).

RSA Implementation

Various programs implement the RSA Algorithm through three steps:

1. The program converts the message into a representative integer between 0 and (n-1). If the message is large, the program will break it down into blocks. Each block is represented by its own integer less than n-1.

2. By raising each of the integer values to the Eth (encrypted) power, the program encrypts the message. The resulting value is divided by *n*. The remainder is saved as the encrypted message. This type of arithmetic is known as *modulo arithmetic*, which retains only the remainder from a division operation. The original message is now an encrypted message, C.

3. To decrypt C, the recipient raises the message to the Dth (decrypted) power. Then, the recipient uses n to perform modulo division on the result. The result is the blocks within the decrypted message, which the program converts back to text.

In practice, the user distributes the encryption key (E, *n*) and keeps the decryption key (D, *n*) private.

The Math of RSA

The RSA Algorithm goes through four steps. First, it finds two large primary numbers (p and q). Next, n is calculated such that n=p*q. Then, E (the public exponent) is selected. E must be less than n and relatively prime to (p-1)*(q-1). Finally, D (the private exponent) is computed such that ED = 1 mod ((p-1)*(q-1)). As mentioned earlier, (E, *n*) is the public key and (D, *n*) is the private key.

RSA is the most popular public key algorithm. In the past, though, it was very expensive to license and use. In September 2000, the RSA patent expired, so it is now available for public use.

Diffie-Hellman—The Primary Alternative to RSA

There are several alternatives to the RSA algorithm. The most popular of the alternatives is the Diffie-Hellman Algorithm. This algorithm is very similar to RSA; however, the strength of each algorithm is based on separate factors. The RSA factor of strength is the difficulty of finding the prime factors of a large integer. The Diffie-Hellman factor of strength is the difficulty of computing discrete logarithms in a finite field generated by a large primary number. Although both algorithms are similar in mathematical theory, their implementation is somewhat different. The implementation was affected by the expiration of the Diffie-Hellman patent in September 1997, which released this algorithm to the public.

Digital Signature Algorithm (DSA)

The *digital signature algorithm (DSA)* was introduced by NIST and made available to the public in 1994. Because it was not proprietary, it was used in many products, such as Linux.

Hash Encryption

Hash encryption converts data from a variable length to a fixed-length, 128-bit piece of data called a hash value. Theoretically, no two data will produce the same hash value. Also, the hash process is irreversible. You cannot recover the original data by reversing the hash process.

Hashes are most often used if there is information you never want to be decrypted or read. For example, Unix passwords are only stored on the system as hashes. When you log on to a Unix system and enter your password, the system calculates the hash and compares it to the one on file for your user ID. If they match, you are granted system access.

Hash Algorithms

Several hash algorithms exist, including MD2, MD4, MD5, and the *Secure Hash Algorithm (SHA)*.

MD2, MD4, and MD5

The MD series is a group of one-way hash algorithms developed by Ron Rivest. MD4 and MD5 are faster than the original MD2 and used more often. MD4 was susceptible to attack, so Rivest developed MD5. MD5 is stronger than MD4 and still produces a 128-bit hash. MD5 is discussed in RFC 1321.

Secure Hash Algorithm (SHA)

SHA was developed by NIST and the NSA and produces a 160-bit hash value. Because it was developed by the government, SHA is the standard hash algorithm for government communications.

SHA is similar to MD5 in structure, though it is slower and more secure. Its increased security stems from the fact that its hash value is 25 percent larger than the value created by MD5.

Digital Signatures (DSs)

Digital signature (DS) is the technique of appending a string of characters to an electronic message in order to authenticate the sender. Some DS techniques also provide an integrity check to ensure the data was not altered during transit. A DS is applied to the message, in essence sealing it from modification. These signatures are based on public key encryption. Because DS is based on an asymmetric scheme, it helps ensure the integrity and confidentiality of the message. The two components of a DS are the original message and the sender's private key that is used to encrypt the message.

DS, as appended to messages, typically employs hexadecimal representations for the body of the signature. This is an integer that uses a single byte for each character. The DS simply takes a text message and treats it as if it were a number consisting of a sequential string of hexadecimal digits. The process of creating a DS is as follows:

1. The original text message is sent through a hashing algorithm, which creates a string of hexadecimal characters known as the *message digest*.

2. The algorithm used to form the message digest seals the message so that if any character in the plaintext message is changed, the digest will change also. The message digest, generated for use with digital signatures, is a fixed length, short enough to be encrypted with the sender's private key.

3. The message digest is encrypted with the sender's private key, resulting in the digital signature.

4. The sender encrypts the digital signature with a new *random key.*

5. The sender encrypts the new random key with the recipient's public key, resulting in a *digital envelope.* A digital envelope is a type of security that uses two layers of encryption to protect a message.

6. The encrypted message, encrypted digital signature, and encrypted digital envelope are sent to the recipient over a network such as the Internet.

7. The recipient decrypts the *digital envelope* with his or her private key in order to obtain the random key.

8. The new random key allows the recipient to decrypt the digital signature and the original message.

9. The recipient then decrypts the digital signature with the sender's public key, exposing the original message digest.

10. The original message digest is assembled using a *cyclic redundancy check,* which samples bits horizontally according to some repetitive scheme across characters in the plaintext message field. The recipient must have the hashing algorithm used by the sender.

11. The decrypted, original message is sent through the algorithm. This produces a new message digest.

12. This new message digest is compared to the original message digest in order to verify the digital signature. Even the change of a single bit in the digest will result in a failure to verify the signature.

The primary function of digital signatures is to provide the same significance as handwritten signatures. DS accomplishes this task by satisfying two needs: identifying the signer and verifying the content.

Identifying the Signer

DS provides greater reliability for identification of the possessor of the private key as the signer of a particular message than does a conventional signature on a paper document. The difficulty arises when trying to associate the holder of a specific private key with an individual person. A solution to this problem is to bring in a third party to electronically verify the identity of the key holder and to certify that information to the recipient. These third parties are known as *certificate authorities (CAs)*.

Verification of Content

DSs are able to provide a seal on an electronic message. By using a hashing algorithm, DSs can verify that the contents of a message remain unchanged from the version that was signed with the private key. The recipient can be assured that the message was not intercepted en route, and the sender can be assured that the recipient did not alter the message. The sender can also not deny (repudiate) that the message was sent.

Digital Certificates

Digital certificates electronically identify an individual. A certificate is a digitally signed statement from a trusted third party that verifies the identity and public key of an individual or computer. They are the electronic equivalents of a driver's license or birth certificate. A digital certificate can be obtained either from a public CA or from a private authority running its own certificate server. Digital certificates are composed of:

➤ Sender's public key

➤ Sender's name

➤ Expiration date of sender's public key

➤ Name of the certificate issuer

➤ Serial number of the certificate

➤ Digital signature of the issuer

CAs guarantee that when a user downloads a file sent from a sender, the sender is the person who signed the file and is not someone who forged the sender's signature. This verification acts like a notary seal on a document. The CA verifies the person's identity and then sends him his digital certificate, which contains information about the sender's identity, and a copy of his public key. The certificate is encrypted by the CA's private key.

When a person signs a document, a software program will append their digital signature and their digital certificate to the document. When the recipient receives the file containing the sender's digital signature and digital certificate, they can verify that no one has forged the document. The software program verifies the digital signature by comparing the sender's public key contained in their digital signature with the copy contained in the sender's digital certificate. The success of authenticating software programs depends on two assumptions—first, that users cannot easily determine the private key from the public key, and second, that someone does not steal the person's certificate and private key.

These encryption and secure exchange systems are used, both individually and combined, to secure transactions in electronic commerce. This segment of online activity is expected to grow tremendously in the next few years. Business-to-consumer electronic commerce sales are estimated to grow to $7 billion in the next few years, and business-to-business transactions will be worth more than $150 billion. With this expected amount of growth, it is important to understand how these encryption technologies work together to ensure secure transaction processing.

Using Encryption Processes

Encryption algorithms and crypto-systems can be combined to allow for secure communications such as email, e-commerce transactions, and network security.

Email

Several encryption technologies exist to provide secure messaging. The most common are PGP and S/MIME.

PGP

Pretty Good Privacy, or *PGP*, was developed by Philip Zimmerman. It provides a confidentiality and authentication service that can be used for email and file-storage applications. PGP uses cryptographic algorithms integrated into a general-purpose application that is independent of operating systems and processors. PGP and its documentation, including source code, are freely available on the Internet.

S/MIME

Secure Multi–Purpose Internet Mail Extensions (S/MIME) is a secure method of sending e-mail that uses the RSA public-key encryption system. S/MIME is included in the latest versions of the Web browsers from Microsoft and Netscape, and has also been endorsed by other vendors that make messaging products. RSA has proposed S/MIME as a standard to the Internet Engineering Task Force (IETF).

MIME is described in RFC 1521 and spells out how an electronic message will be organized. S/MIME describes how encryption information and a digital certificate can be included as part of the message body. S/MIME follows the syntax provided in the Public Key Cryptography Standard (Public Key Cryptography System) format #7.

Web Server Encryption

Secure Sockets Layer (SSL) is the de facto secure protocol for e-commerce transactions. Although SSL does not provide mechanisms for handling payment, it does offer confidentiality in Web sessions, authenticity of Web servers, and, optionally, verification of end users. The second, less used, secure protocol is Secure HTTP (S-HTTP). S-HTTP is a connectionless protocol that wraps messages in a secure digital envelope.

Secure Sockets Layer (SSL)

SSL provides a secure channel between Web clients and Web servers that choose to use the protocol for Web sessions. Unlike the standard Internet protocols such as TCP/IP, SSL must be selectively employed by the Web client and server in order to use the protocol. Usually, by simply clicking on a designated SSL Web page link, a Web client will invoke the protocol to connect to an SSL-enabled server.

SSL is a layered approach to providing a secure channel. That is, SSL is simply another layer in the network protocol stack that rides on top of the TCP/IP stack. SSL provides secure communications, authentication of the server, and data integrity of the message packet. Because SSL resides on top of the TCP/IP layers, it can potentially secure the communications of any number of application-level protocols that communicate over the Internet. Currently, SSL secures only Web sessions.

SSL secures the channel by providing end-to-end encryption of the data that is sent between a Web client and Web server. Although an intermediary may be able to see the data in transmission, the encryption will effectively scramble the data so that it cannot be intelligently interpreted. However, the technology should not be oversold. Data that resides on the Web client's machine and on the Web server's machine before it is encrypted and after it is decrypted is only as secure as the host machines.

In addition to securing the channel via encryption, SSL provides authentication of the merchant's server. This means that if the channel has been successfully secured, the Web client is assured the server has been endorsed by a CA that the Web client trusts. The CA will endorse only the identity of the Web server. This means that end users can be sure of the identity of the Web site they are connected to, but there is no assurance of the quality of the Web content.

SSL uses two different encryption technologies, public key (asymmetric) encryption and private key (symmetric) encryption, to authenticate the Web server and/or client and to encrypt the communication channel. Public key encryption is used to authenticate the server and/or client and to exchange a private session key between the Web server and client. The exchange of the private session key makes symmetric encryption possible in securing communications. The strict use of public key encryption to conduct secure sessions is inefficient. Its performance would be too slow, and thus impractical for Web sessions. Private key encryption and decryption, by contrast, is significantly faster than public key encryption. A performance penalty exists when using SSL or any encryption algorithm in general; however, the delay imposed by private key encryption is acceptable in most Internet applications.

When initiating a secure connection, the consumer's browser sends the server a "Client Hello" that consists of the browser-supported suite of secure protocols and a random challenge string generated by the browser. The random challenge string is unique to this session and will be used at the close of the initialization to verify that a secure session has been established. The suite of secure protocols consists of key exchange algorithms for agreement on a private session key, private key encryption protocols for transaction confidentiality, and hashing algorithms for data integrity.

Before setting up the secure connection, SSL will attempt to authenticate the server. In response to the Client Hello, the server will respond with a "Server Hello" consisting of an X.509 standard server certificate, an acknowledgment that the server can support the protocols requested by the client, and a random connection identifier. As with the random challenge string, the connection identifier will be used at the close of the protocol to determine if a secure session has been set up.

The merchant's certificate must be endorsed by a trusted CA for server authentication. The client's browser will then check the digital signature on the server certificate against the public key of the CA stored in the browser's table of CAs. If the merchant server certificate is endorsed by a CA, it will be signed through use of the CA's private key. The endorsement of the certification authority is verified when the browser checks the signature using the public key stored in its table of CA's public keys.

Once the merchant server has been authenticated by the browser client, the browser will generate a master secret to be shared only between the server and client. This secret serves as a seed to generate a number of keys used for both symmetric (private key) encryption and data integrity. The master secret is encrypted with the server's public key and sent to the merchant.

From this point on, public key encryption is no longer necessary for this session. Efficient private key encryption algorithms such as RC2 (40-bit encryption) and RC4 or RC6 (128-bit) can be used to secure all subsequent messages during this session. From the master secret, both the server and client will generate two sets of symmetric key pairs to secure incoming and outgoing messages. Because the server and client have agreed to a common protocol and they are both using the same master secret, they will generate identical symmetric key pairs. One key pair is used to encrypt outgoing traffic from the client and to decrypt incoming traffic to the server. In other words, the client's outgoing write key equals the server's incoming read key.

The other symmetric key pair is used to encrypt the server's outgoing messages and to decrypt the client's incoming messages. For security purposes, it is important to note that the client browser generates the master shared secret. This provides assurance from the client's perspective that the server is not reusing the same symmetric encryption key pairs for other sessions. In addition, the master secret is randomly generated for each new session. Even if this key were compromised by chance, it could not be used to decrypt other sessions with other merchants or future sessions with the same merchant.

Two final handshakes are used to verify the secure setup of the session. The "Client Finish" encrypts the server's random connection identifier using the client-write key. If the server started with the same shared secret, the server's read key will decrypt the random connection identifier. The server will know that a secure connection has been established if the decrypted connection identifier is the same as the one the server sent during the Server Hello. The "Server Finish" completes the setup of the secure channel.

The server uses the server-write key to encrypt the challenge string sent by the client during the Client Hello. The encrypted challenge key is sent back to the client. The client decrypts the challenge using the client's read key and compares it with the challenge originally sent to the server. If the comparison checks properly, the client will have assurance that a secure connection has been established. Recall that the random challenge was sent to the server during the Client Hello in plaintext form that could possibly have been intercepted by a third party. Although this may have seemed foolish at the time, the final step of encrypting and decrypting the random challenge provides the assurance of security. Because the master secret is known only to the server and client, and was subsequently used as a seed in encrypting and decrypting the random challenge, the client can be assured that a secure connection has been established with the server challenged during the Client Hello.

Through this series of handshakes involving public and private key cryptography, the Web shopper can be assured of a secure connection to an authenticated merchant server.

Secure HyperText Transfer Protocol (S-HTPP)

The *Secure HyperText Transfer Protocol (S-HTPP)* is a secure extension of HTTP. S-HTTP provides a means for communicating securely with a Web server. The protocol was designed to be general enough to provide broad support for a number of different secure technologies, including symmetric encryption for data confidentiality, public key encryption for client/server authentication, and message digests for data integrity.

Unlike SSL, the negotiation of secure properties occurs through an exchange of packet headers in S-HTTP. Whereas SSL used special handshakes to establish the parameters of the secure connection, S-HTTP defines a specific security negotiation header for packets sent during the Web session. The security negotiation headers may define the choice of secure technologies (symmetric encryption, client/server authentication, data integrity), the specific algorithms that the party will support, the direction in which the party desires the property to be enforced (sending or receiving), and the mode in which the property is requested (required, optional, refuse).

Once the secure properties for a session have been negotiated, S-HTTP secures the session by encapsulating the data within a secure envelope. The secure envelope supports confidentiality of the Web session contents, message integrity, and authentication of clients and servers.

Secure Network Protocols

Virtual private networks (VPNs) are becoming popular methods for securing remote access connections.

A VPN is a private data network that makes use of the public telecommunication infrastructure, maintaining privacy through the use of a tunneling protocol and security procedures. A virtual private network can be contrasted with a system of owned or leased lines that can only be used by one company. The purpose of a VPN is to provide the same capabilities at much lower cost by using the shared public infrastructure of the Internet rather than a private one.

Using a virtual private network involves encrypting data before sending it through the public network and decrypting it at the receiving end. An additional level of security involves encrypting not only the data but also the originating and receiving network addresses. Microsoft, 3Com, and several other companies have developed the *Point-to-Point Tunneling Protocol (PPTP)* for virtual private network creation.

Although VPNs offer direct cost savings over other communications methods (such as leased lines and long-distance calls), they can also offer other advantages, including indirect cost savings as a result of reduced training requirements and equipment, increased flexibility, and scalability.

In VPNs, *virtual* implies that the network is dynamic, with connections set up according to organizational needs. It also means that the network is formed logically, regardless of the physical structure of the underlying network (the Internet, in this case). Unlike the leased lines used in traditional corporate networks, VPNs do not maintain permanent links between the end points that make up the corporate network. Instead, when a connection between two sites is needed, it is created; when the connection is no longer needed, it is torn down, making the bandwidth and network resources available for other uses. Thus, the connections making up a VPN do not have the same physical characteristics as the hard-wired connections used on the LAN.

Tunnels can consist of two types of end points, either an individual computer or a LAN with a security gateway, which might be a router or a firewall. Only two combinations of these end points, however, are usually considered in designing VPNs. In the first case, LAN-to-LAN tunneling, a security gateway at each end point serves as the interface between the tunnel and the private LAN. In these cases, users on either LAN can use the tunnel transparently to communicate with each other.

The second case, that of client-to-LAN tunnels, is the type usually set up for a mobile user who wants to connect to the corporate LAN. The client, i.e., the mobile user, initiates the creation of the tunnel in order to exchange traffic with the corporate network. To do so, he runs special client software on his computer to communicate with the gateway protecting the destination LAN.

Four different protocols have been suggested for creating VPNs over the Internet: Point-to-Point Tunneling Protocol (PPTP), Layer 2 Forwarding (L2F), Layer 2 Tunneling Protocol (L2TP), and IP Security Protocol (IPSec).

One reason for the number of protocols is that, for some companies, a VPN is a substitute for remote-access servers, allowing mobile users and branch offices to dial into the protected corporate network via their local ISP. For others, a VPN may consist of traffic traveling in secure tunnels over the Internet between protected LANs. The protocols that have been developed for VPNs reflect this dichotomy. PPTP, L2F, and L2TP are largely aimed at dial-up VPNs, while IPSec's main focus to date has been LAN-to-LAN solutions.

The most commonly used protocol for remote access to the Internet is *Point-to-Point Protocol (PPP)*. PPTP builds on the functionality of PPP to provide remote access that can be tunneled through the Internet to a destination site. As currently implemented, PPTP encapsulates PPP packets using a modified version of the generic routing encapsulation (GRE) protocol, which gives PPTP the flexibility of handling protocols other than IP, such as Internet packet exchange (IPX) and network basic input/output system extended user interface (NetBEUI).

Because of its dependence on PPP, PPTP relies on the authentication mechanisms within PPP, namely password authentication protocol (PAP) and Challenge Handshake Authentication Protocol (CHAP). Because there is a strong tie between PPTP and Windows NT, an enhanced version of CHAP, MS-CHAP, is also used, which utilizes information within NT domains for security. Similarly, PPTP can use PPP to encrypt data, but Microsoft has also incorporated a stronger encryption method called Microsoft Point-to-Point Encryption (MPPE) for use with PPTP.

Aside from the relative simplicity of client support for PPTP, one of the protocol's main advantages is that PPTP is designed to run at OSI Layer 2, or the link layer, as opposed to IPSec, which runs at Layer 3. By supporting data communications at Layer 2, PPTP can transmit protocols other than IP over its tunnels. PPTP does have some limitations, though. For example, it does not provide strong encryption for protecting data, nor does it support any token-based methods for authenticating users.

L2F also arose in the early stages of VPN development. Paralleling PPTP's design, L2F utilized PPP for authentication of the dial-up user, but it also included support for TACACS+ and RADIUS for authentication. L2F differs from PPTP because it defines connections within a tunnel, allowing a tunnel to support more than one connection. There are also two levels of authentication of the user, first by the ISP prior to setting up the tunnel, and then when the connection is set up at the corporate gateway. Because L2TP is a layer-2 protocol, it offers users the same flexibility as PPTP for handling protocols other than IP, such as IPX and NetBEUI.

L2TP was created by an IETF working group as the replacement for PPTP and L2F. L2TP is designed to address the shortcomings of these past protocols and to become an IETF-approved standard. L2TP uses PPP to provide dial-up access that can be tunneled through the Internet to a site. However, L2TP defines its own tunneling protocol, based on the work done on L2F. L2TP transport is defined for a variety of packet media, including X.25, frame-relay, and ATM. To strengthen the encryption of the data it handles, L2TP uses IPSec's encryption methods.

Because it uses PPP for dial-up links, L2TP includes the authentication mechanisms within PPP, namely PAP and CHAP. Similar to PPTP, L2TP supports PPP's use of the extensible authentication protocol for other authentication systems, such as RADIUS. PPTP, L2F, and L2TP do not include encryption or processes for managing the cryptographic keys required for encryption in their specifications. The current L2TP draft standard recommends that IPSec be used for encryption and key management in IP environments; future drafts of the PPTP standard may do the same.

The last, but perhaps most important protocol, IPSec, grew out of efforts to secure IP packets as the next generation of IP (IPv6) was being developed; it can now be used with IPv4 protocols as well. Although the requests for comment (RFCs) defining the IPSec protocols have been part of the IETF's standards track since mid-1995, the protocols are still being refined while engineers learn more from products that appear in the marketplace.

IPSec allows the sender (or a security gateway acting on his behalf) to authenticate or encrypt each IP packet or apply both operations to the packet. Separating the application of packet authentication from encryption has led to two different methods of using IPSec, called modes. In *transport mode*, only the transport-layer segment of an IP packet is authenticated or encrypted. The other approach, authenticating or encrypting the entire IP packet, is called *tunnel mode*. While transport-mode IPSec can prove useful in many situations, tunnel-mode IPSec provides even more protection against certain attacks and traffic monitoring that might occur on the Internet.

IPSec is built around a number of standardized cryptographic technologies that provide confidentiality, data integrity, and authentication. For example, IPSec uses:

➤ *Diffie-Hellman key exchanges*—for delivering secret keys between peers on a public net

➤ *Public key cryptography*—for signing Diffie-Hellman exchanges, to guarantee the identities of the two parties and avoid man-in-the-middle attacks

➤ *Data encryption standard (DES)*—and other bulk encryption algorithms for encrypting data

➤ *Keyed hash algorithms (HMAC, MD5, SHA)*—for authenticating packets

➤ *Digital certificates*—for validating public keys

There are currently two ways to handle key exchange and management within IPSec's architecture: manual keying and IKE for automated key management. Both of these methods are mandatory requirements of IPSec. While manual key exchange might be suitable for a VPN with a small number of sites, VPNs covering a large number of sites or supporting many remote users benefit from automated key management.

IPSec is often considered the best VPN solution for IP environments, because it includes strong security measures—notably encryption, authentication, and key management—in its standard set. Because IPSec is designed to handle only IP packets, PPTP and L2TP are more suitable for use in multiprotocol or non-IP environments, such as those using NetBEUI, IPX, and AppleTalk.

Details of IPSec

IPSec combines the aforementioned security technologies into a complete system that provides confidentiality, integrity, and authenticity of IP datagrams. IPSec actually refers to several related protocols as defined in the new RFC 2401-2411 and 2451 (the original IPSec RFCs 1825-1829 are now obsolete). These standards include:

➤ *IP Security Protocol*—Defines the information to add to an IP packet to enable confidentiality, integrity, and authenticity controls as well as defining how to encrypt the packet data.

➤ *Internet Key Exchange (IKE)*—Negotiates the security association between two entities and exchanges key material. It is not necessary to use IKE, but manually configuring security associations is a difficult and manually intensive process. IKE should be used in most real-world applications to enable large-scale secure communications.

IPSec Packets

IPSec defines a new set of headers to be added to IP datagrams. These new headers are placed after the IP header and before the Layer 4 protocol (typically Transport Control Protocol [TCP] or User Datagram Protocol [UDP]). These new headers provide information for securing the payload of the IP packet as follows:

➤ *Authentication header (AH)*—This header, when added to an IP datagram, ensures the integrity and authenticity of the data, including the invariant fields in the outer IP header. It does not provide confidentiality protection. AH uses a keyed-hash function rather than digital signatures because digital signature technology is too slow and would greatly reduce network throughput.

➤ *Encapsulating security payload (ESP)*—This header, when added to an IP datagram, protects the confidentiality, integrity, and authenticity of the data. If ESP is used to validate data integrity, it does not include the invariant fields in the IP header.

AH and ESP can be used independently or together. For both of these protocols, IPSec does not define the specific security algorithms to use, but rather provides an open framework for implementing industry-standard algorithms. Initially, most implementations of IPSec will support MD5 from RSA Data Security or the SHA as defined by the U.S. government for integrity and authentication. The DES is currently the most commonly offered bulk encryption algorithm, although RFCs are available that define how to use many other encryption systems, including IDEA, Blowfish, and RC4.

In transport mode, only the IP payload is encrypted, and the original IP headers are left intact. This mode has the advantage of adding only a few bytes to each packet. It also allows devices on the public network to see the final source and destination of the packet. This capability allows you to enable special processing (for example, quality of service) in the intermediate network based on the information in the IP header. However, the Layer 4 header will be encrypted, limiting the examination of the packet. Unfortunately, by passing the IP header in the clear, transport mode allows an attacker to perform some traffic analysis. For example, an attacker could see when Cisco's CEO sent a lot of packets to another CEO. However, the attacker would only know that IP packets were sent; the attacker would not be able to determine if they were e-mail or another application.

In tunnel mode, the entire original IP datagram is encrypted, and it becomes the payload in a new IP packet. This mode allows a network device, such as a router, to act as an IPSec proxy. That is, routers perform encryption on behalf of the hosts. The source's router encrypts packets and forwards them along the IPSec tunnel. The destination's router decrypts the original IP datagram and forwards it on to the destination system. The major advantage of tunnel mode is that the end systems do not need to be modified to enjoy the benefits of IPSec. Tunnel mode also protects against traffic analysis. With tunnel mode, an attacker can only determine the tunnel endpoints and not the true source and destination of the tunneled packets, even if they are the same as the tunnel endpoints.

As defined by the IETF, IPSec transport mode can only be used when both the source and the destination systems understand IPSec. In most cases, you deploy IPSec with tunnel mode. Doing so allows you to implement IPSec in the network architecture without modifying the operating system or any applications on your PCs, servers, and hosts.

Security Association

IPSec provides many options for performing network encryption and authentication. Each IPSec connection can provide encryption, integrity, or both. When the security service is determined, the two communicating nodes must determine exactly which algorithms to use (for example, DES or IDEA for encryption; MD5 or SHA for integrity). After deciding on the algorithms, the two devices must share session keys. As you can see, there is quite a bit of information to manage. The *security association* is the method that IPSec uses to track all the particulars concerning a given IPSec communication session. A Security Association (SA) is a relationship between two or more entities that describes how the entities will use security services to communicate securely. The nomenclature gets a little confusing at times because SAs are used for more than just IPSec. For example, IKE SAs describe the security parameters between two IKE devices.

The security association is unidirectional, meaning that for each pair of communicating systems, there are at least two security connections—one from A to B and one from B to A. The security association is uniquely identified by a randomly chosen unique number, called the *security parameter index (SPI)* and the destination IP address of the destination. When a system sends a packet that requires IPSec protection, it looks up the security association in its database, applies the specified processing, and then inserts the SPI from the security association into the IPSec header. When the IPSec peer receives the packet, it looks up the security association in its database by destination address and SPI and then processes the packet as required.

Internet Key Management Protocol

IPSec assumes that a security association is in place, but it does not have a mechanism for creating that association. The IETF chose to break the process into two parts: IPSec provides the packet-level processing, while the *Internet Key Management Protocol (IKMP)* negotiates security associations. After considering several alternatives, including the Simple Key Internet Protocol (SKIP), the IETF chose IKE as the standard method of configuring security associations for IPSec.

IKE creates an authenticated, secure tunnel between two entities and then negotiates the security association for IPSec. This process requires that the two entities authenticate themselves to each other and establish shared keys.

Authentication

Both parties must be authenticated to each other and IKE provides a very flexible framework for authentication that supports multiple authentication methods. The two entities must agree on a common authentication protocol through a negotiation process. The following mechanisms are generally implemented:

➤ *Pre-shared keys*—The same key is pre-installed on each host. IKE peers authenticate each other by computing and sending a keyed hash of data that includes the pre-shared key. If the receiving peer is able to independently create the same hash using its pre-shared key, it knows that both parties must share the same secret, thus authenticating the other party.

➤ *Public key cryptography*—Each party generates a pseudo-random number and encrypts it in the other party's public key. The ability for each party to compute a keyed hash containing the other peer's number, decrypted with the local private key as well as other publicly and privately available information, authenticates the parties to each other. Currently only the RSA public key algorithm is supported.

➤ *Digital signature*—Each device digitally signs a set of data and sends it to the other party. This method is similar to the previous one, except that it provides nonrepudiation. Currently, both the RSA public key algorithm and the digital signature standard (DSS) are supported.

Both digital signature and public key cryptography require the use of digital certificates to validate the public/private key mapping. IKE allows the certificate to be accessed independently (for example, through DNSSEC or by having the two devices explicitly exchange certificates as part of IKE).

Key Exchange

Both parties must have a shared session key in order to encrypt the IKE tunnel. The Diffie-Hellman protocol is used to agree on a common session key. The exchange is authenticated as described previously to guard against man-in-the-middle attacks.

Using IKE with IPSec

These two steps, authentication and key exchange, create the IKE SA, a secure tunnel between the two devices. One side of the tunnel offers a set of algorithms, and the other side must then accept one of the offers or reject the entire connection. When the two sides have agreed on which algorithms to use, they must derive key material to use for IPSec with AH, ESP, or both together. IPSec uses a different shared key than IKE. The IPSec shared key can be derived by using Diffie-Hellman again to ensure perfect forward secrecy, or by refreshing the shared secret derived from the original Diffie-Hellman exchange that generated the IKE SA by hashing it with pseudo-random numbers. The first method provides greater security but is slower. After this process is complete, the IPSec SA is established.

IPSec gives you the power to enable confidentiality, integrity, and authenticity in your network infrastructure. The Internet holds unlimited promise for changing the way we do business, but not without our first addressing the security risks. IPSec provides a key piece of the solution because it allows you to embed security at the network layer. It will work in concert with your other security mechanisms and help your organization become a global networked business.

Public Key Infrastructure (PKI)

The accepted technology standard for identifying individuals is *public key infrastructure (PKI)* using digital certificates, but PKI solutions are often expensive, complex systems that are difficult to deploy, administer, and use. PKI has been touted as the next big thing for years, but it has yet to gain wide acceptance. There are many reasons for this, but trust issues and the lack of easy-to-use applications are two of the main problems.

A PKI enables users of a basically insecure public network such as the Internet to securely and privately exchange data and money through the use of a public and a private cryptographic key pair that is obtained and shared through a trusted authority. The public key infrastructure provides for a digital certificate that can identify an individual or an organization, and directory services that can store and, when necessary, revoke the certificates.

The public key infrastructure assumes the use of *public key cryptography*, which is the most common method for authenticating a message sender or encrypting a message on the Internet. Traditional cryptography has usually involved the creation and sharing of a secret key for the encryption and decryption of messages. This secret or private key system has the significant flaw that if the key is discovered or intercepted by someone else, messages can easily be decrypted. For this reason, public key cryptography and the public key infrastructure is the preferred approach on the Internet.

A public key infrastructure consists of:

➤ CA issues and verifies a digital certificate. A certificate includes the public key or information about the public key.

➤ A registration authority (RA) that acts as the verifier for the CA before a digital certificate is issued to a requestor.

➤ One or more directories where the certificates (with their public keys) are held.

➤ A certificate management system.

Cryptography Attacks

There are seven types of cryptanalytic attacks. Each attack assumes that the cryptanalyst has knowledge of the information encrypted.

➤ *Ciphertext-only attack*—The cryptanalyst has the ciphertext of several messages, all of which have been encrypted using the same encryption algorithm.

➤ *Known-plaintext attack*—The cryptanalyst has access not only to the ciphertext of several messages, but also to the plaintext of those messages.

➤ *Chosen-plaintext attack*—The cryptanalyst not only has access to the ciphertext and associated plaintext for several messages, but he also chooses the plaintext that gets encrypted and obtains the resulting ciphertext. This is more powerful than a known-plaintext attack because the cryptanalyst can choose specific plaintext blocks to encrypt, ones that might yield more information about the key.

➤ *Adaptive-chosen-plaintext attack*—This is a special case of a chosen-plaintext attack. Not only can the cryptanalyst choose the plaintext that is encrypted, but he can also modify his choice based on the results of the previous encryption.

In a chosen-plaintext attack, a cryptanalyst might just be able to choose one large block of plaintext to be encrypted; in an adaptive chosen-plaintext attack, he can choose a smaller block of plaintext and then choose another based on the results of the first, and so forth.

➤ *Chosen-ciphertext attack*—The cryptanalyst can choose different ciphertexts to be decrypted and has access to the decrypted plaintext. For example, the cryptanalyst has access to a tamperproof box that does automatic decryption. His job is to deduce the key.

➤ *Chosen-Key attack*—This attack doesn't mean that the cryptanalyst can choose the key; it means that he has some knowledge about the relationship between different keys.

➤ *Rubber-hose attack*—The cryptanalyst threatens, blackmails, or tortures someone until they give him the key. Bribery is sometimes referred to as a purchase-key attack.

Practice Questions

Question 1

Which of the following is a symmetric encryption algorithm?

- ○ a. 3DES
- ○ b. MD5
- ○ c. RSA
- ○ d. Diffie-Helman

Answer a is correct. 3DES is a symmetric encryption algorithm. Answer b is incorrect because MD5 is a hashing algorithm. Answers c and d are incorrect because RSA and Diffie-Helman are asymmetric algorithms.

Question 2

Which of the following is a hash algorithm?

- ○ a. 3DES
- ○ b. MD5
- ○ c. RSA
- ○ d. Diffie-Helman

Answer b is correct. MD5 is a hash algorithm. Answer a is incorrect because 3DES is a symmetric algorithm. Answers c and d are incorrect because RSA and Diffie-Helman are asymmetric algorithms.

Question 3

Which of the following is an asymmetric algorithm?

- ○ a. 3DES
- ○ b. MD5
- ○ c. RSA
- ○ d. SHA

Answer c is correct. RSA is an asymmetric algorithm. Answer a is incorrect because 3DES is a symmetric algorithm. Answers b and d are incorrect because MD5 and SHA are hashing algorithms.

Question 4

Which of the following is not a core component of a PKI?

○ a. Digital certificate

○ b. CA

○ c. RA

○ d. Firewall

Answer d is correct. A firewall is not a core component of a PKI. Answers a, b, and c are incorrect because digital certificates, CAs, and RAs are core components of a PKI.

Question 5

_____ make up the foundation of the encryption process.

○ a. Hashes

○ b. Email messages

○ c. Certificates

○ d. Algorithms

Answer d is correct. Algorithms make up the foundation of the encryption process. Answers a, b, and c are incorrect because hashes, email messages, and certificates can all use encryption, but they are not the foundation for the encryption process.

Question 6

_____ refers to the method of using multiple processes, processors, or machines working together to try to crack an algorithm.

○ a. Parallelization

○ b. Polyinstantiation

○ c. Encryption

○ d. Hashing

Answer a is correct. Parallelization is the method of using multiple processes, processors, or machines working together to try to crack an algorithm. Answer b is incorrect because polyinstantiation is used to prevent inference violations. Answer c is incorrect because encryption is the process of using an algorithm to change data to an unreadable form. Answer d is incorrect because hashing is the process of using a hash algorithm to transform data to a usually shorter fixed-length value.

Question 7

Which of the following is most commonly used for HTTP traffic encryption?

○ a. SSL

○ b. PGP

○ c. DSA

○ d. IKE

Answer a is correct. SSL is most commonly used for HTTP traffic encryption. Answer b is incorrect because PGP is commonly used for email encryption. Answer c is incorrect because DSA is used for digital signatures. Answer d is incorrect because IKE is commonly used for key exchange in VPNs.

Question 8

Which standard uses AH and ESP?

○ a. RSA

○ b. Ethernet

○ c. SSL

○ d. IPSec

Answer d is correct. IPSec uses AH and ESP. Answers a, b, and c are incorrect because RSA, Ethernet, and SSL do not use AH and ESP.

Question 9

_____ encryption converts data from a variable-length to a fixed-length piece of data.

- ○ a. Email
- ○ b. Asymmetric
- ○ c. Hash
- ○ d. Symmetric

Answer c is correct. Hash encryption converts data from a variable-length to a fixed-length piece of data. Answer a is incorrect because email uses encryption; it is not an encryption technique. Answers b and d are incorrect because asymmetric and symmetric are encryption processes, but they do not convert the data to a fixed-length piece of data.

Question 10

_____ electronically identify an individual.

- ○ a. Hashes
- ○ b. Digital certificates
- ○ c. Encryption algorithms
- ○ d. Machine state

Answer b is correct. Digital certificates can electronically identify an individual. Answers a, c, and d are incorrect because hashes, encryption algorithms, and machine state cannot electronically identify an individual.

Need to Know More?

 www.counterpane.com is the Web site for Counterpane, the company founded by Bruce Schneier. This site serves as an excellent resource for encryption information, especially the Cryptogram newsletter.

 www.securityfocus.com is an excellent resource for security information.

 www.verisign.com is the Web site for Verisign, one of the leading PKI companies. This site offers a wealth of information on the topic.

Security Architecture and Models

Terms you'll need to understand:

✓ Resource manager

✓ Primary storage

✓ Closed system

✓ Information Technology Security Evaluation Criteria (ITSEC)

✓ Trusted Computer System Evaluation Criteria (TCSEC)

✓ Covert channel

✓ Telecommunications Electronics Material Protected from Emanating Spurious Transmissions (TEMPEST)

Techniques you'll need to master:

✓ Understanding principles of common computer and network organizations, architectures, and designs

✓ Understanding principles of common security models, architectures, and evaluation criteria

✓ Understanding common flaws and security issues associated with system architecture designs

The Security Architecture and Models domain contains the concepts, principles, structures, and standards used to design, implement, monitor, and secure operating systems, equipment, networks, applications, and those controls used to enforce various levels of confidentiality, integrity, and availability.

For the CISSP exam, you need to fully understand the security models in terms of confidentiality, integrity, and availability. You also need to understand system models in terms of the international standards: Common Criteria, international (ITSEC), United States Department of Defense (TCSEC), and Internet Engineering Task Force (IETF).

Principles of Common Computer and Network Organizations, Architectures, and Designs

This section will discuss the various principles of computer architectures and designs, including addressing, machine types, storage types, and protection mechanisms.

Addressing

Addressing is how the operating system or program knows how much memory it has and how to call it. Physical addresses are the actual hard-coded addresses to the physical memory. For example, memory block 12k to 20k is a physical address. In most cases, applications do not refer to physical memory. Instead, they refer to virtual memory. Only the operating system can refer to physical memory, and it helps the application by handling the virtual and physical memory mapping.

Symbolic addresses, or *virtual* addresses as they are more commonly called, are addresses that applications use. Symbolic addresses might refer to block 12k to 20k, just like physical addresses, but the block 12k to 20k is actually block 56k to 64k in physical memory. For example, an application may request X amount of memory space where X is greater than the real amount of memory space or is greater than the amount of memory space currently available. The operating system then creates and manages the virtual memory for the application. Virtual memory is not real physical, hard-coded memory. Virtual memory might not even exist physically. All the program knows is that it has X amount of virtual memory to use it as it wishes. The operating system handles the application's virtual memory by keeping a table of what real physical blocks of memory are assigned to the application. The actual blocks of memory might be scattered throughout physical memory and virtual hard drive space. Virtual addressing enables the operating system to handle *multitasking*, the ability to run several programs at one time.

One distinction you should know is address space versus memory space. *Memory space* is a fixed real amount, e.g., 64Mb. *Address space* may be smaller than , equivalent to, or larger than memory space, and specifies where memory is located on the system.

Hardware, Firmware, and Software

The distinction between hardware, firmware, and software is very important. *Hardware* is the computer parts with logical programming chips. *Firmware* is an application or operational code developed to help the hardware function as desired. For example, firewall appliances use firmware to provide firewall functionality. Firmware is usually embedded on a chip or resident in memory. *Software* is an application that can be installed and uninstalled.

Machine Types

Various machine types exist, and for the exam, you should understand the difference between them. A *real machine* is an operating system (OS) that lets you manage physical hardware. The *virtual machine* is an operating layer on top of the OS used to give more control to the OS to automate certain trivial functions, or to provide increased security. The *multistate machine* uses an OS that thinks in states (like a finite state machine) used for real-time programming, artificial intelligence, event programming, and so on. Multitasking is an OS feature that lets several programs run at the same time. Unix is an example of a multitasking OS. *Multi user* is another OS feature that allows multiple users at the same time. MVS is an example of a multiuser OS.

OSI Model

The International Standards Organization (ISO) defines a seven-layer model for network communications protocol. The model is more formally called the Open Systems Interconnection (OSI) model. This model should exist in any network.

The advantage of breaking down the model into layers is twofold:

➤ Each layer can be regarded as a black box. Well-defined inputs and outputs exist, but the inner workings of the layer can be regarded as being independent. Thus, new versions, updates, or better methods can be written without affecting the whole system.

➤ Communication need only take place at the layer appropriate for the task.

The seven layers are (in order):

1. *Physical layer*—The Physical layer is concerned with transmitting raw bits over a communication channel—how many volts to use for 0 and 1, how

many bits per second can be sent, and whether transmission can take place in both directions simultaneously.

2. *Data Link layer*—The Data Link layer groups the bits into units, sometimes called *frames*, and sees that each frame is correctly received. It puts special bit patterns on the start and end of each frame to mark them, and computes checksum by adding up all the bytes in the frame in a certain way. The Data Link layer appends the checksum to the frame.

3. *Network layer*—The primary task of this layer is routing. Two Network-layer protocols are in widespread use, one connection-oriented and one connectionless. The connection-oriented protocol is X.25 and is favored by operators of public networks, such as telephone companies. The connectionless protocol is IP and is part of the DoD (U.S. Department of Defense) protocol suite.

4. *Transport layer*—Packets can be lost on the way from the sender to the receiver. Although some applications can handle their own error recovery, others prefer a reliable connection. The job of the Transport layer is to provide this recovery service. The Transport layer bridges the gap between the Network and Session layers by providing a reliable transport connection. In the case of X.25, because it is connection-oriented, the packets arrive in the correct sequence; but in the case of IP, it is possible for packets to arrive out of order. The job of the Transport layer is to make sure that the packets are received in the same order they are sent out.

5. *Session layer*—The Session layer is an enhanced version of the Transport layer. It provides dialog control to keep track of which party is currently talking, and it provides synchronization facilities. In practice, few applications are interested in the Session layer, and it is rarely supported. It is not even in the DoD protocol suite.

6. *Presentation layer*—Unlike the lower layers, which are concerned with getting the bits from the sender to the receiver reliably and efficiently, the Presentation layer is concerned with the meaning of the bits. Most messages do not consist of random bit strings but of more structured information, such as names, addresses, amounts of money, and so on. In the Presentation layer, it is possible to define records containing fields like these and then have the sender notify the receiver that a message contains a particular record in a certain format.

7. *Application layer*—The Application layer is a collection of miscellaneous protocols for common activities, such as electronic mail, file transfer, and connecting remote terminals to computers over a network.

Operating States

Operating states deal with multitasking and the current state of the application's operations. Operating states are needed because only one application can use a processor at a time. The operating states are blocked, running, and ready. The *blocked state* is when the process is unable to run until some external event happens, like the user pressing a key. The *running state* is when the process (name for the application currently running) is actually using the CPU at that instant. The *ready state* is when the process is runnable but temporarily stopped to let another process finish running. A process in the running state may move to the blocked state (if it needs to wait for a resource), or it may move to the ready state (if its amount of time using the processor, called a *time slice*, is over). A process in the blocked state may only move to the ready state after it has completed whatever it had to do with the resource. A process in the ready state may only move to the running state when it is its turn to use the processor again. Having the CPU handle the management and switching of states allows the system to multitask, that is, run more than one application at a time.

Resource Manager

The resource manager helps control system resources. A resource can be a hardware device (e.g., a tape drive) or a piece of information (e.g., a locked record in a database). A computer will normally have many different resources that can be acquired. Resources come in two types: preemptable and nonpreemptable. A preemptable resource is one that can be taken away from the process that owns it with no ill effects. Memory is an example of a preemptable resource. Consider, for example, a system with 512Kb of user memory, one printer, and two 512K processes that each want to print something. Process A requests and gets the printer, then it starts to compute values to print. Before it has finished with the computation, it exceeds its time quantum and is swapped out. Process B now runs and tries, unsuccessfully, to acquire the printer. Potentially, we now have a deadlock situation because A has the printer and B has the memory, and neither can proceed without the resource held by the other. Fortunately, it is possible to preempt (take away) the memory from B by swapping it out and swapping A in. Now A can run, do its printing, and then release the printer. Thus, no deadlock occurs.

Storage Types

Various storage types exist and are selected depending on your needs: primary, secondary, network, and read. Few storage terms describe storage areas on the system. *Primary storage* refers to system memory. *Secondary storage* refers to disk or tape. *Network storage* also has its own terminology, network attached storage and storage area networks. *Read storage* refers to storing data on the hardware of your system. *Virtual storage* is using system virtual memory for storage.

Principles of Common Security Models, Architectures, and Evaluation Criteria

Certification/accreditation, security models, and evaluation criteria are very important, especially in government and military functions. To establish a heightened level of security, hardware and applications used in these areas should meet a certain set of standards. To ensure these standards are met, evaluation criteria and certification levels have been developed.

Accreditation and Certification

Accreditation and certification are the technical evaluation of a system's security features, made as part of, and in support of. the approval/accreditation process. They establish the extent to which a particular computer system's design and implementation meet a specified set of security requirements.

Closed and Open Systems

A *closed system* means that products from one vendor cannot work with another vendor. You must purchase specific components from the manufacturer. For example, for many years, Sun systems used only specific parts. In an *open system*, you can purchase any standards-compliant part for the system.

Confinement, Bounds, and Isolation

Numerous restraints are placed on a system. *Confinement* restraints ensure that a user cannot write into the security object. *Bounds* are declared limits of a storage construct such as an array, segment, or stack. *Isolation* is the containment of users and resources in an automated system in such a way that users and processes are separate from one another as well as from the protection controls of the operating system.

IETF Security Architecture (IPSec)

The IETF Security Architecture is a standard for secure online communications. There are many different uses of IPSec; however, VPNs are currently where IPSec development is focused.

ITSEC Classes and Required Assurance Functionality

The Information Technology Security Evaluation Criteria (ITSEC) were created by the European Community as a result of "normalizing" the British, German, and French ITSECs into a single EEC-wide ITSEC. These criteria are based on a recognition by their developers that the U.S. Trusted Computer Security Evaluation Criteria (TCSEC) idea of having a single set of measurements for both security functionality and assurance isn't as useful as separately measuring functionality and assurance. Thus, instead of one level—such as the TCSEC's C2 or B1 (which implies a certain combination of functionality and assurance), the ITSEC assigns two levels to each system: an "F" (functionality) level and an "E" (European assurance) level. In this way, a system could have all of the security functions required for the highest level (F6), but some of those functions might not be assured to the highest possible level, and thus the system assurance might be somewhat lower (e.g., E4). When you come across a system that is ITSEC-certified, it will have a rating that looks like this: F4/E4.

The ITSEC also has the idea of evaluating entire systems rather than just computing platforms (such as Windows NT or Solaris). The idea is that an entire system—hardware, operating system, database management system (DBMS), and application—should be evaluated because a system's security level may be greater (or less) than the security level of each of its component parts, or the total security functionality required for a certain "F" level may be distributed across different components in the composite system rather than repeated in all of the components.

Objects and Subjects

An *object* is a passive entity that contains or receives information. Access to an object potentially implies access to the information it contains. Examples of objects are records, blocks, pages, segments, files, directories, directory trees, and programs, as well as bits, bytes, words, fields, processors, video displays, keyboards, clocks, printers, network nodes, and so on. A *subject* is an active entity, generally in the form of a person, process, or device, that causes information to flow among objects or changes the system state. The relationship between an object and a subject is on an access control basis. It is common for applications to use access control matrices to describe the security levels that subjects have to different objects.

Reference Monitors and Kernels

A *reference monitor* is an access control concept that refers to an abstract machine that mediates all accesses to objects by subjects. A *security kernel* is the hardware, firmware, and software elements of a trusted computing base that implements the reference monitor concept. The kernel must mediate all accesses, be protected from modification, and be verifiable as correct. Establishing trust in such a kernel dictates that it be "small" and amenable to complete analysis in order to validate that it correctly performs those functions—and only those functions—necessary to implement the specified security model.

Security Models

Numerous security models exist to help explain and mathematically demonstrate system security.

Bell-LaPadula Model

This model was proposed by Bell and LaPadula for enforcing access control in government and military applications. In such applications, subject and objects are often partitioned into different security levels. A subject can only access objects at certain levels determined by the subject's security level. For instance, the following are two typical access specifications: "Unclassified personnel cannot read data at confidential levels" and "top-secret data cannot be written into the files at unclassified levels." This kind of access control is also called *mandatory access control*, which, according to the United States Department of Defense TCSEC, is "a means of restricting access to objects based on the identity of subject and/or groups to which they belong. The controls are discretionary in the sense that a subject with a certain access permission is capable of passing that permission (perhaps indirectly) to any other subject."

The Bell-LaPadula model supports mandatory access control by determining the access rights from the security levels associated with subjects and objects. It also supports discretionary access control by checking access rights from an access matrix.

Each object is associated with a security level of the form (classification level, set of categories). Each subject is also associated with a maximum and current security level, which can be changed dynamically. The set of classification levels is ordered by a < relationship. For instance, it can be the set top-secret, secret, confidential, unclassified, where:

unclassified < confidential < secret < top-secret

A category is a set of names such as Nuclear and NATO. Security level A dominates B if and only if A's classification set is a superset of B's. For instance, top-secret, {Nuclear, NATO}, dominates secret, {NATO}, because top-secret > secret and the set {Nuclear, NATO} contains {NATO}.

Clark-Wilson

The Clark-Wilson model, published in 1987 and updated in 1989, involves two primary elements for achieving data integrity—the well-formed transaction and separation of duties. *Well-formed transactions* prevent users from manipulating data, thus ensuring the internal consistency of data. *Separation of duties* prevents authorized users from making improper modifications, thus preserving the external consistency of data by ensuring that data in the system reflects the real-world data it represents.

The Clark-Wilson model differs from the other models that are subject and object oriented by introducing a third access element—programs—resulting in what is called an *access triple*, which prevents unauthorized users from modifying data or programs. In addition, this model uses integrity verification and transformation procedures to maintain internal and external consistency of data. The verification procedures confirm that the data conforms to the integrity specifications at the time the verification is performed. The transformation procedures are designed to take the system from one valid state to the next. The Clark-Wilson model is believed to address all three goals of integrity.

Biba
The first model to address integrity in computer systems was based on a hierarchical lattice of integrity levels defined by Biba in 1977. The Biba integrity model is similar to the Bell-LaPadula model for confidentiality in that it uses subjects and objects; in addition, it controls object modification in the same way that Bell-LaPadula controls disclosure.

Biba's integrity policy consists of three parts. The first part specifies that a subject cannot execute objects that have a lower level of integrity than the subject. The second part specifies that a subject cannot modify objects that have a higher level of integrity. The third part specifies that a subject may not request service from subjects that have a higher integrity level.

TCSEC Classes
The Trusted Computer Security Evaluation Criteria (DOD 5200.28-STD, a.k.a. TCSEC, a.k.a. the Orange Book because the cover of the publication is orange) were developed by the U.S. Defense Department's National Security Agency. TCSEC is a set of criteria for determining both the security functionality and the degree of assurance that the functionality works as documented that is required for a system to meet a certain defined security level. More accurately, the TCSEC takes into account these five aspects of security: the system's security policy, the accountability mechanisms on the system, the operational and lifecycle assurance of the system's security, and the documentation developed and maintained about the system's security aspects.

A TCSEC level indicates that the system has a set of predefined security features in all of these categories; TCSEC levels range from D (minimal protection, i.e., no real security enforced), to C (discretionary access policy enforced), to B (mandatory access policy enforced), to A (formally proven security). These criteria were designed for measuring the security of computing platforms—i.e., operating systems and their underlying hardware.

Policy for TCSEC is as follows:

➤ There must be an explicit, well-defined security policy to be enforced by the system

➤ Objects must be adequately marked

➤ Subjects must be appropriately identified

➤ Audits should be periodically performed

➤ Hardware and software mechanisms should be independently evaluated

➤ Continuous protection should be in place

Common Flaws and Security Issues Associated with System Architectures and Designs

Even with certification/accreditation and evaluation criteria, systems still contain flaws and security issues. Some of these flaws include covert channels, initialization and failure states, input checks, and electromagnetic radiation.

Channel Issues

A *channel* is an information transfer path within a system. It may also refer to the mechanism by which the path is effected. A *covert channel* is a communication channel that allows a process to transfer information in a manner that violates the system's security policy. A *covert storage channel* is a channel that involves the direct or indirect writing of a storage location by one process and the direct or indirect reading of the storage location by another process. Covert storage channels typically involve a finite resource (e.g., sectors on a disk) that is shared by two subjects at different security levels. A *covert timing channel* is a channel in which one process signals information to another by modulating its own use of system resources (e.g., CPU time) in such a way that this manipulation affects the real response time observed by the second process. An *exploitable channel* is any channel that is usable or detectable by subjects external to the trusted computing base.

Initialization and Failure States

What happens if you crash the system during initialization, and what happens during failure? If not designed properly, the system could open some serious security holes during initialization and failure.

Input and Parameter Checking

Do certain parameters and input do what they are supposed to do and not more? If not designed properly, a system could allow a user to input code or system commands that would violate the system's security. Proper input and parameter checks will help alleviate this issue. Currently, Web applications are prime targets for input and parameter vulnerabilities.

Maintenance Hooks and Privileged Programs

Superzap is an IBM utility program used to install zaps or fixes to MVS operating system or application program code. Superzap could be used as an all-powerful program capable of flipping bits in object code to change program functionality. *Su* is a linux/unix program that allows a user to operate as another user, including root. These types of programs are examples of maintenance hooks and privileged programs that operate without access control, which makes them extremely dangerous. If not properly controlled, they could be used to gain unauthorized access.

Programming (Techniques, Compilers, APIs, and Library Issues)

Compiler functionality has grown over the past several years to encompass not only code generation but also complex transformations and optimizations necessary to elicit high performance from modern architectures and systems. As compiler-generated run-time systems and dynamic optimization have assumed an increasing share of the resource management responsibility previously encapsulated in the kernel, it has become clear that a comprehensive view of end-system security must address vulnerabilities introduced through reliance on compiler-based services. Even at the user level, the technology for assuring compiler and run-time enforced protections is apparently lacking, as evidenced by the growing documentation of Java vulnerabilities.

Electromagnetic Radiation

All electronic devices emit electromagnetic radiation. It is possible to monitor this radiation and understand, for example, what is being displayed on a monitor.

TEMPEST was the name of a classified (secret) U.S. government project to study (probably for the purpose of both exploiting and guarding against) the susceptibility of some computer and telecommunications devices to emitting electromagnetic radiation (EMR) in a manner that can be used to reconstruct intelligible data. For example, using TEMPEST technology and techniques, attackers may be able to identify from a distance what is displaying on a monitor and thus gain access to confidential information.

TEMPEST's name is believed to have been a code name used during development by the U. S. government in the late 1960s, but at a somewhat later stage, it became an acronym for Telecommunications Electronics Material Protected from Emanating Spurious Transmissions. Today, in military circles, the term has been officially supplanted by Emsec (for Emissions Security); however, the term TEMPEST is still widely used in the civilian arena.

Practice Questions

Question 1

> A communication channel that allows a process to transfer information in a manner that violates the system's security policy is a(n) _____.
>
> ○ a. ITSEC
>
> ○ b. Bell-LaPadula
>
> ○ c. TEMPEST
>
> ○ d. Covert channel

Answer d is correct. A covert channel is a communication channel that allows a process to transfer information in a manner that violates the system's security policy. Answer a is incorrect because ITSEC is security evaluation criteria. Answer b is incorrect because Bell-LaPadula is a security model. Answer c is incorrect because TEMPEST deals with electromagnetic radiation.

Question 2

> Which of the following is not a common system flaw?
>
> ○ a. Covert channels
>
> ○ b. Lack of input checks
>
> ○ c. Use of ITSEC
>
> ○ d. Use of privileged programs

Answer c is correct. ITSEC is a set of security criteria. Answers a, b, and d are incorrect because covert channels, lack of input checks, and use of privileged programs are all common system flaws.

Question 3

> Which of the following is not a TCSEC level?
>
> ○ a. F
>
> ○ b. C
>
> ○ c. B
>
> ○ d. D

Answer a is correct. F is not a TCSEC level. Answers b, c, and d are incorrect because C, B, and D are all TCSEC levels.

Question 4

> Which of the following is not a security model?
>
> ○ a. Bell-LaPadula
>
> ○ b. Biba
>
> ○ c. Clark-Wilson
>
> ○ d. Smith-Kline

Answer d is correct. Smith-Kline is not a security model. Answers a, b, and c are incorrect because Bell-LaPadula, Biba, and Clark-Wilson are all security models.

Question 5

> How many layers are in the OSI model?
>
> ○ a. Five
>
> ○ b. Seven
>
> ○ c. Nine
>
> ○ d. Three

Answer b is correct. There are seven layers in the OSI model. Answers a, c, and d are thus incorrect.

Question 6

What is the name of the European evaluation criteria?

○ a. ITSEC

○ b. TEMPEST

○ c. IPSec

○ d. TCSEC

Answer a is correct. ITSEC is the European evaluation criteria. Answer b is incorrect because TEMPEST deals with electromagnetic radiation. Answer c is incorrect because IPSec is a communications protocol. Answer d is incorrect because TCSEC is the U.S. evaluation criteria.

Question 7

Which of the following is not an operating state?

○ a. Blocked

○ b. Running

○ c. Ready

○ d. Open

Answer d is correct. Open is not an operating state. Answers a, b, and c are incorrect because blocked, running, and ready are all operating states.

Question 8

A _____ is an access control concept that refers to an abstract machine that mediates all access to objects by subjects.

○ a. Closed system

○ b. Security perimeter

○ c. Reference monitor

○ d. Covert channel

Answer c is correct. A reference monitor is an access control concept that refers to an abstract machine that mediates all access to objects by subjects. Answer a is incorrect because a closed system means that products from one vendor cannot work with another vendor. Answer b is incorrect because a security perimeter deals with security techniques used at the network edge. Answer d is incorrect because a covert channel is a communication channel that allows a process to transfer information in a manner that violates the system's security policy.

Question 9

An application installed on a system is:

○ a. Hardware

○ b. Software

○ c. Firmware

○ d. Memory

Answer b is correct. Software is an application installed on a system. Answer a is incorrect because hardware is computer parts with logical programming chips. Answer c is incorrect because firmware is an application or operational code developed to help hardware function as desired. Answer d is incorrect because memory is a component of a system where data is stored for quick access.

Question 10

The study of electromagnetic radiation is called:

○ a. DAC

○ b. TEMPEST

○ c. MAC

○ d. TCSEC

Answer b is correct. TEMPEST is the study of electromagnetic radiation. Answer a is incorrect because DAC is discretionary access control. Answer c is incorrect because MAC is mandatory access control. Answer d is incorrect because TCSEC is the U.S. evaluation criteria.

Need to Know More?

 www.itsec.gov.uk/docs/formal.htm features the ITSEC documents that detail all the criteria.

 www.radium.ncsc.mil/tpep/library/tcsec/ interprets the TCSEC criteria.

 www.securityfocus.com is an excellent security resource site.

Operations Security

Terms you'll need to understand:

✓ Directive controls

✓ Preventive controls

✓ Detective controls

✓ Corrective controls

✓ Recovery controls

✓ War dialing

✓ Social engineering

✓ Dumpster diving

Techniques you'll need to master:

✓ Understanding administrative management

✓ Understanding control types

✓ Understanding monitoring techniques

The Operations Security domain is used to identify the controls over hardware, media, and operators with access to any computing resources. Auditing and monitoring are key to controlling this area.

For the CISSP exam, you need to know the resources that must be protected, the privileges that must be restricted, the control mechanisms available, and the principles of good practice.

Administrative Management

Following a few basic administrative steps goes a long way toward developing a strong security infrastructure. To begin with, each job should have a written description that details the job requirements and specifications. These descriptions should be updated whenever the responsibilities of the position change. When creating these job descriptions, proper segregation of duties should be built in. For example, developers should not have the ability to change production code or move code to production machines. Proper change control procedures dictate that changes should be requested and documented, and code should be passed to Quality Assurance (QA) or another independent group to complete the migration process.

When hiring employees, background checks should be performed to ensure they are not hiding anything during the interview process. User access privileges should be granted using the *least privilege principle*. That is, users should only be given the access and privileges necessary to perform their job duties. Additionally, people should be rotated through jobs so no one person becomes too powerful. If job rotation is not possible, each person should be required to take at least a week's vacation all at one time. Job rotation also helps prevent (or detect) certain fraud schemes, such as an employee "skimming" funds or creating bogus user accounts with Administrator privileges.

When an employee is dismissed, take precautions to disable all network and system access. If an employee needs to retrieve some files from the system, have an administrator retrieve the necessary files. This process helps prevent the employee from seeking revenge by deleting or modifying important files.

Operations Concepts

Several operations concepts are important to ensure strong security is in place. *Antivirus management* is one of those key areas. Proper deployment and periodic updates are necessary to help ensure systems are protected against viruses. With the recent rash of virus attacks, antivirus programs have become more important.

Another issue is *system backups*. All critical information should be properly backed-up. In the event of system crash, failure, or sabotage, you need recent backups to restore the system quickly and to get up and running. Without backups, you could lose millions of dollars worth of data or engineering time.

Privileged operations and the functions those operations perform should be closely monitored. All key events, such as Administrator or root logon, should be logged and accounted for. With vigilance, anything out of the ordinary can be quickly identified and investigated, catching an unauthorized user quickly before any real damage can be done. These logs and other critical records should be archived and stored for a period of time. Thus, if a problem is identified in the future, the logs still exist and can be reviewed and used during court proceedings. With due care and diligence, networks can be properly secured.

Another key concept is understanding how to handle sensitive information and media. All sensitive information should be clearly marked, and procedures should be documented on how to handle this information. Sensitive information should be properly stored and kept separate from general public information. Additionally, when destroying sensitive information, a very thorough method should be used. Shredding or burning paper and using magnets for computer disks are good methods for destroying information.

Control Types

Controls are processes or procedures that help secure data and resources. There are four main types of controls: preventive, detective, corrective, and recovery. *Preventive controls* are used to prevent security incidents. Using strong passwords is an example of a preventive control. *Detective controls* help identify security incidents. Reviewing log files or file permissions for abnormalities is a detective control. *Corrective controls* help fix problems after they arise. A good example of a corrective control is changing file permissions after discovering a problem. *Recovery controls* help rebuild a system, application, or network after a security incident has occurred.

Operations Controls

Operations controls help ensure a stable, secure processing environment. *Resource protection* is key to strong operations controls. Without proper protection of critical resources, secure processes may be irrelevant. Why harden operating systems from network attacks if it is easier to physically access the system? *Change control management* is also an important operations control. Here, proper procedures should be in place to control how code is moved from development to staging to production. One person alone should not have this power. Using proper separation of duties, several people should be involved in this process. One person moves the code from development to staging, and after thorough testing, another individual moves the code from staging to production.

Hardware controls ensure the security of computer hardware. System cases should be locked, stored in a secure data center, etc. *Input-output controls* consist of people controlling input to the systems and then people distributing output of the system to respective parties. *Media controls* cover the processes and procedures in place to properly mark, handle, store, and destroy storage media such as paper, disks, hard drives, and CDs.

Resource Protection

Resource protection is critical not just for data files, but for any resource key to your environment. Communications hardware and software should be protected to keep unwanted individuals from accessing your internal network through misconfigured or improperly protected configurations.

Processing equipment is another area of concern. If not properly protected, these resources can be used for unauthorized purposes. Check-processing equipment can be easily used to write unauthorized checks if proper controls are not in place to limit access to the equipment.

Password files should also be properly protected. In the wrong hands, password files can lead to the complete compromise of your network. Application program libraries and source code should be protected. If this information is made public, any competitive advantage the company holds will be quickly lost.

Vendor software, operating systems, and system utilities should also be properly protected. If not configured or implemented securely, theses applications can leave holes in your network that are easily exploited by attackers.

System logs, audit trails, and violation reports are subject to protection. Because these reports have the ability to identify attacks and security incidents, the perpetrator may try to erase his tracks. Proper protection of these documents and files will provide strong evidence that something wrong has occurred.

Auditing

Auditing is the best way to understand what exposures you have in your network and resources. Audits can check for compliance to government or corporate regulations. They can be as simple as reviewing the previous day's IDS logs or as complex as a multi-month in-depth examination. They can be conducted daily, weekly, monthly, or annually. They can be conducted by internal or external parties. Whatever the issue, an audit will help identify and document threats, vulnerabilities, and exposures.

Security audits entail an in-depth examination of your security infrastructure, policies, people, and procedures. The purpose is to identify areas of weakness within the infrastructure and provide recommendations for appropriate solutions. A successful audit can only be achieved with the complete cooperation of all parties involved.

Many people have an initial negative perception of audits in general and security-related audits or assessments in particular. However, an audit of security-relevant events is important for ensuring that access to information and resources follows established security policies. The best way to know your network access controls are working is through an independent audit or assessment.

There are two basic security functions of auditing. First, a security audit ensures compliance to procedures established within your company security policy. Second, a security audit allows you to reconstruct an audit trail to determine the location or source of security-related events.

The purpose of reconstructing security-related events through audit trails is simply to detect, deter, and reveal any attempts, internal or external, to circumvent network protection mechanisms and network audit monitoring. Audit trails need to be transparent to network users, to support all audit applications, to be complete and accurate in reconstructing network events, and to protect against file manipulation by attackers.

Events to audit include logon and logoff activities, attempts to conduct file manipulation, or attempts to change system or network privileges. Each event should include the type or name of the event, the date and time of occurrence, the degree of success, and any program or file names involved. Management should develop and implement procedures for conducting the audit or assessment, select events to audit, review audit trails daily, maintain and safeguard audit data, and review audit parameters periodically. Always remember that audit trails require protection.

An audit or assessment to reconstruct security-related events should have specific requirements and goals for reviewing users' daily compliance to security policies. These may include:

➤ Determining any patterns of user access to specific objects or files on the network

➤ Evaluating any patterns of individual users

➤ Determining the performance level of various protection mechanisms on the network, especially their effectiveness

➤ Discovering any attempts, especially repeated attempts, by users to bypass the protection mechanisms on the network

➤ Evaluating the effectiveness of the audit or assessment as a deterrent to perpetrators' attempts to bypass any network protection mechanisms

➤ Understanding the network or system, including configuration and functionality

➤ Verifying the phases of processing that a system must perform and the relationship between each phase

➤ Verifying that network processes actually perform with expected results

Security Maintenance and Monitoring

The goal of maintenance and monitoring is to keep the systems and network up-to-date, properly configured, and analyzed for suspicious activity. Although this does not sound like much work, you may be surprised at how much time, energy, and resources can go into performing these three simple steps.

Security is a process. Implementing a few point solutions and then leaving them alone will not make you secure. In fact, it will leave you with a very strong, false sense of security.

Additionally, this process can never stop. If you do stop monitoring and maintaining your systems, it is just a manner of time before someone (whether an external or internal attacker) takes advantages of holes and vulnerabilities left on your network and systems.

The first thing you need to do is ensure that you stay up-to-date with all patches and updates. Secondly, you need to monitor security sites and mailing lists to keep abreast of newly discovered attacks and vulnerabilities in systems you run in your organization. Third, you must monitor system configurations and log files to look for unusual changes or signs of attack, and react accordingly.

Penetration Testing

Penetration testing is both a review of existing vulnerabilities and a security baseline that provides a snapshot of your security posture. With this information about your current level of network security, penetration tests can help effectively and objectively communicate the state of your network security and make decisions about areas to protect or improve.

A penetration test demonstrates management's due diligence to assure site availability, data integrity, and information protection for your organization and your customers. It does not guarantee that your site cannot be successfully attacked or compromised. The final report does, however, give you a profile of your security posture at a given snapshot in time. This profile can be used as a guide for tracing unwanted network activity as well as for securing weak links in your network and system infrastructure, thus helping you mitigate the risk of future system and network compromises.

When engaging in a penetration test, it is important to examine internal and external connectivity to determine the effectiveness of current safeguards, the extent of any network-level vulnerabilities present, and the ability to detect and respond to attack.

When possible, the penetration test should be more comprehensive than a simple network scan. The best test creates a thorough list of security vulnerabilities plus the potential means of gaining unauthorized access for the entire network, probing your network both from the external perspective of an Internet or dial-in hacker and the internal perspective of a disgruntled employee or an internal contractor.

A penetration test that will provide you with the best information should include the following:

➤ *Network mapping* and *target analysis* to determine network topology, correlate the network's Internet presence with information collected from public and corporate records, and provide insight into the probability of a successful attack.

➤ *Host and service discovery* to determine how many hosts are on the network and which network services each host is currently running.

➤ *Vulnerability analysis* to determine all potential vulnerabilities that exist for each network service running on each identified host. The analysis should confirm the presence of vulnerabilities on specific systems by exploiting identified potential vulnerabilities. Taking it one step further, this analysis should determine what additional vulnerabilities could be exploited when the first-level vulnerabilities help attackers gain initial access. This is often referred to as secondary exploitation.

➤ *Vulnerability measurement* and *data collection* to identify methods of entry into your corporate network through exploitation of network vulnerabilities.

➤ *Data analysis* and *security design* review to compare test results with current operational requirements identifying critical deficiencies.

➤ *Recommendations* to identify the right safeguards, plus, findings and specific recommendations for each system that can be used by your client to determine policies across their business.

Common methods used during penetration tests include war dialing, sniffing, eavesdropping, radiation monitoring, dumpster diving, and social engineering. *War dialing* is the process of systematically dialing a range of phone numbers in the target organization looking for dial-in modems that may give you unauthorized access to the network. *Sniffing* is the process of capturing packets traveling across the network and reading their contents in the hope of capturing userid/password combinations or other critical information. *Radiation monitoring* allows an attacker to capture emissions from items such as monitors and identify what is being displayed. *Dumpster diving* is the activity of digging through an individual's or organization's trash to find critical information and documents that were not properly disposed of. *Social engineering* is one of the best attack techniques; it focuses on the weaknesses in the human factor. Calling individuals and pretending to be help desk personnel to gain user passwords is one social engineering technique.

Practice Questions

Question 1

> Which of the following is not a security/operations reason to use job rotation?
>
> ○ a. Employees need variety.
>
> ○ b. It helps identify possible fraud schemes.
>
> ○ c. It keeps one person from getting too much power.
>
> ○ d. It provides pre-trained backups.

Answer a is correct. Although job rotation can provide variety, its main purposes are to help identify possible fraud schemes, keep one person from getting too much power, and provide pre-trained backups. Answers b, c, and d are thus incorrect.

Question 2

> Which of the following does not require special resource protection such as encryption, physical security, strong access controls, and so on?
>
> ○ a. Password files
>
> ○ b. Operating system
>
> ○ c. Communications hardware/software
>
> ○ d. Security policies

Answer d is correct. Password files, operating systems, and communications hardware/software all require protection. Security policies should be available for all employees to review. Answers a, b, and c are thus incorrect.

Question 3

> Reviewing access logs is an example of which control type?
>
> ○ a. Detective control
>
> ○ b. Preventive control
>
> ○ c. Corrective control
>
> ○ d. Recovery control

Answer a is correct. Reviewing access logs is an example of detective control. Answer b is incorrect because a preventive control is implemented to keep security incidents from occurring. Answer c is incorrect because a corrective control is implemented to correct an identified issue before it can be used to cause harm. Answer d is incorrect because a recovery control helps an organization recover from a security incident.

Question 4

> Maintaining strong passwords is an example of what control type?
>
> ○ a. Detective control
>
> ○ b. Preventive control
>
> ○ c. Corrective control
>
> ○ d. Recovery control

Answer b is correct. Preventive controls maintain strong passwords. Answer a is incorrect because a detective control helps identify possible security incidents. Answer c is incorrect because a corrective control is implemented to correct an identified issue before it can be used to cause harm. Answer d is incorrect because a recovery control helps an organization recover from a security incident.

Question 5

> Maintaining backups in case a system needs to be restored is which type of control?
>
> ○ a. Detective control
>
> ○ b. Preventive control
>
> ○ c. Corrective control
>
> ○ d. Recovery control

Answer d is correct. Recovery controls maintain backups in case a system needs to be restored. Answer a is incorrect because a detective control helps identify possible security incidents. Answer b is incorrect because a preventive control is implemented to keep security incidents from occurring. Answer c is incorrect because a corrective control is implemented to correct an identified issue before it can cause harm.

Question 6

> What is the activity of digging through an individual's or organization's trash to find critical information and documents that were not properly disposed of?
>
> ○ a. Dumpster diving
>
> ○ b. Social engineering
>
> ○ c. Radiation monitoring
>
> ○ d. Sniffing

Answer a is correct. Dumpster diving is the activity of digging through an individual's or organization's trash to find critical information and documents that were not properly disposed of. Answer b is incorrect because social engineering focuses on the weaknesses in the human factor. Answer c is incorrect because radiation monitoring allows an attacker to capture emissions from items such as monitors and identify what is being displayed. Answer d is incorrect because sniffing is the process of capturing packets traveling across the network and reading their contents in the hope of capturing userid/password combinations or other critical information.

Question 7

> Which of the following items do not need to be monitored?
>
> ○ a. Patches
>
> ○ b. Applications
>
> ○ c. Security sites and mailing lists
>
> ○ d. System configuration and log files

Answer b is correct. Applications do not need to be monitored. Patches, security sites, security mailing lists, system configuration, and log files all need to be monitored. Answers a, c, and d are thus incorrect.

Question 8

> When dealing with media, which of the following is not important?
>
> ○ a. Marking
>
> ○ b. Handling
>
> ○ c. Destruction
>
> ○ d. Writing

Answer d is correct. The method used to get the data onto the media type is not as important as proper marking, handling, and destruction. Answers a, b, and c are thus incorrect.

Question 9

> Audits can be performed:
>
> ○ a. Daily
>
> ○ b. Weekly
>
> ○ c. Annually
>
> ○ d. All of the above

Answer d is correct. Audits can be performed whenever possible. They can be formal projects or quick tasks that just take a minute. Answers a, b, and c are thus incorrect.

Question 10

> When an employee is dismissed, which of the following should you not do?
>
> ○ a. Let him back on his computer
>
> ○ b. Lock his account
>
> ○ c. Remove network access
>
> ○ d. Disable email

Answer a is correct. You should not let employees back on their computers when they have been dismissed. Answers b, c, and d are all things that should be done when an employee is terminated.

Need to Know More?

 www.itaudit.org is an excellent resource for IT audit information.

 http://packetstorm.securify.com is a great resource for tools and exploits to use during a penetration test.

 www.securityfocus.com is an excellent security resource site.

Business Continuity Planning (BCP) and Disaster Recovery Planning (DRP)

9

Terms you'll need to understand:

✓ Contingent events

✓ Nondisasters

✓ Disasters

✓ Catastrophes

✓ Warm sites

✓ Hot sites

✓ Cold sites

Techniques you'll need to master:

✓ Understanding Business Continuity Planning (BCP)

✓ Understanding risk evaluation

✓ Understanding BCP/DRP

✓ Understanding backup procedures and alternatives

The Business Continuity Planning (BCP) and Disaster Recovery Planning (DRP) domain addresses the preservation of business in the face of major disruptions to normal business operations. BCP and DRP involve the preparation, testing, and updating of specific processes and procedures to protect critical business processes from the effect of major system and network failures.

For the CISSP exam, you need to know the difference between business continuity planning and disaster recovery. You should understand BCP in the areas of project scope and planning, business impact analysis, recovery strategies, recovery plan development, and implementation. You should understand DRP in terms of recovery plan development, implementation, and restoration.

Risk Evaluation

The first part of the BCP/DRP process is to evaluate the organization's risks and understand loss potentials. Here, you need to identify threats from both internal and external sources. These threats include natural, manmade, technological, or political disasters. You should then determine the probability of these events and their severity. Once the threats are identified, you need to perform a cost benefit analysis with the associated loss potential to see which events should be adequately protected against.

When identifying threats, several threat categories should also be identified. *Primary* threats are the most important. These are direct threats the organization may face. *Secondary* or *collateral* threats can materialize in the face of primary threats, such as flooding in the event of a hurricane. You should select the events that are most likely to occur and that will have the greatest impact.

Once these events are selected, identify safeguards and controls to prevent or minimize the effect of the loss potential. These safeguards may include increasing physical protection or even relocating assets.

Business Continuity Planning (BCP)

The primary goal of BCP is to reduce the risk of financial loss by improving the ability to recover and restore operations efficiently and effectively. Disaster recovery planning focuses on emergency response procedures, extended backup operations, and restoring computing facilities in the event they are damaged or destroyed. A *contingent event* is a chance event, an uncertainty. It is something that has a possibility of occurrence but may or may not actually come about. Contingency planning for computer security is concerned with providing alternatives for those chance events that could be detrimental to the normally performed functions. At best, contingency planning should provide reasonable security within the economic constraints mandated by the nature of the processes performed. Comprehensive risk analysis is needed to provide a basis for cost justification.

When creating recovery plans, certain event descriptions are often used. *Nondisasters* are disruptions in service stemming from system malfunction or other failure. These events require action in order to recover operational status and resume service. *Disasters* are disruptions that cause the entire facility to be inoperative for a lengthy period of time, usually more than one day. These events require action to recover operational status, usually the use of an alternate processing facility. *Catastrophes* are major disruptions entailing the destruction of the data processing facility. Short-term and long-term recovery plans are required to cover a wide variety of disaster scenarios. An alternate processing facility is needed to satisfy immediate operational needs, just as in the case of a disaster.

Two absolutely essential prerequisites that must be in effect to set the stage for contingency planning are:

1. *Information backup*—It is essential to maintain backup data files to permit reconstruction and restoration of the primary computer files if necessary.

2. *Management commitment*—It is important for management to exhibit ongoing interest and concern about the BCP/DRP effort and to provide financial and other resources as needed. Failure of a contingency plan is usually management failure. Management must also establish the policies and goals that guide the planning effort and monitor the results to ensure ongoing effectiveness.

The primary goals of the disaster recovery plan are to improve staff responsiveness, ease confusion, and provide for logical decisions during a crisis. The overall recovery plan should extend to all aspects and components needed to restore the vital operations of the enterprise.

Planning

The initial phase of contingency planning must be to define and establish the goals that are expected for the activity. These goals should be to direct the proper allocation of resources in order to counter threats, to devise effective strategies for backup, to assist economic justification, and to ensure the effectiveness of the program. In order to provide adequate direction for the planning process, the goals should contain the following:

➤ A statement of importance for business resumption following disruption or loss of the computer facility

➤ A statement of priorities for the relative importance of the functions or applications performed

➤ A statement of organizational responsibility

➤ A statement of urgency and timing

One of the most important objectives of contingency planning is to take care of the routine procedures and free up personnel to function more effectively during a crisis. A team approach is essential to reduce confusion and allocate required activities efficiently.

The economics of backup and, in particular, disaster recovery should be carefully considered when developing strategies. Disaster recovery measures are usually not activated for short-term problems.

Development of a comprehensive contingency plan can be accomplished in several different ways. Plans can be developed by an in-house staff or by outside consultants, and a combination of the two is often very effective.

Management must choose how to develop the plan, commit the resources to ensure that it is accomplished, and set target dates for these accomplishments. Finally, management must insist on adequate feedback to ensure that the contingency plans are indeed workable and that procedures are kept current.

Once management has approved the plan, a BCP/DRP team should be created to further develop and carry out the plan. Individual roles and responsibilities should be clearly documented, as should everything else that takes place during a disaster. The last thing you want is to have mass chaos ensue because people do not know their roles.

One person, or several key people, should be in charge of declaring when to put the plan into action, and formal procedures should be in place to notify the rest of the team and set the plan into action.

Once the plan is created and documented, the plan should be tested—and should continue to be tested at least annually. The worst thing you can have is a plan that you are not sure actually works. In the event of a disaster, you want the BCP/DRP team to work like a well-oiled machine.

Documentation

A written plan must be developed to reflect the chosen strategies and activities for business resumption and to ensure prompt and proper reaction to service disruptions. The written plan is very important. In fact, you do not have a formal BCP/DRP until it is reviewed and approved by management and the team participants. The written plan should include:

➤ Assignment of individual and team responsibilities in order to expedite the mobilization of personnel

➤ Damage assessment and containment

➤ Activation of short- and long-term backup plans

➤ Access to data backup facilities

➤ Recovery of critical systems and files

➤ Notification to staff, customers, suppliers, and so on

➤ Availability of alternative support services (telephone, office facilities, transportation supplies, housing, meals, and so on)

➤ Restoration of primary data processing facility or movement to a new permanent site

➤ Orderly resumption of moving back to the main site for operations

Overall, the plan should have four phases: activation, restoration, testing, and maintenance. The plan activation phase is concerned with prompt restoration of the organization's business functions after a disaster. Restoration involves the restoration of computer operations and support activities to a permanent location, which can either be the original site or a new location. Testing is the third phase and involves reviewing and testing plans every 6 months (or at least annually) to ensure continuing compatibility and operational readiness. The last phase is maintenance. Maintain copies of the detailed contingency plans at several locations away from the main site.

Backup Locations

A crucial element of any contingency plan is adequate data and resources, and backups are the way to ensure everything will be available during an emergency. Hardware backup alone will usually be inadequate to ensure continuity of activities; you also need to back up data. Procedures to back up computer hardware should include both on-site and off-site protective strategies. On-site backup represents the first line in defense contingency planning.

The purpose of on-site backup measures is to minimize dependency on unique hardware components in order to encourage flexibility in processing, and thereby to facilitate backup. For remote backup sites, you have several options:

➤ *Hot sites*—Sites that are fully configured and ready to operate within several hours. The equipment and systems software must be compatible with the primary installation being backed up.

➤ *Warm sites*—Sites that are partially configured, usually with selected peripheral equipment, such as disk drives and tape drives and controllers, but without the main computer.

➤ *Cold sites*—Sites that have the basic environment (electrical wiring, air conditioning, flooring, and so on). The cold site is ready to receive equipment but does not offer any components at the site in advance of the need. Activation of the site may take several weeks.

The major distinctions between the types of backup sites are activation time and cost.

Some of the considerations relating to backup schedules include the following:

➤ Frequency of backup cycle

➤ Anticipation of failure

➤ Retention intervals for master files

➤ Preservation of transaction files coincident with master files

➤ Selection of backup techniques for relative fields

➤ Selection of specialized backup for DBMS

Specialized backup procedures include the following:

➤ *Electronic vaulting*—Electronic vaulting is a system that immediately transmits copies of each online transaction or change to a remotely located computer facility where the data is preserved for backup.

➤ *Mirror processing*—Mirror processing goes one step further than electronic vaulting and performs updates to a backup copy of the database so that the backup files are more readily available for use in an emergency.

➤ *Hierarchical storage management (HSM)*—Hierarchical storage management uses software that dynamically manages the storage and retrieval of online data files through storage media devices that vary in speed (and cost).

Backup plans for data processing must extend beyond the central data processing activities to the sources and recipients of information.

The most convenient form of primary backup is a copy of the current software file rather than the previous generation of a software file. Software backup versions should be maintained at both the main computing facility and at a secure offsite storage location because they must be accessible for short-term disruptions and for disasters.

Alternatives for Backup Equipment

In an emergency, the hardware vendor is usually the best source for replacement equipment. However, vendors often require a waiting period that is not acceptable for critical operations. Another source of equipment replacement is the used hardware market.

Another option is on-the-shelf hardware, available for purchase at your local computer store. This option is the ideal situation, in which replacement of equipment can occur quickly because components are readily available in inventory. A commonly used option in large corporations or in a group of small businesses is mutual aid agreements. Here, reciprocal agreements between two or more organizations with similar equipment or applications are used as a source of equipment in an emergency. These agreements are not usually enforceable, so they are at best a secondary backup for a disaster.

A dedicated, self-developed hot site is the best and most reliable form of backup, but it is also the most expensive. This setup is ideal for critical applications that cannot afford even one day of downtime. Third-party hot sites are a viable alternative if in-house developed hot sites are too costly. Third parties, such as SunGard, offer fully operational areas with a guaranteed configuration of equipment and software. These sites are usually available to subscribers with notice of 24 hours or less.

Longer-term operational needs for backup can be addressed by subscribing to a cold-site service. The cold site provides all of the environmental support needed for a computer facility: power, climate control, raised flooring, telephone wiring, access security, and so forth. However, the cold site does not serve immediate backup needs.

Several vendors of backup processing facilities offer computer-ready trailers, known as mobile backup sites, that can be set up in a subscriber's parking lot or another site following a disaster. Mobile backup sites have advantages over the other solutions:

➤ They can serve to back up multiple sites from a single source, which has a special appeal for decentralized organizations.

➤ They can avoid or minimize travel to recover a computer operation. This is particularly desirable following a natural disaster when employees may be reluctant to travel and leave injured relatives or damaged property.

Practice Questions

Question 1

> The primary goal of BCP/DRP is:
>
> ○ a. To reduce the risk of financial loss by improving the ability to recover and restore operations efficiently and effectively
>
> ○ b. To give management something to do
>
> ○ c. To find the cheapest alternative site for backup processing
>
> ○ d. To document what to do in the event of a disaster

Answer a is correct. Although cost and documentation are important components, the overall goal of business continuity planning is to reduce the risk of financial loss. Answers b, c, and d are thus incorrect.

Question 2

> A contingent event is:
>
> ○ a. An offsite storage location
>
> ○ b. A planned event
>
> ○ c. A natural disaster
>
> ○ d. A chance event

Answer d is correct. A contingent event is a chance event that is unplanned. Although a contingent even can be a natural disaster, it can also be another kind of disaster, or chance event, as well. Answer c is thus incorrect. Answers a and b are also incorrect.

Question 3

> Two essential prerequisites for creating a BCP/DRP are:
>
> ○ a. Threat events and probability of occurrence
>
> ○ b. Information backup and management commitment
>
> ○ c. Team leaders and documentation
>
> ○ d. Hot site availability

Answer b is correct. Although threats, probabilities, team leaders, documentation, and hot sites are all part of a plan, you first need backups and management commitment to begin the entire planning process. Answers a, c, and d are thus incorrect.

Question 4

A written plan should not include:

- ○ a. Damage assessment and containment
- ○ b. Activation procedures of short- and long-term backup plans
- ○ c. Access to data backup facilities
- ○ d. Budget information

Answer d is correct. Everything else should be included in the plan. Answers a, b, and c are thus incorrect.

Question 5

Which of the following is software that dynamically manages the storage and retrieval of online data files through storage media devices?

- ○ a. Tape backup
- ○ b. Electronic vaulting
- ○ c. Hierarchical storage management
- ○ d. Mirror processing

Answer c is correct. Hierarchical storage management uses software that dynamically manages the storage and retrieval of online data files through storage media devices. Answer a is incorrect because tape backup is the process of copying data to tape. Answer b is incorrect because electronic vaulting is a system that immediately transmits copies of each online transaction or change to a remotely located computer facility where the data is preserved for backup. Answer d is incorrect because mirror processing updates to a backup copy of the database so that the backup files are more readily available for use in an emergency.

Question 6

> Sites that are fully configured and ready to operate within several hours are:
>
> ○ a. Hot sites
> ○ b. Cold sites
> ○ c. Warm sites
> ○ d. Medium sites

Answer a is correct. Hot sites are sites that are fully configured and ready to operate within several hours. Answer b is incorrect because cold sites are sites that have the basic environment and are ready to receive equipment, but do not offer any components at the site in advance of the need. Answer c is incorrect because warm sites are sites that are partially configured, usually with selected peripheral equipment, such as disk drives and tape drives and controllers, but without the main computer. Answer d is not a real option, and is thus incorrect.

Question 7

> Which of the following is a system that immediately transmits copies of each online transaction or change to a remotely located computer facility where the data is preserved for backup?
>
> ○ a. Tape backup
> ○ b. Electronic vaulting
> ○ c. Hierarchical storage management
> ○ d. Mirror processing

Answer b is correct. Electronic vaulting is a system that immediately transmits copies of each online transaction or change to a remotely located computer facility where the data is preserved for backup. Answer a is incorrect because tape backup is the process of copying data to tape. Answer c is incorrect because hierarchical storage management uses software that dynamically manages the storage and retrieval of online data files through storage media devices. Answer d is incorrect because mirror processing updates to a backup copy of the database so that the backup files are more readily available for use in an emergency.

Question 8

Sites that have the basic environment and are ready to receive equipment, but do not offer any components at the site in advance of the need are called _____.

- ○ a. Hot sites
- ○ b. Cold sites
- ○ c. Warm sites
- ○ d. Medium sites

Answer b is correct. Cold sites are sites that have the basic environment and are ready to receive equipment, but do not offer any components at the site in advance. Answer a is incorrect because hot sites are sites that are fully configured and ready to operate within several hours. Answer c is incorrect because warm sites are sites that are partially configured, usually with selected peripheral equipment, such as disk drives and tape drives and controllers, but without the main computer. Answer d is not a real option and is thus incorrect.

Question 9

The major distinction between types of backup sites is:

- ○ a. Time and cost
- ○ b. Location
- ○ c. Space
- ○ d. None of the above

Answer a is correct. Time and cost are the key differentiators between types of backup sites. Location and space are decision factors, but they are not differentiators. Answers b, c, and d are thus incorrect.

Question 10

Sites that are partially configured, usually with selected peripheral equipment, such as disk drives and tape drives and controllers, but without the main computer are called _____.

○ a. Hot sites

○ b. Cold sites

○ c. Warm sites

○ d. Medium sites

Answer c is correct. Warm sites are sites that are partially configured, usually with selected peripheral equipment, such as disk drives and tape drives and controllers, but without the main computer. Answer a is incorrect because hot sites are sites that are fully configured and ready to operate within several hours. Answer b is incorrect because cold sites are sites that have the basic environment and are ready to receive equipment, but do not offer any components at the site in advance of the need. Answer d is not a real option and is thus incorrect.

Need to Know More?

 www.dr.org/ppover.htm is an excellent resource for BCP/DRP information.

 www.securityfocus.com is an excellent security resource site.

 www.sungard.com is the leading offsite recovery provider. This site provides a lot of information on backup sites.

Law, Investigation, and Ethics

Terms you'll need to understand:

✓ Patent

✓ Trademark

✓ Copyright

✓ Criminal law

✓ Civil law

✓ Administrative law

✓ Federal Interest Computer

✓ Due care

✓ Hearsay

✓ Military and intelligence attacks

✓ Business attacks

✓ Financial attacks

✓ Terrorist attacks

✓ Grudge attacks

✓ Fun attacks

Techniques you'll need to master:

✓ Understanding intellectual property

✓ Understanding computer-relevant laws

✓ Understanding the categories of laws

✓ Understanding evidence handling

✓ Understanding major categories of computer crime

✓ Understanding the Code of Ethics

The Law, Investigation, and Ethics domain addresses computer crime laws and regulations, investigative techniques, and methods to gather evidence.

For the CISSP exam, you need to know various computer-relevant laws (including laws applicable for that crime and laws prohibiting computer crime), methods to gather and preserve evidence (evidence handling), the methods for determining whether a computer crime has been committed, as well as the major categories of computer crime. Also important to understand for the exam are the RFC 1087 and the ISC2 Code of Ethics.

This chapter contains a lot of information, but it is focused on particular areas, as it caters to your needs for the exam. Many legal terms are discussed, but they are discussed in the context of information security and the CISSP exam, which does not necessarily include all formal legal definitions and applications.

We will begin this chapter by defining some of those relevant definitions regarding intellectual property. Later, we will address each of the areas mentioned above in order to provide you with as clear an understanding as possible of those areas for your exam preparation. Please understand that the ISC2 Code of Ethics is quoted in its entirety. All candidates should be familiar with this Code of Ethics, because they must abide by its standards in all professional dealings.

Understanding Intellectual Property

This section covers the areas of intellectual property that are relevant to the exam. Understanding the definitions of each item is important, and will also assist you in understanding some of the other areas that we discuss and review later in this chapter.

Patents, Trademarks, Copyrights, and Trade Secrets

As described earlier, the definitions listed here are discussed in the context of information security and the CISSP exam, which does not necessarily include all formal legal definitions and applications.

A *patent* is the protection of an invention that has been sufficiently documented and explained so as to allow the Federal Patent Office to verify its originality and to grant a patent. This patent then limits the development and use of that design to the patent holder for a period of time. The patent holder may then grant a license to others for the design information, usually for a fee.

A *trademark* is any distinguishing name, character, logo, or other symbol that establishes an identity for a product, service, or organization. Trademarks can be registered, meaning they have been filed in the appropriate jurisdiction. This registration prevents others from being able to use that trademark. A wealth of information on trademarks can be found at **www.ggmark.com/welcome.html**.

A *copyright* is a legal right granted to an author (or other "creator") to exclusive publication, distribution, or sale of a created work. It allows an author to protect how an idea is expressed. An author does not generally have to file for copyright protection, as the law states that the copyright comes into force as soon as the idea is expressed in a tangible form. Many people will register their copyright, however, in order to provide immediate protection and a definite date of record in case there is ever a dispute. Registration of a copyright is done through either a federal copyright registry, or by mailing a copy of the work through registered mail.

A *trade secret* is proprietary information that is "used, made, or marketed by one having the exclusive legal rights," according to Webster's Collegiate Dictionary. This means that the company has ownership rights to exclusive use of the information. A trade secret is specific proprietary information that meets specific criteria under the law. To qualify as a trade secret, the information must conform to all three of the requirements listed below:

➤ The information *must* be genuine, but not absolute or exclusively secret. This means that an organization doesn't need to enforce extensive security measures to protect that information, even though elements of the secret, and maybe the secret itself, may become discoverable. The owner may license the secret to others, and as long as reasonable operational and legal protections are in place, it remains a protected asset.

➤ It must provide the owner competitive or economic advantages. The secret must have real business value to the owner. If there is no real business value other than to protect it from the public, the information cannot be classified as a trade secret.

➤ The owner must take reasonable steps to protect that information. However, there is no checklist of what reasonable might be. The court will apply a reasonableness test to the specific situation and arrive at a conclusion. Many plaintiffs have lost their claims to trade secret status due to the lack of a specific safeguard.

Computer-Relevant Laws

This section covers computer-relevant laws you should know for the exam. Several laws have been enacted to help protect companies and individuals from computer crimes and privacy violations. The following laws are important for the exam and will be discussed in detail next:

➤ Computer Fraud and Abuse Act of 1986

➤ Computer Security Act of 1987

➤ Privacy Act of 1974

➤ Electronic Communications Privacy Act of 1986

Each of these laws will be defined and described in this section. Following those descriptions, I will also address some of the major categories and types of laws and differences in relevant international laws to assist you in your review and preparation for the exam.

Computer Fraud and Abuse Act of 1986 (Amended 1996)

The original act was very narrow in defining what a computer crime was. The act covered only:

➤ Classified national defense or foreign relations information

➤ Records of financial institutions or credit reporting agencies

➤ Government computers

Unauthorized access or access in excess of authorization became a felony for classified information and a misdemeanor for financial information. It also became a misdemeanor to access a government computer with or without authorization should the government's use of the computer be affected, such as the system be unavailable due to a "crash."

The amendments in 1996 clarified the law and added three new crimes:

➤ Use of a "federal interest computer" that furthers an intended fraud

➤ Altering, damaging, or destroying information in a federal interest computer that prevents the use of the computer or information and causes a loss of at least $1000 or impairs medical treatment

➤ Trafficking in computer passwords, if it affects interstate or foreign commerce or permits unauthorized access to government computers

Acts Considered Felonies Under 18 U.S.C. 1030 (Computer Fraud and Abuse Act 1986)

There are three felonies and four misdemeanors identified in the code. Although this information is relevant to the "Evidence Handling" section later in this chapter, I am addressing it here so that its relevance to the actual definition of the act is understood as well.

The felonies are as listed:

➤ Unauthorized access to a computer that stores classified information:

  ➤ Unauthorized access to computer

➤ Obtaining classified information

➤ Injuring U.S. or giving advantage to a foreign nation

➤ Use of the computer to defraud others:

➤ Unauthorized access to a federal interest computer

➤ Intent to defraud

➤ Obtain something of value

➤ Extortion

➤ Use of the computer in interstate commerce or communications intending that the transmission will damage the computer system or prevent its use:

➤ Damage to computer system

➤ Withhold or deny use

➤ Cause loss greater than $1,000

➤ Unauthorized modification of medical information

If any of the following are proven, the felonies identified above are reduced to a misdemeanor:

➤ Lack of intent to cause damage or deny service

➤ Unauthorized access to a computer obtaining financial information

➤ Unauthorized access to a federal interest computer

➤ Trafficking passwords on a federal interest computer

Computer Security Act of 1987

This act states that the security and privacy of federal computer systems are in the public interest. It gives to NIST (National Institute of Standards and Technology) the computer security mission, including the development of standards. The act requires that each U.S. federal agency provide its employees with training in computer security awareness and practice, and set up a security plan for each of its systems.

Federal Privacy Act of 1974

As taken from the Act:

"Conditions of Disclosure: No agency shall disclose any record that is contained in a system of records by any means of communication to any person, or to another agency, except pursuant to a written request by, or with the prior written consent of, the individual to whom the record pertains, unless disclosure of the record would be:

➤ To those officers and employees of the agency who maintain the record and who have a need for the record in the performance of their duties

➤ Required under section 552 of this title

➤ For a routine use as defined in subsection (a)(7) of this section and described under subsection (e)(4)(D) of this section

➤ To the Bureau of the Census for purposes of planning or carrying out a census or survey or related activity pursuant to the provisions of title 13

➤ To a recipient who has provided the agency with advance, adequate, written assurance that the record will be used solely as a statistical research or reporting record, and the record is to be transferred in a form that is not individually identifiable

➤ To the National Archives and Records Administration as a record that has sufficient historical or other value to warrant its continued preservation by the United States Government, or for evaluation by the Archivist of the United States or the designee of the Archivist to determine whether the record has such value

➤ To another agency or to an instrumentality of any governmental jurisdiction within or under the control of the United States for a civil or criminal law enforcement activity if the activity is authorized by law, and if the head of the agency or instrumentality has made a written request to the agency that maintains the record specifying the particular portion desired and the law enforcement activity for which the record is sought

➤ To a person pursuant to a showing of compelling circumstances affecting the health or safety of an individual if upon such disclosure notification is transmitted to the last known address of such individual

➤ To either House of Congress, or, to the extent of matter within its jurisdiction, any committee or subcommittee thereof, any joint committee of Congress or subcommittee of any such joint committee

➤ To the Comptroller General, or any of his authorized representatives, in the course of the performance of the duties of the General Accounting Office

➤ Pursuant to the order of a court of competent jurisdiction

➤ To a consumer reporting agency in accordance with section 3711(e) of title 31."

This means that is it illegal for any organization to release information that it has acquired about you:

➤ Without your express consent

➤ Unless it is required directly for their job and will not be disclosed publicly

➤ Unless it is requested officially by a court of the jurisdiction

Electronic Communications Privacy Act of 1986

On the basis of its own investigations and of published studies, the Congress makes the following findings:

"(a) Wire communications are normally conducted through the use of facilities which form part of an interstate network. The same facilities are used for interstate and intrastate communications. There has been extensive wiretapping carried on without legal sanctions, and without the consent of any of the parties to the conversation. Electronic, mechanical, and other intercepting devices are being used to overhear oral conversations made in private, without the consent of any of the parties to such communications. The contents of these communications and evidence derived therefrom are being used by public and private parties as evidence in court and administrative proceedings and by persons whose activities affect interstate commerce. The possession, manufacture, distribution, advertising, and use of these devices are facilitated by interstate commerce.

"(b) In order to protect effectively the privacy of wire and oral communications, to protect the integrity of court and administrative proceedings, and to prevent the obstruction of interstate commerce, it is necessary for Congress to define on a uniform basis the circumstances and conditions under which the interception of wire and oral communications may be authorized, to prohibit any unauthorized interception of such communications, and the use of the contents thereof in evidence in courts and administrative proceedings.

"(c) Organized criminals make extensive use of wire and oral communications in their criminal activities. The interception of such communications to obtain evidence of the commission of crimes or to prevent their commission is an indispensable aid to law enforcement and the administration of justice.

"(d) To safeguard the privacy of innocent persons, the interception of wire or oral communications where none of the parties to the communication has consented to the interception should be allowed only when authorized by a court of competent jurisdiction and should remain under the control and supervision of the authorizing court. Interception of wire and oral communications should further be limited to certain major types of offenses and specific categories of crime with assurances that the interception is justified and that the information obtained thereby will not be misused."

Essentially, this means that unless you have the permission of either party involved in a communication of any form, or you are a law enforcement office with express permission from an authorized court, you are not permitted to intercept any communication regardless of how it was transmitted.

Major Categories and Types of Laws

In regards to security, you'll need to know three major types of laws: criminal, civil, and administrative. *Criminal law* governs individual conduct that violates the government laws that are enacted for the protection of the public. *Tort law* is a form of civil law that takes effect when damage, injury, or wrongful acts are done willfully or negligently against an individual or business that result in damage or loss. In *civil law*, there is no prison time, but financial restitution, among other things, is used to compensate the victim. Compensation typically consists of the actual damages to the victim in the form of attorney/legal fees, lost profits, and investigative costs. Compensation may also consist of punitive damages. These are established by a jury and are intended to punish an offender for their actions. The law establishes statutory damages that are paid to the victim.

Administrative law is also known as *regulatory law* and establishes the standards of performance and conduct from government agencies to organizations.

Differences in International Computer Crime-Related Laws

There are some differences in international laws. Nations typically have different views regarding the seriousness of computer crime and how they interpret technology and crime issues. This sometimes leads to problems, because what is illegal in one country is not always illegal in another.

In addition, evidence rules generally differ in various legal systems, which poses problems in evidence collection. Added to this are the different technical capabilities of the various law enforcement units. Finally, some governments may not wish to cooperate and assist each other in international cases. This means that the computer criminal may be "untouchable" by the country where the offense has occurred.

Evidence Handling

This section discusses how to collect, analyze, and handle evidence, including the evidence life cycle, conducting investigations, surveillance, and seizure.

Evidence Life Cycle

This section covers the "Understanding Evidence Handling" technique listed at the beginning of the chapter.

The evidence life cycle is important to understand in relation to security incident response procedures. The evidence life cycle has five states: collection and identification; analysis; storage, protection, and transportation; presentation in court; and return to victim/owner.

Collection and Identification

As the evidence is gathered, it must be properly identified and marked. The collection must be recorded in a logbook detailing the particular price of evidence, who found it, where it was found, and when it was found. The location must be specific to provide correlation later in court.

When marking evidence, the following guidelines should be followed:

➤ If it will not damage the evidence, mark the actual piece of evidence with your initials, the date, and the case number, if known. Seal this in the appropriate container and again write your initials, the date, and the case number on the container.

➤ If the actual evidence cannot be marked, seal the evidence in an appropriate container and mark it with your initials, the date, and the case number.

➤ The container should be sealed with evidence tape, and your marking should go over the tape to indicate any tampering with the evidence.

➤ Be careful not to damage the evidence while marking it.

➤ When handling evidence, use static-free gloves for computer components in order to preserve any fingerprints and not damage the component. Otherwise, regular gloves may be worn.

Analysis

The analysis step is pretty self-explanatory. Here, you examine the evidence itself for clues, links, or information that pertain to the crime and the person who committed it.

Storage, Prevention, and Transportation

All evidence must be properly handled and prepared for storage. This requirement has two purposes:

➤ To protect the evidence from being damaged during transportation and storage prior to court

➤ To protect the evidence for its return to the owner

Once the evidence is properly preserved, it should transported to a storage facility where it can be locked up and guarded until needed for a trial or returned to its owner.

Presentation in Court

Each piece of evidence collected must be presented in court. During the transportation of the evidence from storage to court, the same care must be followed as when it was first collected.

Return to Victim/Owner

Once the trial is over, the evidence must be returned to its owner. However, the police typically destroy some "contraband" items. Other materials, even though rightfully the owner's, may be under the control of the court and may not be returned to the owner in every situation.

Admissible Evidence

The concept of admissibility is based upon the following:

➤ *Relevancy of evidence*—the evidence must prove or disprove a material fact

➤ *Reliability of evidence*—the evidence and the process to produce the evidence must be proven to be reliable

Relevance

Relevance means that the evidence proves or disproves that a crime occurred. It documents the time frame of the crime, identifies how it was committed, links in suspects through acts or methods, and demonstrates motives for the crime.

Foundation of Admissibility

The foundation of admissibility is based on witnesses who testify to the fact that evidence is trustworthy through the identification of the custodian of the information, and the familiarity of the custodian with the information and with Electronic Data Processing (EDP) procedures in general. It must also document how the evidence is collected and illustrate how errors are prevented and corrected if they occur. If necessary, the custodian must be able to explain why media is erased, how the information is regularly used in the operation of the business, and how unnecessary operations are eliminated.

Legally Permissible

The evidence must have been collected using legal means. For example, information/evidence that is collected using unconstitutional means, unlawful search and seizure, secret recordings (except where authorized by a court), questionable privacy violations, or forced confessions/statements will be inadmissible in court.

Conducting Computer Crime Investigations

Investigations are the key processes to help identify and discover what happened during a security incident. Defined procedures and a prepared incident response team are crucial. The steps in a computer crime investigation are:

1. File a report indicating that an event has occurred.

2. Review affected systems (this step is performed by a CERT team if available.)

3. Investigate the report to determine if a crime has occurred.

4. Determine if disclosure of the incident is required.

5. Inform senior management when started, what occurred, source, and operation.

6. Identify company elements involved.

7. Review security/audit policies and procedures.

8. Determine the need for law enforcement.

9. Protect chain of custody of evidence.

Types of Surveillance

As it pertains to the exam, surveillance generally falls into two categories: physical and computer. Physical surveillance is done at the time of the abuse through either Closed-Circuit Television (CCTV) or after the fact through undercover operations. (Undercover operations would only be undertaken by law enforcement agencies.)

Computer surveillance is accomplished passively through the use of audit logs or actively using electronic monitoring tools, including keyboard sniffing or line monitoring. To do this, you must have either a warrant or a statement in your security policy that informs users that they are being monitored or that the corporation has the right to monitor.

Entrapment and Enticement

Enticement, as it pertains to the exam, is the process of luring an intruder to look at selected files. If the user downloads them, this could be used as evidence against them. Law enforcement officers usually conduct entrapment, where they induce a person to commit a crime they were not previously contemplating.

Search and Seizure Rules and Procedures

Search and seizure of computer evidence is often done quickly due to the nature of the evidence. The fact that the evidence is online means that it can be easily erased without any trace of its existence. Computer evidence can be obtained through a seizure by several means:

➤ Voluntary or consensual

➤ Subpoena

➤ Search warrant

A court issues the subpoena to an individual with the instructions to bring the evidence to court. A search warrant is issued to a law enforcement officer allowing them to take the equipment.

By seizing the equipment, it is possible to preserve the evidence, and once seized, the evidence must follow the custody chain of evidence. This includes proper labeling and preservation of the evidence and a log entry to show where it was taken from, who took it, and who has had contact with it since it was seized.

Federal Interest Computer

A federal interest computer is defined as a computer that is exclusively for the use of a financial institution or the U.S. government, or, if it is not exclusive, one used for a financial institution or the U.S. government where the offense adversely affects the use of the financial institution's or the government's operation of the computer. Or, it can also be defined as a computer that is one of two or more computers used to commit the offenses, not all of which are located in the same state.

This is defined in Title 18 USC, Chapter 47, Section 1030, which was enacted as part of the Computer Fraud and Abuse Act of 1986.

Due Care

The officers and directors of the company are expected to act carefully in fulfilling their tasks of monitoring and directing the activities of corporate management. A director shall act:

➤ In good faith

➤ With the care an ordinarily prudent person in a like position would exercise under similar circumstances

➤ In a manner he or she reasonably believes is in the best interest of the enterprise

Without taking due care in corporate actions to protect the company's information assets, an officer and/or director may open the organization to some legal liability.

Hearsay

One consideration of the legal value of computer-generated evidence is that such evidence, at least on the federal level, is often considered hearsay. *Hearsay evidence* is that which is not gathered from the personal knowledge of the witness, but through other sources. The value of the evidence is dependent upon the quality and competence of the source. In strict legal terms, hearsay covers a wide variety of topics. For the exam, understanding hearsay in this context is important.

All business records are considered hearsay because there is no way to prove that they in themselves are accurate, reliable, and trustworthy. However, should the business documents be used regularly in business activity and presented by an individual who is a component in their formation and use, it may be possible to submit business documents as records. To do so, the corresponding witness must:

➤ Have custody of the records in question on a regular basis

➤ Rely on those records in the regular course of business

➤ Know that they were prepared in the regular conduct of business

A memory or disk dump can be admitted as evidence if it acts merely as a statement of fact. A system or hex dump is not considered hearsay because it is used to identify the state of the systems, not the truth of the contents.

Major Categories of Computer Crime

Many types of computer crime exist, but the major categories included on the exam are discussed next.

Military and Intelligence Attacks

Computer criminals and intelligence agents are after sensitive military and law enforcement files containing military data and investigation reports.

Business Attacks

Businesses are reporting more and more information loss through competitive intelligence gathering and computer-related attacks. These attacks can be very costly due to the loss of trade secrets and reputation.

Financial Attacks

Banks and large corporations are often targeted to provide hackers with the funds they need or want. However, although banks provide one of the greatest targets, toll fraud is also a very large financial attack, often costing telephone companies millions of dollars.

Terrorist Attacks

More and more terrorist groups are using online capabilities to assist in their bombing attacks. In fact, some are moving more towards information terrorism than using physical destruction.

Grudge Attacks

These are targeted at individuals and companies who have done something that the attacker doesn't like. One example is a disgruntled employee who causes damage through a logic bomb after being fired.

"Fun" Attacks

These are attacks perpetrated by individuals who are not in it for the money but for the thrill of being able to break into a computer and tell all of their friends. Although they may not do anything with the information they have access to, they are dangerous nonetheless. Script kiddies fall into this category.

Code of Ethics

Ethics are a very important component of the CISSP exam. Because the CISSP is a professional certification, individuals are required to follow and uphold a certain code of ethics for the profession. RFC 1087 and the ISC2 Code of Ethics are the leading standards that should be followed.

RFC 1087 Ethics and the Internet

This text is taken directly from the RFC, available at **www.faqs.org/rfcs/ rfc1087.html**. RFC 1087 is an important discussion of ethics and the Internet that candidates should be familiar with.

"At great human and economic cost, resources drawn from the U.S. Government, industry, and the academic community have been assembled into a collection of interconnected networks called the Internet. Begun as a vehicle for experimental network research in the mid-1970's, the Internet has become an important national infrastructure supporting an increasingly widespread, multi-disciplinary community of researchers ranging, among other things, from computer scientists and electrical engineers to mathematicians, physicists, medical researchers, chemists, astronomers, and space scientists.

"As is true of other common infrastructures (e.g., roads, water reservoirs and delivery systems, and the power generation and distribution network), there is widespread dependence on the Internet by its users for the support of day-to-day research activities. The reliable operation of the Internet and the responsible use of its resources is of common interest and concern for its users, operators, and sponsors. Recent events involving the hosts on the Internet and in similar network infrastructures underscore the need to reiterate the professional responsibility every Internet user bears to colleagues and to the sponsors of the system. Many of the Internet resources are provided by the U.S. Government. Abuse of the system thus becomes a Federal matter above and beyond simple professional ethics."

Internet Activities Board (IAB) Statement of Policy

"The Internet is a national facility whose utility is largely a consequence of its wide availability and accessibility. Irresponsible use of this critical resource poses an enormous threat to its continued availability to the technical community.

"The U.S. Government sponsors of this system have a fiduciary responsibility to the public to allocate government resources wisely and effectively. Justification for the support of this system suffers when highly disruptive abuses occur. Access to and use of the Internet is a privilege and should be treated as such by all users of this system.

"The IAB strongly endorses the view of the Division Advisory Panel of the National Science Foundation Division of Network, Communications Research and Infrastructure that, in paraphrase, characterized as unethical and unacceptable any activity that purposely:

➤ Seeks to gain unauthorized access to the resources of the Internet

➤ Disrupts the intended use of the Internet

➤ Wastes resources (people, capacity, computer) through such actions

➤ Destroys the integrity of computer-based information

➤ Compromises the privacy of users

"The Internet exists in the general research milieu. Portions of it continue to be used to support research and experimentation on networking. Because experimentation on the Internet has the potential to affect all of its components and users, researchers have the responsibility to exercise great caution in the conduct of their work. Negligence in the conduct of Internet-wide experiments is both irresponsible and unacceptable.

"The IAB plans to take whatever actions it can in concert with federal agencies and other interested parties to identify and set up technical and procedural mechanisms to make the Internet more resistant to disruption. Such security, however, may be extremely expensive and may be counterproductive if it inhibits the free flow of information that makes the Internet so valuable. In the final analysis, the health and well-being of the Internet is the responsibility of its users who must, uniformly, guard against abuses that disrupt the system and threaten its long-term viability."

International Information Systems Security Certifications Consortium (ISC2) Code of Ethics

The information below is the ISC2 Code of Ethics, available at **www.isc2.org/ code.html**. All candidates should be familiar with this Code of Ethics, since they must abide by its standards in all professional dealings.

"All information systems security professionals who are certified by ISC2 recognize that such certification is a privilege that must be both earned and maintained. In support of this principle, all Certified Information Systems Security Professionals (CISSPs) commit to fully support this Code of Ethics. CISSPs who intentionally or knowingly violate any provision of the code will be subject to action by a peer review panel, which may result in the revocation of certification.

"There are only four mandatory canons in the code. By necessity, such high-level guidance is not intended to substitute for the ethical judgement of the professional.

"Additional guidance is provided for each of the canons. While this guidance may be considered by the Board in judging behavior, it is advisory rather than mandatory. It is intended to help the professional in identifying and resolving the inevitable ethical dilemmas that will confront him/her.

"The Code of Ethics Preamble is as follows:

➤ Safety of the commonwealth, duty to our principals and to each other requires that we adhere, and be seen to adhere, to the highest ethical standards of behavior.

➤ Therefore, strict adherence to this code is a condition of certification.

"The Code of Ethics Canons are as follows:

➤ Protect society, the commonwealth, and the infrastructure

➤ Act honorably, honestly, justly, responsibly, and legally

➤ Provide diligent and competent service to principals

➤ Advance and protect the profession

"The following additional guidance is given in furtherance of these goals.

"Objectives for Guidance

"In arriving at the following guidance, the committee is mindful of its responsibility to:

➤ Give guidance for resolving good versus good and bad versus bad dilemmas

➤ To encourage right behavior such as:

  ➤ Research

  ➤ Teaching

  ➤ Identifying, mentoring, and sponsoring candidates for the profession

  ➤ Valuing the certificate

➤ To discourage such behavior as:

  ➤ Raising unnecessary alarm, fear, uncertainty, or doubt

  ➤ Giving unwarranted comfort or reassurance

  ➤ Consenting to bad practice

  ➤ Attaching weak systems to the public net

  ➤ Professional association with non-professionals

  ➤ Professional recognition of or association with amateurs

  ➤ Associating or appearing to associate with criminals or criminal behavior

"However, these objectives are provided for information only; the professional is not required or expected to agree with them.

"In resolving the choices that confront him, the professional should keep in mind that the following guidance is advisory only. Compliance with the guidance is neither necessary nor sufficient for ethical conduct.

"Compliance with the preamble and canons is mandatory. Conflicts between the canons should be resolved in the order of the canons. The canons are not equal and conflicts between them is not intended to create ethical binds. The canons are as follows.

"Protect Society, the Commonwealth, and the Infrastructure

➤ Promote and preserve public trust and confidence in information and systems.

➤ Promote the understanding and acceptance of prudent information security measures.

➤ Preserve and strengthen the integrity of the public infrastructure.

➤ Discourage unsafe practice.

"Act Honorably, Honestly, Justly, Responsibly, and Legally

➤ Tell the truth; make all stakeholders aware of your actions on a timely basis.

➤ Observe all contracts and agreements, express or implied.

➤ Treat all constituents fairly. In resolving conflicts, consider public safety and duties to principals, individuals, and the profession in that order.

➤ Give prudent advice; avoid raising unnecessary alarm or giving unwarranted comfort. Take care to be truthful, objective, cautious, and within your competence.

➤ When resolving differing laws in different jurisdictions, give preference to the laws of the jurisdiction in which you render your service.

"Provide Diligent and Competent Service to Principals

➤ Preserve the value of their systems, applications, and information.

➤ Respect their trust and the privileges that they grant you.

➤ Avoid conflicts of interest or the appearance thereof.

➤ Render only those services for which you are fully competent and qualified.

"Advance and Protect the Profession

➤ Sponsor for professional advancement those best qualified. All other things equal, prefer those who are certified and who adhere to these canons. Avoid professional association with those whose practices or reputation might diminish the profession.

➤ Take care not to injure the reputation of other professionals through malice or indifference.

➤ Maintain your competence; keep your skills and knowledge current. Give generously of your time and knowledge in training others."

Understanding this code of ethics will help you understand what is expected of a CISSP.

Practice Questions

Question 1

> An invention which has been sufficiently documented and explained so as to allow a federal office to verify its originality is known as a:
>
> ○ a. Patent
>
> ○ b. Trademark
>
> ○ c. Copyright
>
> ○ d. Trade secret

Answer a is correct. A patent is an invention which has been sufficiently documented and explained so as to allow a federal office to verify its originality. Answer b is incorrect because a trademark is any distinguishing name, character, logo or other symbol that establishes an identity for a product, service or organization. Answer c is incorrect because copyright allows an author to protect how an idea is expressed. Answer d is incorrect because a trade secret is proprietary information that is used, made, or marketed by one having the exclusive legal rights.

Question 2

> The following quote is from which computer-related law?
>
> "To safeguard the privacy of innocent persons, the interception of wire or oral communications where none of the parties to the communication has consented to the interception should be allowed only when authorized by a court of competent jurisdiction and should remain under the control and supervision of the authorizing court. Interception of wire and oral communications should further be limited to certain major types of offenses and specific categories of crime with assurances that the interception is justified and that the information obtained thereby will not be misused."
>
> ○ a. Electronic Communications Privacy Act of 1986
>
> ○ b. Computer Fraud and Abuse Act of 1986
>
> ○ c. Computer Security Act of 1987
>
> ○ d. Privacy Act of 1974

Answer a is correct. The quoted text is from the Electronic Communications Privacy Act of 1986. Answers b, c, and d are thus incorrect.

Question 3

Proprietary information that is used, made, or marketed by one having the exclusive legal rights is known as:

○ a. Patent

○ b. Trademark

○ c. Copyright

○ d. Trade secret

Answer d is correct. A trade secret is proprietary information that is used, made, or marketed by one having the exclusive legal rights. Answer a is incorrect because a patent is an invention that has been sufficiently documented and explained so as to allow a federal office to verify its originality. Answer c is incorrect because a copyright allows an author to protect how an idea is expressed. Answer d is incorrect because a trademark is any distinguishing name, character, logo or other symbol that establishes an identity for a product, service or organization.

Question 4

Which of the following allows an author to protect how an idea is expressed?

○ a. Patent

○ b. Trademark

○ c. Copyright

○ d. Trade secret

Answer c is correct. A copyright allows an author to protect how an idea is expressed. Answer a is incorrect because a patent is an invention that has been sufficiently documented and explained so as to allow a federal office to verify its originality. Answer b is incorrect because a trademark is any distinguishing name, character, logo or other symbol that establishes an identity for a product, service or organization. Answer d is incorrect because a trade secret is proprietary information that is used, made, or marketed by one having the exclusive legal rights.

Question 5

What is the act where officers induce a person to commit a crime he or she was not previously contemplating?

○ a. Due care

○ b. Hearsay

○ c. Enticement

○ d. Entrapment

Answer d is correct. Entrapment occurs when officers induce a person to commit a crime he or she was not previously contemplating. Answer a is incorrect because due care specifies a person should act carefully and in good faith in fulfilling their tasks. Answer b is incorrect because hearsay is evidence that is not gathered from the personal knowledge of the witness but through other sources. Answer c is incorrect because enticement is the process of luring an intruder to do something.

Question 6

Evidence that is not gathered from the personal knowledge of the witness, but through other sources is known as:

○ a. Due care

○ b. Hearsay

○ c. Enticement

○ d. Entrapment

Answer b is correct. Hearsay is evidence that is not gathered from the personal knowledge of the witness, but through other sources. Answer a is incorrect because due care specifies a person should act carefully and in good faith in fulfilling their tasks. Answer c is incorrect because enticement is the process of luring an intruder to do something. Answer d is incorrect because entrapment is the act where officers induce a person to commit a crime they were not previously contemplating.

Question 7

Which attack is after sensitive military and law enforcement files containing military data and investigation reports?

- ○ a. Military and intelligence attacks
- ○ b. Business attacks
- ○ c. Grudge attacks
- ○ d. "Fun" attacks

Answer a is correct. Military and intelligence attacks are after sensitive military and law enforcement files containing military data and investigation reports. Answer b is incorrect because business attacks are after competitive information, trade secrets, or to just harm the business's reputation. Answer c is incorrect because grudge attacks are targeted at individuals and companies who have done something that the attacker doesn't like. Answer d is incorrect because "fun" attacks are perpetrated by individuals who are not in it for the money, but for the thrill of being able to break into a computer and tell all of their friends.

Question 8

Attacks that are targeted at individuals and companies who have done something that the attacker doesn't like are known as:

- ○ a. Military and intelligence attacks
- ○ b. Business attacks
- ○ c. Grudge attacks
- ○ d. "Fun" attacks

Answer c is correct. Grudge attacks are targeted at individuals and companies who have done something that the attacker doesn't like. Answer a is incorrect because military and intelligence attacks are after sensitive military and law enforcement files containing military data and investigation reports. Answer b is incorrect because business attacks are after competitive information, trade secrets, or to just harm the business's reputation. Answer d is incorrect because "fun" attacks are perpetrated by individuals who are not in it for the money, but for the thrill of being able to break into a computer and tell all of their friends.

Question 9

Which of the following is not a means to seize computer information and equipment?

- ○ a. Voluntary or consent
- ○ b. Subpoena
- ○ c. Search warrant
- ○ d. Injunction

Answer d is correct. An injunction is a court order to stop a specific action. Voluntary, subpoenas, and search warrants are all possible way to seize computer information and equipment. Answers a, b, and c are thus incorrect.

Question 10

Which of the following is not a step in the evidence life cycle?

- ○ a. Collection and identification
- ○ b. Reporting
- ○ c. Analysis
- ○ d. Return to owner

Answer b is correct. Reporting is not a step in the evidence life cycle. Collection and identification, analysis, and return to owner are all steps in the evidence life cycle. Answers a, c, and d are thus incorrect.

Need to Know More?

 http://austlii.law.uts.edu.au/au/other/crime/123.html contains the text of one of the leading computer crime laws, the Computer Crime and Abuse Act.

 www.cybercrime.gov is an excellent resource for computer crimes, laws, and investigation information.

 www.securityfocus.com is an excellent security resource site.

Physical Security

Terms you'll need to understand:

✓ CCTV

✓ FM-200

✓ Motion detectors

Techniques you'll need to master:

✓ Understanding physical security threats

✓ Understanding elements of physical security

✓ Understanding facility management

✓ Designing strong physical security

The Physical Security domain addresses the threats, vulnerabilities, and countermeasures that can be utilized to physically protect resources and sensitive information.

For the CISSP exam, you need to know the elements involved in choosing a secure site and setting up its design and configuration. You also need to know the methods for securing the facility against unauthorized access, theft of equipment and information, and the environmental safety measures for protecting people, the facility, and its resources.

Physical Security Threats

Physical security requires that buildings be safeguarded in a way that minimizes the risk of resource theft and destruction. To accomplish this, you must be concerned about building construction, room assignments, emergency procedures, regulations governing equipment placement and use, power supplies, product handling, and relationships with outside contractors and agencies.

The physical building must be satisfactorily secured to prevent the entry of those people who are not authorized to enter the site and use equipment. A building does not need to feel like a fort to be safe. Well-conceived plans to secure a building can be initiated without adding undue burden.

What are you trying to protect with physical security? There are many threats to information assets—some created by nature and some created by man—that can be mitigated with the implementation of proper physical security controls. The following list includes some of the more common, and more devastating, physical security threats:

➤ *Fire*—Fire is one of the most devastating physical security threats. If not contained, a strong fire can quickly destroy an entire building.

➤ *Water (rising/falling)*—Although usually not a deadly threat, water and computers do not mix well. Flooding can easily render powerful and expensive computer systems useless.

➤ *Earth movement (earthquakes, slides, volcanoes)*—These natural disasters can cause significant damage to buildings and computer systems.

➤ *Storms (wind, rain, snow, sleet, ice)*—Storms can knock out electricity and cause flooding, broken windows, and so on.

➤ *Sabotage/Vandalism*—Sabotage/vandalism is one of the more dangerous manmade threats. Often, the sabotage/vandalism is not found until it is too late.

➤ *Explosions*—Explosions are very dangerous physical threats. Besides being able to destroy systems, they often lead to loss of life.

➤ *Building collapse*—As with explosions, building collapses are very dangerous and often deadly.

➤ *Toxic materials*—Computer systems and employees should never need to be near toxic materials.

➤ *Utility loss (power, heating, cooling, air, water)*—Utility loss, while inconvenient, is generally not life-threatening. Generators and other back-up supplies can easily mitigate this risk.

➤ *Communications loss (voice, data)*—Communications loss, like utility loss, is generally not life-threatening, but it can lead to a significant revenue loss for the company.

➤ *Equipment failure*—Equipment failure is part of normal business activity, but it can lead to loss of life or loss of revenue. Proper maintenance and care should be taken with all equipment.

➤ *Personnel loss (strikes, illness, access, transport)*—Without proper personnel, physical security may not be as strong. Additionally, some personnel can exploit weaknesses in the physical security infrastructure to gain unauthorized access to resources or information.

Elements of Physical Security Controls

Although physical security threats do exist, these risks can be mitigated by implementing physical security processes, procedures, and technology. The main goals are threat prevention, detection, and suppression. The main physical security elements are:

➤ *Fire (sprinklers, halon, extinguishers)*—Sprinklers and fire extinguishers are the best methods for stopping a fire that has started in the building.

➤ *Water (leakage and flooding)*—Working on raised floors and keeping security systems out of basements and ground floors are good mitigating factors.

➤ *Detection control*—Implementing strong detection controls, such as access controls and motion sensors, can help detect attempted, unauthorized access.

➤ *Electrical (UPS and generators)*—Uninterruptable power supply (UPS) and generators are the best mitigators for loss of power.

➤ *Public, Private, and Restricted Areas (perimeter security, prevention, detection)*— Proper classification and labeling of physical areas helps determine where physical security should be focused.

➤ *Environmental (location, HVAC [Heating, Ventilation, and Air Conditioning])*— Selecting a good location and using proper environmental controls such as air conditioning helps protect from some environmental threats.

Facility Management and Planning Requirements for IT/IS

Certain standards have been created to help protect buildings and systems from physical security threats.

Floor Slab

The floor must be capable of a live load of 150 pounds per square foot with a good fire rating (flame spread rating less than or equal to 25).

Raised Flooring

The construction of the raised flooring must be grounded in order to reduce the likelihood of static discharges and also, in the event of an electrical failure, to ensure that any current sent through the floor frame will be appropriately grounded. The surface of the floor must be of a nonconductive type to prevent electrical injuries.

Walls

The walls must be a floor-to-ceiling slab (i.e., deck-to-deck) with a one-hour minimum fire rating. Any adjacent walls where records such as paper, media, and so forth, are stored must have a two-hour minimum fire rating.

Ceiling

The ceiling must have the same fire rating as the walls, and must be waterproof to prevent water leakage from above. Because it is part of the floor above, the ceiling must have an appropriate live load rate for the materials being stored above.

Windows

When installing either exterior or interior widows, the glass must be fixed in place, meaning that the window cannot open. It must be shatterproof (Lexan is good for this) and translucent.

Doors

The doors should be designed appropriately. Because most doorways open out to facilitate easy escape in an emergency, the door hinges are outside the doorframe. Appropriate care must be taken to protect the door hardware. The doorframe must be constructed to prevent the frame from being forced to open the door.

The door's fire rating must be equal to the walls where the door is placed, and the door must have emergency egress hardware (panic bars, and so forth), as appropriate. The lock mechanism on the door should fail open in the event of an emergency in order to facilitate escape. If the lock must fail closed, then a firefighter's key or some other emergency access must be available.

Other

Water, steam, and gas lines that run through the facility must have appropriate shut-off valves. The Emergency Power-Off (EPO) for the electrical system must be located near the exit doors to facilitate power shutoff when exiting during an emergency.

Air Conditioning (AC)

The AC units for the area must be dedicated to the area and controllable from within the area. The AC must be on a power source independent from the rest of the room and have its own EPO. The AC unit must keep positive pressure in the room in order to force smoke and other gases out of the room. The air intakes must be protected to prevent tampering. Finally, the area must be monitored for environmental conditions to maintain the correct environment.

Pertinent Personnel Access Controls

Any potential employee should have his or her background thoroughly investigated prior to acceptance into the company. Employers should check:

➤ Confirmation of previous employment

➤ Employment history (provided by applicant)

➤ Education history (provided by applicant)

➤ References

➤ Background investigation

➤ Credit history

➤ Security clearances

➤ Ratings/supervision

In addition to the administrative controls identified above, the following physical controls should be implemented within the organization.

Access Control

The access control categories are as follows:

➤ Universal code/card

➤ Possible magnetic card strip, magnetic dot, embedded wire, or proximity access

➤ Group coding

➤ Personal identification systems

➤ User-activated proximity systems, including the following:

> ➤ *Wireless keypad*—The user identifies him or herself by depressing a series of keys on the keypad. The coded representation of the keys is then transmitted to a remote control device. (This type of device is prone to *shoulder surfing*, allowing someone else to see the code that is entered.)

> ➤ *Preset code*—The code is present in the device itself. A single-button system, such as a garage-door opener, would be capable of transmitting a single representation. Multiple-button units store multiple codes.

> ➤ *System sensing*—Using this technology, the bearer has no action to take except to walk by a card reader wearing the card. The card reader senses the card and takes the appropriate action. Some systems require a battery, while the radio frequency (RF) field of the reader energizes other systems.

> ➤ *Passive devices*—Theses systems contain no battery. They sense the electromagnetic field of the reader and retransmit using different frequencies through tuned circuits in the portable device.

> ➤ *Field powered devices*—These units contain active electronic circuits, code storage electronics, digital sequencer, RF transmitter, and a power supply. The power supply extracts power from the electromagnetic field supplied by the reader.

> ➤ *Transponders*—These are fully portable, two-way radio sets combining a radio transceiver, code storage, control logic, and a battery. The reader transmits, and the portable unit receives the interrogating signal. When received, the portable unit responds by transmitting the coded data to the reader.

Facility

The following physical controls are important for the building:

➤ Fences and gates

➤ Turnstiles

➤ Mantraps

➤ Guards

Identification

The following types of identification can be used as physical controls:

➤ *Photo identification*—Clearly identifies what the wearer looks like. However, people often change their appearances.

➤ *Magnetic ID cards*—Identifies that the card has access. There is no way of proving the holder of the card is the actual owner of the card.

➤ *Biometric systems*—Clearly identifies the individual by reading physical characteristics of the person.

There are varieties of measurements available to distinguish among people. These include:

➤ Voice prints

➤ Fingerprints

➤ Hand geometry

➤ Blood vein patterns (wrist/hand/eye)

➤ Retina scan

➤ Iris scan

➤ Keystroke recorders

➤ Signature readers

Biometric devices rank as follows (most secure to least secure):

➤ Retina pattern devices

➤ Fingerprint devices

➤ Handprint devices

➤ Voice pattern devices

➤ Keystroke pattern devices

➤ Signature devices

However, as far as order of acceptance, the order is just the opposite.

CCTV

Closed-circuit television (CCTV) is a television system in which signals are not publicly distributed; cameras are connected to a television monitor in a limited area, such as a store or an office building. CCTV is used for video surveillance systems.

Other Access Control

All entryways must be protected and able to handle visitors, delivery services, and other unusual situations. In addition, internal entryways into sensitive areas should be protected.

Procedures

The access control procedures need to be able to address employees, employees from other company sites, employees who forget their ID, contractors, visitors (including logs and temporary IDs), and service and maintenance personnel.

Determining Site Location

Determining building location is one of the most important decisions a company makes.

If starting from scratch, you can consider the geographical location of your new site. Study long-term weather patterns, including frequency of heavy winds (i.e., tornadoes, hurricanes), snow, and lightning. The likelihood of earthquakes should also play a major role. Additionally, make sure the neighborhood is safe. You do not want employees to be scared for their own personal safety. Also, be on the lookout for industrial storage, airports, railroad tracks, and so on. The following list includes areas you should avoid when determining the location of a new building site:

➤ Flight paths for the local airport

➤ Nearby chemical or explosives plants

➤ Neighboring elevated highways

➤ Railway freight lines

➤ Mine shafts

➤ Toxic waste dumps

➤ Sources of dust and smoke (e.g., industrial incinerators)

➤ New or planned building activity (the vibration of pile drivers will harm your systems)

Another important factor to consider is how easy would it be to reach the site in an emergency. Ask yourself the following questions:

➤ Is there redundant road access?

➤ Are there several sources of help to fight fires?

➤ Is there police support and emergency rescue within easy reach?

You should also examine the socioeconomic profile of the proposed location. Ask yourself the following:

➤ Are there poor areas around the site?

➤ What's the crime rate?

➤ Is it improving or declining?

Designing Strong Physical Security

In designing strong physical security, the following considerations are useful and can help build a resilient and fairly resistant building.

Protecting the Building and Equipment

For location and access, avoid spaces crossed either horizontally or vertically by water and steam pipes or air-conditioning ducts. Allow only one access door to any secured area and no through access. All rooms should be sealed to keep out dust and smoke. Paint the partitions and ceiling with an off-white paint that also provides a vapor barrier. Equipment rooms and storerooms should not have hung ceilings. Use fluorescent light fixtures to save money. Avoid a raised access floor if possible. All doors should look alike. A sensor should be built into the doorframe to indicate when the door is not closed. A push-button cipher lock is usually sufficient for access control. Automatically unlock the door during a power failure.

The electrical-power control panel should be inside the room with circuit breakers for the major pieces of equipment and lighting. It is always required to use wire rated to carry more current than its associated circuit breaker.

A few other considerations include using a resilient vinyl floor. A floor drain is necessary if the room is sprinklered. There should be a telephone, an office paging speaker, and an audible fire alarm in each equipment room.

Abnormally high or low power electrical line voltage can occur often during a business day. Electrical static superimposed on the power lines in sufficient quantity can disrupt electronic equipment. This static usually damages data.

There are three methods to protect against power problems: power line conditioners, UPS, and backup power sources. Power line conditioners use capacitors, inductors, varistors, and tapped transformers to smooth out voltage spikes, surges, and sags, as well as electromagetic and radio-frequency noise.

Air that is too humid also causes problems. Above 80 percent relative humidity, a process of silver migration—similar to electro-plating—starts to occur. It ruins the electrical efficiency of the connection. A good humidity specification is 50+/-10 percent relative humidity. Purified air in the equipment room is desirable, but generally no longer mandatory.

There should be no wood, trash, paper, carpet, fabric, or clothing, and especially no combustible liquids or cleaning fluids in the equipment room. Most computer circuits use only 2 or 5 volts of direct current—about the same as a flashlight—which cannot cause overheating, much less a fire. Early smoke detection and selectively shutting down equipment until the source of heat is eliminated so that actual combustion will not occur is a good practice. In the event of a major fire or if an explosion occurs, it will be almost impossible to save anything inside an equipment room. The fist response should be automatic suppression, followed by hand-held fire extinguishers used only by trained personnel.

Computer rooms should be continuously monitored for temperature, humidity, water leaks, and especially smoke and fire. A recording hygrometer is generally adequate for monitoring humidity. Ionization detectors are the most sensitive to smoke. Photo-cell smoke detectors combined with rate-of-rise temperature sensors are more sensitive to explosions, burning liquids, and burning materials. They, too, should be mounted on the ceiling.

For fire suppression systems, FM-200 is similar to Halon but with no atmospheric ozone-depleting potential. Neither system does much against an electrical fire. Unless electrical power is switched off, the danger exists that water will increase the number of low-resistance shorting paths, intensifying the fire and causing even greater damage to computer equipment. Fast-acting sensors should be installed to shut down electrical power before water sprinklers are turned on. A shut-off valve should be inside the room so the water can be stopped as soon as it is no longer needed. There should be a hand-held fire extinguisher wall-mounted inside every equipment room door.

Smoke alarms should be transmitted automatically to the local fire department. You should clearly define who can silence the alarms. Whenever a smoke detector activates, air circulation should be shut down in the affected area.

All power sources, wiring, and control cables to the alarm systems and process cooling systems should be concealed.

Protecting Wiring

Wiring should not be ignored in the physical security process. Fiber optic cabling is significantly superior to copper because it is totally insensitive to electrical or magnetic interference. It is difficult and expensive to wiretap. Copper wire is easy to monitor by anyone with access anywhere along its length. The best way to protect the integrity of data is with encryption.

Poor copper wire performance is a common problem because of bad contacts and excessive strain or twisting. Data wiring should be certified by someone with the knowledge, experience, and equipment to do this properly. Category 5 cable should be used for high-speed, broadband data transmission.

Any area that contains IP wiring, equipment, or terminals should be locked at all times. Any fire in a utility closet or riser shaft is a serious threat. The best protection is good housekeeping to ensure that no combustible materials are allowed in or near these areas.

Securing Storage Areas

The information stored on tapes and disks is mission critical. Therefore, tight physical security is required for handling and storing all tapes and disks. Magnetic media must be kept away from strong magnetic fields. Magnetic tape is especially vulnerable to heat. Fire heating refers only to how long paper inside will not char.

Dealing with Existing Facilities

It is often better and less expensive to build new facilities than to renovate existing ones. Rewiring and retrofitting older building can be very expensive and will still not always provide the best functionality.

Protecting External Services

Items that require continuous attention to security are interfaces to remote data processing or storage services. Other sensitive interfaces connect to microwave and satellite systems.

Surveillance Devices

There are three categories of data center surveillance:

➤ Guards

➤ Dogs

➤ Visual recording devices

The physical presence of a guard provides a deterrent capacity. Guards can also perform control functions that are a vital part of any security system. The use of guards, however, is limited by their reliability.

Guard dogs are capable of doing what an electronic detector alone cannot do as an automatic response mechanism. Dogs can frighten and sometimes stop intruders. An electronic detector, while possibly alerting a response service and sounding an alarm, may not immediately stop an intruder.

Visual recording devices are powerful surveillance devices. There are two main categories: photographic and electronic. With photographic devices, the motion picture camera and the single-exposure sequence camera are used. Closed circuit TV and video recorder, utilizing a VCR, has the economic advantage of recording and storing events. Camcorders, VHS and 8mm, can also record sound without additional peripheral equipment and do not require intermediate steps of off-premises file processing.

Fire Detectors

Fire detectors often respond to incremental changes in temperature or the products of combustion. Heat-activated sensing devices are usually either fixed temperature detectors or rate-of-rise detectors. These provide a quick alarm, but they may increase the possibility of false alarms. A line-type installation is operated by a pneumatic tube or heat-sensitive cable, while the spot installation locates each sensor in zones at specified distances apart.

Flame-activated devices are another option for fire detectors. Here, flame-radiation-frequency-activated devices that sense the pulsations or flicker of the flame can be used. Additionally, flame-energy-activated devices that sense a portion of the infrared energy in the flame can be used. Radiation-frequency flame detectors are expensive, but response time is less than 5 milliseconds.

Smoke-activated devices are a third type of fire detector. These devices are often considered early-warning devices. There are two main types: photoelectric and radioactive. Photoelectric devices use an electric current that changes when there is a variation in the light intensity. The beam type focuses a beam of light across the protected area, the area-sampling type uses a pipe system to draw air and the spot type contains the light source, receiver, and photoelectric all in one housing.

With radioactive smoke detection devices, as smoke particles or other products of combustion enter this chamber, the normal ionization current is disturbed and causes an alarm signal to be generated.

Motion Detectors

Motion detectors are an important security measure for sensitive areas. Wave pattern sensors are classified according to the frequency of the generated wave and include low-frequency, ultrasonic, and microwave devices. If the reflected wave pattern is modified by any motion within the protected area, the frequency of the returning wave is changed and the motion detectors are programmed to activate the alarm circuit. These devices can monitor areas ranging from 600 to 10,000 square feet.

Capacitance devices monitor an electrical field that is generated around the immediate area of the specific object requiring security measures. These devices provide point or spot protection and are typically used for file cabinets, safes, or other metallic containers. They can also be connected to a metal grid covering windows and doors to detect unauthorized entry.

Audio amplification devices are passive and do not generate any wave patterns. There are two different applications for audio detectors, one for normal room protection and the other for vault protection.

Control

Control assures that an alarm signal generated by either a surveillance or a sensing unit reaches its intended receiving device and that appropriate measures are in force with regard to access and egress. With alarm systems, there are five main types. *Local alarms* are connected directly to an audible alarm on the premises. *Central station alarms* are operated by private security organizations. *Proprietary alarms* are similar to central station alarms except that the receiving and monitoring functions are performed directly on the protected property. *Auxiliary station alarms* automatically cause an alarm originating in a data center to be transmitted over the local municipal fire or police alarm circuits for relaying to both the local police/fire station and the appropriate headquarters. A *remote station alarm* is a direct connection between the signal-initiating device at the protected property and the signal-receiving device located at a remote station, such as the firehouse. A remote system differs from an auxiliary system in that it does not use the municipal fire or police alarm circuits.

The choice of fire extinguishing agents is important. *Wet pipes* always contain water in the pipes connected to the nozzle devices, and, therefore, are considered a closed head system. With *dry pipes*, no water is stored in the pipes—it is held back by a clapper valve. When the dry pipe device is triggered, air is blown out and water will flows. The main advantage is a time delay before the water actually flows, thus providing an opportunity to shut down the systems if the fire is minor, with little chance of causing damage. A *deluge* is similar to the dry pipe system, except that the sprinkler head is open. This device delivers a large volume of water quickly.

Preaction systems are a combination of wet and dry pipe systems, using a closed head. Initially, the pipes are dry. A heat-activated sensor opens an automatic water control valve that sounds an alarm and allows the pipes to fill with water. The water is not discharged until a fusible link melts (as in the wet pipe system). The preaction system is used when it is desirable to prevent an accidental discharge of water by providing an advance alarm.

Gas discharge systems are also used. This system eliminates the necessity of mixing water and electricity. Carbon dioxide or Halon 1301 are used, though not very much anymore. Additionally, FM-200, also known as HFC-227, is the common solution today.

Physical Security Checklist

The following checklist provides an excellent review of the physical security measures that should be in place.

Create a Secure Environment: Building and Room Construction

Ask yourself the following questions when creating a secure environment:

➤ Does each secure room or facility have low visibility (e.g., no unnecessary signs)?

➤ Has the room or facility been constructed with full-height walls?

➤ Has the room or facility been constructed with a fireproof ceiling?

➤ Are there two or fewer doorways?

➤ Are doors solid and fireproof?

➤ Are doors equipped with locks?

➤ Are window openings in secure areas kept as small as possible?

➤ Are windows equipped with locks?

➤ Are keys and combinations to door and window locks secured responsibly?

➤ Have alternatives to traditional lock and key security measures (e.g., bars, anti-theft cabling, magnetic key cards, and motion detectors) been considered?

➤ Has both automatic and manual fire equipment been properly installed?

➤ Are personnel properly trained for fire emergencies?

➤ Are acceptable room temperatures always maintained (i.e., between 50 and 80 degrees Fahrenheit)?

➤ Are acceptable humidity ranges always maintained (i.e., between 20 and 80 percent)?

➤ Are eating, drinking, and smoking regulations in place and enforced?

➤ Has all non-essential, potentially flammable material (e.g., curtains and stacks of computer paper) been removed from secure areas?

Guard Equipment

The following questions are related to guarding equipment:

➤ Has equipment been identified as critical or general use, and segregated appropriately?

➤ Is equipment housed out of sight and out of reach from doors and windows, and away from radiators, heating vents, air conditioners, and other duct work?

➤ Are plugs, cables, and other wires protected from foot traffic?

➤ Are up-to-date records of all equipment brand names, model names, and serial numbers kept in a secure location?

➤ Have qualified technicians (staff or vendors) been identified to repair critical equipment if and when it fails?

➤ Has contact information for repair technicians (e.g., telephone numbers, customer numbers, maintenance contract numbers) been stored in a secure but accessible place?

➤ Are repair workers and outside technicians required to adhere to the organization's security policies concerning sensitive information?

Rebuff Theft

The following questions are guidelines for avoiding theft:

➤ Has all equipment been labeled in an overt way that clearly and permanently identifies its owner (e.g., the school name)?

➤ Has all equipment been labeled in a covert way that only authorized staff would know to look for (e.g., inside the cover)?

➤ Have steps been taken to make it difficult for unauthorized people to tamper with equipment (e.g., by replacing case screws with Allen-type screws)?

➤ Have security staff been provided up-to-date lists of personnel and their respective access authority?

➤ Are security staff required to verify the identity of unknown people before permitting access to facilities?

➤ Are security staff required to maintain a log of all equipment taken in and out of secure areas?

Attend to Portable Equipment and Computers

Ask the following questions regarding portable equipment and computers:

➤ Do users know not to leave laptops and other portable equipment unattended outside of the office?

➤ Do users know and follow proper transportation and storage procedures for laptops and other portable equipment?

Regulate Power Supplies

The following questions are guidelines for regulating power supplies:

➤ Are surge protectors used with all equipment?

➤ Are UPSs in place for critical systems?

➤ Have power supplies been "insulated" from environmental threats by a professional electrician?

➤ Has consideration been given to the use of electrical outlets so as to avoid overloading?

➤ Are the negative effects of static electricity minimized through the use of anti-static carpeting, pads, and sprays as necessary?

Protect Output

The following are guidelines for protecting output:

➤ Are photocopiers, fax machines, and scanners kept in open view?

➤ Are printers assigned to users with similar security clearances?

➤ Is every printed copy of confidential information labeled as "confidential"?

➤ Are outside delivery services required to adhere to security practices when transporting sensitive information?

➤ Are all paper copies of sensitive information shredded before being discarded?

Practice Questions

Question 1

> Which of the following is not a physical security threat?
>
> ○ a. Earthquake
>
> ○ b. Hurricane
>
> ○ c. Fire
>
> ● d. Password cracker

Answer d is correct. A password cracker is not a physical security threat. Answers a, b, and c are incorrect because earthquakes, hurricanes, and fire are all physical security threats.

Question 2

> The floor should be capable of carrying a live load of how many pounds per square foot?
>
> ● a. 150
>
> ○ b. 100
>
> ○ c. 200
>
> ○ d. 250

Answer a is correct. A floor should be capable of carrying a live load of 150 pounds per square foot. Answers b, c, and d are thus incorrect.

Question 3

> Which of the following is the most secure biometric device?
>
> ○ a. Voice pattern recognition
>
> ○ b. Fingerprint scanner
>
> ● c. Retina scanner
>
> ○ d. Signature scanner

Answer c is correct. A retina scanner is the most secure biometric device. Answers a and b are incorrect because voice pattern recognition and fingerprint scanners are not the most secure biometric devices. Answer d is incorrect because even though signature scanners usually provide the highest acceptance rate, they are not the most secure biometric devices.

Question 4

Which of the following is not a commonly used surveillance device?

○ a. Guard

○ b. Dog

○ c. Video recorder

● d. Telescope

Answer d is correct. A telescope is not a commonly used surveillance device. Answers a, b, and c are incorrect because guards, dogs, and video recorders are commonly used surveillance devices.

Question 5

Which of the following fire extinguishing devices always contains water?

● a. Wet pipes

○ b. Dry pipes

○ c. Proaction

○ d. Water extinguisher

Answer a is correct. Wet pipes always contain water in the pipes connected to the nozzle devices, and therefore are considered a closed head system. Answer b is incorrect because dry pipes do not always contain water. Answers c and d are not real options and are thus incorrect.

Question 6

Which fire-extinguishing agent commonly replaces Halon 1301?

- ○ a. FM-100
- ○ b. AM-200
- ● c. FM-200
- ○ d. AM-100

Answer c is correct. FM-200 is a common replacement for Halon 1301 fire suppression systems. Answers a, b, and d are not real options, and are thus incorrect.

Question 7

Which of the following is not an aspect of a computer room that must be continuously monitored?

- ○ a. Temperature
- ○ b. Humidity
- ○ c. Fire
- ● d. Population

Answer d is correct. You do not have to monitor the population of the computer room. Answers a, b, and c are incorrect because temperature, humidity, and fire must all be continuously monitored.

Question 8

Which kind of wiring is insensitive to electrical or magnetic interference?

- ○ a. Copper
- ● b. Fiber optic
- ○ c. Coaxial cable
- ○ d. Ethernet

Answer b is correct. Fiber optic cable is insensitive to electrical or magnetic interference. Answers a, c, and d are incorrect because copper, coaxial cable, and Ethernet are all sensitive to electrical or magnetic interference.

Question 9

> Which of the following sites would be a desirable building location?
>
> ○ a. Next to the airport
>
> ○ b. Next to the active freight train line
>
> 🖙 c. Next to a suburban neighborhood
>
> ○ d. Next to a proposed freeway expansion site

Answer c is correct. The most desirable building location would be next to a suburban neighborhood. Answers a, b, and d all introduce significant physical risks and are thus incorrect.

Question 10

> Which of the following is not something that should be performed for a potential employee?
>
> ○ a. Background check
>
> ○ b. Reference check
>
> ○ c. Education history
>
> 🖙 d. Marital status verification

Answer d is correct. Marital status is not something that needs to be checked for a potential employee. Answers a, b, and c are incorrect because background checks, reference checks, and education history should all be reviewed.

Need to Know More?

 www.cccure.org/Documents/Physical_Security/fm3-19.30.pdf provides the Army's physical security guidelines.

 www.reliablefire.com/halon/halon.html provides excellent information on fire suppression systems.

 www.securityfocus.com is an excellent security resource site.

Sample Test

Question 1

A communication channel that allows a process to transfer information in a manner that violates the system's security policy is a(n):

○ a. ITSEC

○ b. Bell-LaPadula

○ c. TEMPEST

◉ d. Covert channel

Question 2

Reviewing access logs is an example of which control type?

◉ a. Detective control

○ b. Preventive control

○ c. Corrective control

○ d. Recovery control

Question 3

Two essential prerequisites for creating a disaster recovery plan are:

○ a. Threat events and probability of occurrence

◉ b. Information backup and management commitment

○ c. Team leaders and documentation

○ d. Hot site availability and backups

Question 4

Which of the following allows an author to protect how an idea is expressed?

○ a. Patent

○ b. Trademark

◉ c. Copyright

○ d. Trade secret

Question 5

Which of the following fire extinguishing devices always contains water?

◉ a. Wet pipes

○ b. Dry pipes

○ c. Proaction

○ d. Water extinguisher

Question 6

What is a table that identifies which access rights each user has to a particular system object?

○ a. MAC

○ b. DAC

◉ c. ACL

○ d. Lattice

Question 7

Which cabling method uses an RJ-45 connector?

○ a. Coaxial cable

● b. Unshielded twisted pair

○ c. Fiber optic cable

○ d. Wireless

Question 8

What should you not do after dismissing an employee?

○ a. Escort them out the door

● b. Let them return to their desk unsupervised

○ c. Disable all accounts and logons

○ d. Follow the termination checklist

Question 9

Which viruses infect executable code found in certain system areas on a disk?

○ a. Trap doors

○ b. Trojan horses

○ c. Macro viruses

● d. Boot-sector viruses

Question 10

Which security concept masks information in a way that makes it unintelligible to anyone other than the intended recipient?

○ a. Authentication

● b. Encryption

○ c. Auditing

○ d. Certificate

Question 11

Which of the following is not a common system flaw?

○ a. Covert channels

○ b. Lack of input checks

◉ c. Use of ITSEC

○ d. Use of privileged programs

Question 12

Maintaining strong passwords is an example of what control type?

○ a. Detective control

◉ b. Preventive control

○ c. Corrective control

○ d. Recovery control

Question 13

A written BCP/DRP plan should not include:

○ a. Damage assessment and containment

○ b. Activation procedures of short- and long-term backup plans

○ c. Access to data backup facilities

◉ d. Budget information

Question 14

What is the act in which officers induce a person to commit a crime he or she was not previously contemplating?

○ a. Due care

○ b. Hearsay

○ c. Enticement

◉ d. Entrapment

Question 15

Which fire extinguishing agent is commonly replacing Halon 1301?

○ a. FM-100

○ b. AM-200

● c. FM-200

○ d. AM-100

Question 16

Which of the following allows attackers to imitate a different user or system?

○ a. Sniffers

○ b. Spamming

● c. Spoofing

○ d. Crackers

Question 17

An Ethernet network often uses what type of topology?

○ a. Diamond

○ b. Ring

● c. Bus

○ d. Star

Question 18

A(n) _____ can assist only in the prevention of deliberate breaches of security such as theft, fraud, sabotage, and misuse.

● a. Organization structure

○ b. Encapsulation

○ c. Training program

○ d. Change control

Question 19

A backdoor application entry point added by the developer is a:

- ● a. Trap door
- ○ b. Trojan horse
- ○ c. Macro virus
- ○ d. Boot-sector virus

Question 20

_____ encryption converts data from a variable length to a fixed-length piece of data.

- ○ a. Symmetric
- ○ b. Asymmetric
- ● c. Hash
- ○ d. Email

Question 21

Which of the following is not a TCSEC level?

- ● a. F
- ○ b. C
- ○ c. B
- ○ d. D

Question 22

Maintaining backups in case a system needs to be restored is what type of control?

- ○ a. Detective control
- ○ b. Preventive control
- ○ c. Corrective control
- ● d. Recovery control

Question 23

A process that dynamically manages the storage and retrieval of online data files to storage media devices is:

- ○ a. Tape backup
- ○ b. Electronic vaulting
- ◉ c. Hierarchical storage management
- ○ d. Mirror processing

Question 24

Evidence that is not gathered from the personal knowledge of the witness but through other sources is known as:

- ○ a. Due care
- ◉ b. Hearsay
- ○ c. Enticement
- ○ d. Entrapment

Question 25

Which of the following is not an aspect of a computer room that must be continuously monitored?

- ○ a. Temperature
- ○ b. Humidity
- ○ c. Fire
- ◉ d. Population

Question 26

What access control technique allows the resource owner to control other user's access to the object?

- ○ a. MAC
- ◉ b. DAC
- ○ c. Lattice
- ○ d. RBAC

he following is a protocol that one program can use to request a service from a program on another computer?

- a. Secure RPC
- ○ b. CHAP
- ○ c. SLIP
- ○ d. PPTP

Question 28

Security awareness programs cannot:

- ○ a. Make employees aware of issues
- ○ b. Show them the proper procedures to follow
- ● c. Enforce security policy
- ○ d. Make them aware of risks

Question 29

When the computer programming, processing, and data that computers work on are spread out over more than one computer, you have implemented a:

- ● a. Distributed computing environment
- ○ b. Nondistributed computing environment
- ○ c. Agent
- ○ d. Applet

Question 30

Which of the following is a symmetric encryption algorithm?

- ● a. 3DES
- ○ b. MD5
- ○ c. RSA
- ○ d. Diffie-Helman

Question 31

Which of the following is not a security model?

- ○ a. Bell-LaPadula
- ○ b. Biba
- ○ c. Clark-Wilson
- ● d. Smith-Kline

Question 32

The activity of digging through an individual or organization's trash to find critical information and documents that were not properly disposed of is called _____.

- ● a. Dumpster diving
- ○ b. Social engineering
- ○ c. Radiation monitoring
- ○ d. Sniffing

Question 33

Sites that are fully configured and ready to operate within several hours are:

- ● a. Hot sites
- ○ b. Warm sites
- ○ c. Cold sites
- ○ d. Medium sites

Question 34

Which attack is after sensitive military and law enforcement files containing military data and investigation reports?

- ● a. Military and intelligence attacks
- ○ b. Business attacks
- ○ c. Grudge attacks
- ○ d. "Fun" attacks

Question 35

Which wiring is insensitive to electric or magnetic interference?

○ a. Copper

● b. Fiber optic

○ c. Coaxial cable

○ d. Ethernet

Question 36

What access control technique is nondiscretionary?

● a. MAC

○ b. DAC

○ c. Lattice

○ d. RBAC

Question 37

Which protocol maps an IP address to a physical machine address?

○ a. SLIP

○ b. PPP

○ c. Frame relay

● d. ARP

Question 38

Ensuring data and resources are accessible when they need to be defines the concept of:

○ a. Confidentiality

○ b. Integrity

● c. Availability

○ d. Authorization

Question 39

A program that gathers information or performs some other service without your immediate presence and on some regular schedule is a(n)?

○ a. Applet

○ b. ActiveX control

◉ c. Agent

○ d. C++ control

Question 40

Which of the following is a hash algorithm?

○ a. 3DES

◉ b. MD5

○ c. RSA

○ d. Diffie-Helman

Question 41

How many layers are in the OSI model?

○ a. Five

◉ b. Seven

○ c. Nine

○ d. Three

Question 42

During the monitoring process, which of the following is not a mandatory requirement?

○ a. Patches

◉ b. Applications

○ c. Security sites and mailing lists

○ d. System configuration and log files

Question 43

A system that entails immediately transmitting copies of each online transaction or change to a remotely located computer facility where the data is preserved for backup is:

- ○ a. Tape backup
- ◉ b. Electronic vaulting
- ○ c. Hierarchical storage management
- ○ d. Mirror processing

Question 44

Attacks that are targeted at individuals and companies who have done something that the attacker doesn't like are known as:

- ○ a. Military and intelligence attacks
- ○ b. Business attacks
- ◉ c. Grudge attacks
- ○ d. "Fun" attacks

Question 45

Which of the following sites would be a desirable building location?

- ○ a. Next to the airport
- ○ b. Next to the active freight train line
- ◉ c. Next to a suburban neighborhood
- ○ d. Next to a proposed freeway expansion site

Question 46

Which of the following monitors networks and computer systems for signs of intrusion or misuse?

- ◉ a. IDS
- ○ b. MAC
- ○ c. Bell-LaPadula
- ○ d. TACACS

Question 47

Which layer of the OSI model handles TCP?

○ a. Physical

○ b. Network

◉ c. Transport

○ d. Data Link

Question 48

Providing a means of determining who can access which system resources describes what concept?

○ a. Confidentiality

○ b. Integrity

○ c. Availability

◉ d. Authorization

Question 49

Which programming language was developed for specific use on the Internet and a wide variety of platforms?

○ a. Fortran

○ b. C++

○ c. C

◉ d. Java

Question 50

Which of the following is an asymmetric algorithm?

○ a. 3DES

○ b. MD5

◉ c. RSA

○ d. SHA

Answer Key

1. d	18. a	35. b
2. a	19. a	36. a
3. b	20. c	37. d
4. c	21. a	38. c
5. a	22. d	39. c
6. c	23. c	40. b
7. b	24. b	41. b
8. b	25. d	42. b
9. d	26. b	43. b
10. b	27. a	44. d
11. c	28. c	45. c
12. b	29. a	46. a
13. d	30. a	47. c
14. d	31. d	48. d
15. c	32. a	49. d
16. c	33. a	50. c
17. c	34. a	

Question 1

Answer d is correct. A covert channel allows a process to transfer information in a manner that violates the system's security policy. Answer a is incorrect because ITSEC is a set of security evaluation criteria. Answer b is incorrect because Bell-LaPadula is a security model. Answer c is incorrect because TEMPEST deals with electromagnetic radiation.

Question 2

Answer a is correct. A detective control is used to review access logs. Answer b is incorrect because a corrective control is implemented to correct an identified issue before it can be used to cause harm. Answer c is incorrect because a preventive control is implemented to keep security incidents from occurring. Answer d is incorrect because a recovery control helps fix an issue identified during an audit or security review.

Question 3

Answer b is correct. Although threats, probabilities, team leaders, documentation, and hot sites are all part of a plan, you first need backups and management commitment to begin the entire planning process. Answers a, c, and d are thus incorrect.

Question 4

Answer c is correct. A copyright allows an author to protect how an idea is expressed. Answer a is incorrect because a patent is the legal protection of an invention that has been sufficiently documented and explained so as to allow a federal office to verify its originality. Answer b is incorrect because a trademark is any distinguishing name, character, logo or other symbol that establishes an identity for a product, service, or organization. Answer d is incorrect because a trade secret is proprietary information that is used, made, or marketed by one having the exclusive legal rights.

Question 5

Answer a is correct. Wet pipes always contain water in the pipes connected to the nozzle devices, and therefore are considered a closed head system. Answers b, c, and d are incorrect because dry pipes, proaction, and water extinguisher do not always contain water.

Question 6

Answers c is correct. ACL is a table that identifies which access rights each user has to a particular system object. Answers a and b are incorrect because MAC and DAC are access control techniques that use security classification or file owner listings as access rights. Answer d is incorrect because a lattice deals with information flow in multi-user environments.

Question 7

Answer b is correct. Unshielded twisted pair uses an RJ-45 connector. Answer a is incorrect because coaxial cable uses a BNC connector. Answer c is incorrect because fiber optic uses an SC connector. Answer d is incorrect because wireless networks do not have specific connectors.

Question 8

Answer b is correct. You should not allow an employee to return to his desk unsupervised after he has been dismissed. Answers a, c, and d are all steps of an effective termination policy, and thus are incorrect answers.

Question 9

Answer d is correct. A boot-sector virus infects executable code found in certain system areas on a disk. Answer a is incorrect because a trap door is a back door to an application or system created by the developer. Answer b is incorrect because a Trojan horse is a program or virus in which malicious or harmful code is contained inside apparently harmless programming, data, or messages in such a way that it can get control and do its chosen form of damage. Answer c is incorrect because macro viruses infect applications such as Word and Excel by planting malicious macros.

Question 10

Answer b is correct. Encryption allows information to be masked so that only the intended recipient can view the actual contents. Answers a and d are incorrect because authentication involves the concept of verifying authenticity; this may or may not involve certificates. Answer c is incorrect because auditing is the process of logging and/or reviewing the logs of system activity.

Question 11

Answer c is correct. ITSEC is a set of security criteria. Covert channels, lack of input checks, and use of privileged programs are all common system flaws. Answers a, b, and d are thus incorrect.

Question 12

Answer b is correct. A preventive control is implemented to keep security incidents from occurring. Answer a is incorrect because a detective control helps identify possible security incidents. Answer c is incorrect because a corrective control is implemented to correct an identified issue before it can be used to cause harm. Answer d is incorrect because a recovery control helps recover from a security incident.

Question 13

Answer d is correct. A written BCP/DRP plan should not include budget information. Everything else should be included in the plan. Answers a, b, and c are thus incorrect.

Question 14

Answer d is correct. Entrapment is the act in which officers induce a person to commit a crime he or she was not previously contemplating. Answer a is incorrect because due care specifies a person should act carefully and in good faith in fulfilling their tasks. Answer b is incorrect because hearsay is evidence that is not gathered from the personal knowledge of the witness, but through other sources. Answer c is incorrect because enticement is the process of luring an intruder to do something.

Question 15

Answer c is correct. FM-200 is a common replacement for Halon 1301 fire supression systems. The other options are not common replacements for Halon 1301. Answers a, b, and d are thus incorrect.

Question 16

Answer c is correct. Spoofing allows attackers to imitate a different user or system. Answer a is incorrect because sniffers capture network packets. Answer b is incorrect because spammers send unsolicited email messages. Answer d is incorrect because crackers allow attackers to break passwords.

Question 17

Answer c is correct. A bus topology is often used in an Ethernet network. Answer a is incorrect because diamond is not a network topology. Answer b is incorrect because ring topology is often used in Token Ring implementations. Answer d is incorrect because star topologies are used in switched environments.

Question 18

Answer a is correct. An organization structure can assist only in the prevention of deliberate breaches of security such as theft, fraud, sabotage, and misuse Encapsulation, training programs, and change control all help prevent other security breaches in addition to theft, fraud, sabotage, and misuse. Answers b, c, and d are thus incorrect.

Question 19

Answer a is correct. A trap door is a back door to an application or system created by the developer Answer b is incorrect because a Trojan horse is a program or virus in which malicious or harmful code is contained inside apparently harmless programming, data, or message in such a way that it can get control and do its chosen form of damage. Answer c is incorrect because macro viruses infect applications such as Word and Excel by planting malicious macros. Answer d is incorrect because a boot-sector virus infects executable code found in the master boot record.

Question 20

Answer c is correct. Hash encryption converts data from a variable length to a fixed length piece of data. Asymmetric and symmetric are encryption processes, but they do not convert the data to a fixed length piece of data. Answers a and b are thus incorrect. Answer d is incorrect because email uses encryption; it is not an encryption technique.

Question 21

Answer a is correct. F is not a TCSEC level. Answers b, c, and d are all TCSEC levels, and are thus incorrect answers.

Question 22

Answer d is correct. Recovery control maintains backups in case a system needs to be restored. Answer a is incorrect because a detective control helps identify possible security incidents. Answer b is incorrect because a preventive control is implemented to keep security incidents from occurring. Answer c is incorrect because a corrective control is implemented to correct an identified issue before it can be used to cause harm.

Question 23

Answer c is correct. Hierarchical storage dynamically manages the storage and retrieval of online data files to storage media devices. Answer a is incorrect because tape backup is the process of copying data to tape. Answer b is incorrect because electronic vaulting is a system that immediately transmits copies of each on-line transaction or change to a remotely located computer facility where the data is preserved for backup. Answer d is incorrect because mirror processing updates to a backup copy of the database so that the backup files are more readily available for use in an emergency.

Question 24

Answer b is correct. Hearsay is evidence that is not gathered from the personal knowledge of the witness but through other sources. Answer a is incorrect because due care specifies a person should act carefully and in good faith in fulfilling their tasks. Answer c is incorrect because enticement is the process of luring an intruder to do something. Answer d is incorrect because entrapment is the act where officers induce a person to commit a crime they were not previously contemplating.

Question 25

Answer d is correct. You do not always have to monitor the population of the computer room. You should monitor temperature, humidity, and fire. Answers a, b, and c are thus incorrect.

Question 26

Answer b is correct. DAC allows the resource owner to control other user's access to the object. Answer a is incorrect because MAC is a nondiscretionary access control technique that uses defined security classifications. Answer c is incorrect because lattice deals with information flow in multi-user environments. Answer d is incorrect because RBAC allows security officers to specify access security policies based on an organization's structure.

Question 27

Answer a is correct. Secure RPC is a protocol that one program can use to request a service from a program on another computer. Answer b is incorrect because CHAP is a password authentication protocol. Answer c is incorrect because SLIP is a TCP/IP protocol used for communication between two machines that were previously configured for communication with each other. Answer d is incorrect because PPTP is a tunneling protocol.

Question 28

Answer c is correct. Awareness programs help educate, but they cannot enforce security policy. Security programs can make employees aware of issues, show them the proper procedures to follow, and make them aware of risks. Answers a, b, and d are thus incorrect.

Question 29

Answer a is correct. A distributed computing environment is implemented when the computer programming, processing, and data that computers work on are spread out over more than one computer. Answer b is incorrect because a nondistributed computing environment is where the computer programming, processing, and data are not spread out over more than one computer. Answer c is incorrect because an agent is a program that gathers information or performs some other service without your immediate presence and on some regular schedule. Answer d is incorrect because an applet is a small application program.

Question 30

Answer a is correct. 3DES is a symmetric encryption algorithm. Answer b is incorrect because MD5 is a hashing algorithm. RSA and Diffie-Helman are asymmetric algorithms. Answers c and d are thus incorrect.

Question 31

Answer d is correct. Smith-Kline is not a security model. Bell-LaPadula, Biba, and Clark-Wilson are all security models. Answers a, b, and c are thus incorrect.

Question 32

Answer a is correct. Dumpster diving is digging through an individual's or organization's trash to find critical information and documents that were not properly disposed of. Answer b is incorrect because social engineering focuses on the weaknesses in the human factor. Answer c is incorrect because radiation monitoring allows an attacker to capture emissions from items such as monitors and to be able to identify what is being displayed. Answer d is incorrect because sniffing is the process of capturing packets traveling across the network and reading their contents in the hope of capturing userid/password combinations or other critical information.

Question 33

Answer a is correct. Hot sites are sites that are fully configured and ready to operate within several hours. Answer b is incorrect because warm sites are sites that are partially configured, usually with selected peripheral equipment, such as disk drives and tape drives and controllers, but without the main computer. Answer c is incorrect because cold sites are sites that have the basic environment and are ready to receive equipment but do not offer any components at the site in advance of the need. There is no such thing as a medium site; answer d is thus incorrect.

Question 34

Answer a is correct. Military and intelligence attacks are after sensitive military and law enforcement files containing military data and investigation reports. Answer b is incorrect because business attacks are after competitive information, trade secrets, or to just harm the business's reputation. Answer c is incorrect because grudge attacks are targeted at individuals and companies who have done something that the attacker doesn't like. Answer d is incorrect because "fun" attacks are perpetrated by individuals who are not in it for the money, but for the thrill of being able to break into a computer and tell all of their friends.

Question 35

Answer b is correct. Fiber optic cable is insensitive to electrical or magnetic interference. Copper, coaxial cable, and Ethernet are all sensitive to electrical or magnetic interference. Answers a, c, and d are thus incorrect.

Question 36

Answer a is correct. MAC is nondiscretionary. Answer b is incorrect because DAC is discretionary access control. Answer c is incorrect because lattice deals with information flow in multi-user environments. Answer d is incorrect because RBAC allows security officers to specify access security policies based on an organization's structure.

Question 37

Answer d is correct. ARP maps an IP address to a physical machine address. Answer a is incorrect because SLIP is used for communications between machines, such as your system and your ISP. Answer b is incorrect because PPP is a protocol for communication between two computers using a serial interface. Answer c is incorrect because Frame Relay is a telecommunications service.

Question 38

Answer c is correct. Availability means that data and resources are accessible when they need to be. Answer a is incorrect because confidentiality protects data from being viewed by unauthorized individuals. Answer b is incorrect because integrity protects data from being modified, retaining the consistency and original meaning of the information. Answer d is incorrect because authorization provides a means of determining who can access what system resources.

Question 39

Answer c is correct. An agent is a program that gathers information or performs some other service without your immediate presence and on some regular schedule. Answer a is incorrect because an applet is a small application program. A control (ActiveX or C++) is a component of the ActiveX language and environment. Answers b and d are thus incorrect.

Question 40

Answer b is correct. MD5 is a hash algorithm. Answer a is incorrect because 3DES is a symmetric encryption algorithm. RSA and Diffie-Helman are asymmetric algorithms. Answers c and d are thus incorrect.

Question 41

Answer b is correct. There are seven layers in the OSI model. Answers a, c, and d are thus incorrect.

Question 42

Answer b is correct. Applications do not need to be monitored. Patches, security sites, security mailing lists, system configuration, and log files all need to be monitored. Answers a, c, and d are thus incorrect.

Question 43

Answer b is correct. Electronic vaulting is a system that entails immediately transmitting copies of each online transaction or change to a remotely located computer facility where the data is preserved for backup. Answer a is incorrect because tape backup is the process of copying data to tape. Answer c is incorrect because hierarchical storage management uses software that dynamically manages the storage and retrieval of online data files to storage media devices. Answer d is incorrect because mirror processing updates to a backup copy of the database so that the backup files are more readily available for use in an emergency.

Question 44

Answer d is correct. "Fun" attacks are attacks that are perpetrated by individuals who are not in it for the money but for the thrill of being able to break into a computer and tell their friends. Answer a is incorrect because military and intelligence attacks are after sensitive military and law enforcement files containing military data and investigation reports. Answer b is incorrect because business attacks are after competitive information or trade secrets, or just to harm the business's reputation. Answer c is incorrect because grudge attacks are targeted at individuals and companies who have done something that the attacker doesn't like.

Question 45

Answer c is correct. The most desirable building location would be next to a suburban neighborhood. Next to the airport, next to an active freight train line, and next to a proposed freeway expansion site would not be ideal building locations. Answers a, b, and d are thus incorrect.

Question 46

Answer a is correct. IDS monitors networks and computer systems for signs of intrusion or misuse. Answer b is incorrect because MAC is an access control technique. Answer c is incorrect because Bell-LaPadula is an access control model. Answer d is incorrect because TACACS is a centralized access control methodology.

Question 47

Answer c is correct. TCP works at the Transport layer. Answer b is incorrect because IP works at the Network layer. The Data Link and Physical layers deal with getting the data packets to the physical communications medium. Answers a and d are thus incorrect.

Question 48

Answer d is correct. Authorization provides a means of determining who can access what system resources. Answer a is incorrect because confidentiality protects data from being viewed by unauthorized individuals. Answer b is incorrect because integrity protects data from being modified, retaining the consistency and original meaning of the information. Answer c is incorrect because availability means that data and resources are accessible when they need to be accessed.

Question 49

Answer d is correct. Java was developed for specific use on the Internet and a wide variety of platforms. Fortran, C++, and C were not developed specifically for use over the Internet on a wide variety of platforms. Answers a, b, and c are thus incorrect.

Question 50

Answer c is correct. RSA is an asymmetric algorithm. Answer a is incorrect because 3DES is a symmetric algorithm. MD5 and SHA are hashing algorithms. Answers b and d are thus incorrect.

Glossary

access control
Provides the means to control the behavior, use, and content of a system.

accountability
Allows administrators and managers to track who performed which operation. Ties actions and operations to a specific person.

Address Resolution Protocol (ARP)
A protocol for mapping an Internet protocol address to a physical machine address that is recognized in the local network.

administrative law
Also known as regulatory law, it establishes the standards of performance and conduct from government agencies to organizations.

agents
A program that gathers information or performs some other service without your immediate presence and on some regular schedule.

aggregation
The process of combining small pieces of information to gain insight into the "whole."

asymmetric algorithms
An encryption process where different keys are used for encryption and decryption.

authentication
Determining whether users are who they say they are.

authorization
Determining whether a user can access a requested resource.

availability
Ensuring data is accessible to those who use the data when they need to use it.

brute force
Trying all possible words and character combinations to find the correct password, passphrase, or PIN.

business attacks

Information loss through competitive intelligence gathering and computer-related attacks. These attacks can be very costly due to the loss of trade secrets and reputation.

catastrophes

Major disruptions entailing the destruction of the data processing facility.

Challenge Handshake Authentication Protocol (CHAP)

A more secure procedure for connecting to a system than the Password Authentication Protocol (PAP).

civil law

Takes effect when damage, injury, or wrongful acts are done willfully or negligently.

Closed-Circuit Television (CCTV)

A television system in which signals are not publicly distributed; cameras are connected to a television monitor in a limited area, such as a store or an office building.

closed system

Products from one vendor cannot work with another vendor. You must purchase specific components from the manufacturer.

cold sites

Sites that have the basic environment (electrical wiring, air conditioning, flooring, etc.). The cold site is ready to receive equipment but does not offer any components at the site in advance of the need.

confidentiality

Ensuring that only authorized people have the ability to see the data.

contingent event

A chance event, an uncertainty. It is something that has a possibility of occurrence but may or may not actually come about.

copyright

A legal right granted to an author (or other "creator") to exclusive publication, distribution, or sale of a created work.

corrective controls

Help fix problems after they arise.

covert channel

Channel that involves the direct or indirect writing of a storage location by one process and the direct or indirect reading of the storage location by another process.

crackers

Programs that break passwords.

criminal law

Government law that is enacted for the protection of the public.

denial of service (DoS)

An incident in which a user or organization is deprived of the services of a resource they would normally expect to have.

detective controls

Help identify security incidents.

digital signature
The technique of appending a string of characters to an electronic message in order to authenticate the sender.

disasters
Disruptions causing the entire facility to be inoperative for a lengthy period of time, usually more than one day.

discretionary access control (DAC)
Restricts a user's access to an object (i.e., a file). The owner of the file controls other user's access.

distributed computing
The computer programming, processing, and data that computers work on are spread out over more than one computer, usually over a network in a client-server environment.

due care
Acting in good faith, with the care an ordinarily prudent person in a like position would exercise under similar circumstances, and in a manner he or she reasonably believes is in the best interest of the enterprise.

dumpster diving
Analyzing the trash of a potential "victim" to gain information that will be useful in an attack.

federal interest computer
A computer that is exclusively for the use of a financial institution or the U.S. government, or, if it is not exclusive, one used for a financial institution or the U.S. government where the offense adversely affects the use of the financial institution's or the government's operation of the computer.

financial attacks
Banks and large corporations are often targeted to provide hackers with the funds they need or want. However, although banks provide one of the greatest targets, toll fraud is also a very large financial attack, often costing telephone companies millions of dollars.

firewalls
Help control which protocols and applications can gain access to a network.

FM-200
A common solution used in gas discharge fire suppression systems.

"fun" attacks
Perpetrated by individuals who are not in it for the money but for the thrill of being able to break into a computer and tell all of their friends.

grudge attacks
Targeted at individuals and companies who have done something that the attacker doesn't like.

hash
Hashing is the transformation of a string of characters into a usually shorter, fixed-length value or key that represents the original string.

hearsay
That which is not gathered from the personal knowledge of the witness but through other sources.

High-Level Data Link Control (HDLC)
A group of protocols or rules for transmitting data between network points.

hot sites

Sites that are fully configured and ready to operate within several hours. The equipment and systems software must be compatible with the primary installation being backed up.

inference

A unilateral activity in which an unclassified user legitimately accesses unclassified information from which that user is able to deduce secret information.

Information Technology Security Evaluation Criteria (ITSEC)

The ITSEC were created by the European Community as a result of "normalizing" the British, German, and French ITSECs into a single EEC-wide ITSEC.

Integrated Services Digital Network (ISDN)

A set of CCITT/ITU (Consultative Committee for International Telegraph and International Telecommunications Union) standards for digital transmission over ordinary telephone copper wire as well as over other media.

integrity

Ensuring the data has not been modified in any way, whether in transit or in storage.

International Standards Organization/ Open Systems Interconnection (ISO/ OSI) layers and characteristics

The OSI model has seven layers that help define network operations. Starting from bottom to top, the layers are physical, data link, network, transport, session, presentation, and application.

intrusion detection

Monitor networks and computer systems for signs of intrusion or misuse.

IPSec

IPSec is designed to provide interoperable, high quality, crypto-graphically-based security. The set of security services offered include connectionless integrity, data origin authentication, replay protection, confidentiality (encryption), and limited traffic flow confidentiality.

lattice-based access control

Based on the information flow in multi-user computer systems.

layering

Facilitates the verification of the correctness of the application by allowing examination of one layer at a time, but it also simplifies future changes by allowing the higher layers to be modified for new releases without the need to redesign the lower layers.

man-in-the-middle attacks

The attacker places himself in the flow of traffic and intercepts communications.

mandatory access control (MAC)

All users and resources are classified and assigned a security label.

military and intelligence attacks
Computer criminals and intelligence agents are after sensitive military and law enforcement files containing military data and investigation reports.

motion detectors
Devices that sense motion and either alert authorities, set off an alarm, or turn on a light when triggered.

Network Address Translation (NAT)
The translation of an IP address used within one network to a different IP address known within another network.

neural networks
A system of programs and data structures that approximate the operation of the human nervous system.

nondisasters
Disruptions in service stemming from system malfunction or other failure.

nonrepudiation
Provides a means of proving that a transaction occurred so it cannot later be denied.

Password Authentication Protocol (PAP)
A procedure used by PPP servers to validate a connection request.

patent
The protection of an invention that has been sufficiently documented and explained, so as to allow the Federal Patent Office to verify its originality and to grant a patent.

Point-to-Point Protocols (PPP)
A protocol for communication between two computers using a serial interface, typically a personal computer connected by phone line to a server.

polyinstantiation
Allows different versions of the same information item to exist at different classification levels.

preventive controls
Used to prevent security incidents.

primary storage
System memory.

public key infrastructure (PKI)
Accepted technology standard for identifying individuals using digital certificates.

recovery controls
Help rebuild a system, application, or network after a security incident has occurred.

resource manager
Helps control system resources.

role-based access control
Each user is assigned one or more roles, and each role is assigned one or more privileges that are permitted to users in that role.

rule-based access control
The system will intercept every access request and compare the resource-specific access conditions with the rights of the user in order to make an access decision.

Secure Remote Procedure Call (S-RPC)

A protocol that one program can use to request a service from a program located in another computer in a network without having to understand network details.

Serial Line Internet Protocol (SLIP)

A TCP/IP protocol used for communication between two machines that were previously configured for communication with each other.

sniffers

Capture packets and their contents, which may contain passwords, credit card numbers, social security numbers, or other sensitive information.

social engineering

Capitalizing on the weakness of individuals to gain access or critical information that can lead to system compromise.

spamming

The sending of unsolicited email messages.

spoofing

A user appears to be someone else or manipulates packets so they appear to come from another system or network.

symmetric algorithms

An encryption process where one key is used for both encryption and decryption.

Synchronous Data Link Control (SDLC)

A transmission protocol that is equivalent to layer 2 of the OSI model of network communication. This level of protocol makes sure that data units arrive successfully from one network point to the next and flow at the right pace.

Telecommunications Electronics Material Protected from Emanating Spurious Transmissions (TEMPEST)

Solution to the susceptibility of some computer and telecommunications devices to emit electromagnetic radiation (EMR) in a manner that can be used to reconstruct intelligible data.

terrorist attacks

Attacks launched by terrorists for political reasons. Some are moving more towards information terrorism than using physical destruction.

trademark

Any distinguishing name, character, logo, or other symbol that establishes an identity for a product, service, or organization.

transparency

Relates to how intrusive the firewall is to system users.

Trusted Computer System Evaluation Criteria (TCSEC)

A U.S. Department of Defense (DoD) set of criteria for determining both the security functionality and the degree of assurance that the functionality works as documented that is required for a system to meet a certain defined security level.

tunneling

Using the Internet as part of a private secure network. The "tunnel" is the particular path that a given company message or file might travel through the Internet.

Virtual Private Network (VPN)

A private data network that makes use of the public telecommunication infrastructure, maintaining privacy through the use of a tunneling protocol and security procedures.

war dialing

Calling a large group of phone numbers to find active modems or PBXs.

warm sites

Sites that are partially configured, usually with selected peripheral equipment, such as disk drives and tape drives and controllers, but without the main computer.

Index

Execute privileges, 9
Expert systems, 89–90
Explosions, threats from, 200
External services, protecting, 209

F

Failures, security implications of, 138
Faxes, security of, 52
Federal computer systems, security and privacy of, 179
Federal interest computers, 186
Federal Privacy Act of 1974, 179–181
Felonies, computer-related, 178–179
Fiber optic cable, 31, 209, **217**, **230**
    connector for, 31
Field powered security devices, 204
File infectors, 84
Filter rule set, 41
Financial institutions, federal interest computers, 186
Fire detectors, 210
Fire extinguishing agents, 211–212, **216–217**, **222**, **225**
Fire suppression systems, 208
Fires, 200–201
Firewalls, 39–42
    application gateway architecture, 41
    application proxies, 40
    circuit gateways, 40
    NAT use, **56**
    packet filtering, 40
    router architecture, 40–41
    stateful packet filter architecture, 41
Firmware, 131
Flooding, 53
Floor slab, securing, 202, **215**
FM-200, 208, **225**
Footprint of usage, 19
Forecasting, 86
Frame relay, 48–49
Frames, 47
Fraud
    Computer Fraud and Abuse Act of 1986, 178–179
    eliminating, 53
    protecting against, 67–68
    toll fraud, 187
Function calls, 38

G

Glass houses, 80
Government/military applications
    access control model for, 11–12
GRE (generic routing encapsulation) protocol, 115
Grudge attacks, 188, **196**, **232**
Guard dogs, for surveillance, 210
Guards, 210
Guidelines, 70

H

Hardware, 131
Hardware backups, 165–166
Hardware controls, 150
Hash encryption, 106–107, **124**, **127**, **226**, **231**
Hash function, 51–52

HDLC, 47–48
    variations of, 48
Hearsay, 187, **195**, **227**
Heuristics, 85
Hierarchical storage management, 166, **169**, **227**
High Level Data Link Control. *See* HDLC.
Hiring practices, 148
    security implications of, 68–69, **75**
Host and service discovery, 153
Host-to-host security, IPSec for, 35
Host-to-subnet security, IPSec for, 35
Hosts, links between, 37
Hot sites, 165, 167, **170**, **229**
HTTP traffic, encryption of, **54**
Hubs, for star networks, 32
Humidity, 208

I

IAB (Internet Activities Board) statement policy, 189–190
IDEA (International Data Encryption Algorithm), 103
Identification, 13–14, 63
    of individuals, 109–110, 121–122, **127**.
        See also Digital certificates; PKI.
    of message signer, 108–109
    as physical controls, 205
IDS, 18–20, **25**, 39, **232**
    anomaly detection, 19
    system monitoring, 20
IETF Security Architecture, 134. *See also* IPSec.
IKE, 118, 120–121
    with IPSec, 121
IKMP, 35, 120–121
Implementation definition, 91
Individuals
    identifying, 121–122, **127**. *See also* PKI.
    physical identification of, 205
    privacy of, 179–181
Inference engines, 89–90
Inferences, 86, **94**
    polyinstantiation and, 86–87, **95**
Information backup, 163, **168–169**
Information/data, 66–67. *See also* Data.
Information valuation, 66
Information warehouse, 85
InformationTechnology Security Evaluation Criteria. *See* ITSEC.
Initialization, system crashes during, 138
Input, security issues with, 139
Input checks, 139
Input-output controls, 150
Integrated Services Digital Network. *See* ISDN.
Integrity. *See also* Data integrity.
    Biba integrity model, 12
    Clark-Wilson model, 12
    of email messages, 44–45
Intellectual property, 176–177, **193–194**, **222**
Internal auditor, 68
International Information Systems Security Certification Consortium (ISC2) Code of Ethics, 190–192
International laws for computer-related crimes, 182

99   2097451568